# Jesus and His Enemies

# Jesus and His Enemies

## Narrative Conflict in the Four Gospels

Robert R. Beck

ORBIS BOOKS
Maryknoll, New York 10545

Founded in 1970, Orbis Books endeavors to publish works that enlighten the mind, nourish the spirit, and challenge the conscience. The publishing arm of the Maryknoll Fathers and Brothers, Orbis seeks to explore the global dimensions of the Christian faith and mission, to invite dialogue with diverse cultures and religious traditions, and to serve the cause of reconciliation and peace. The books published reflect the views of their authors and do not represent the official position of the Maryknoll Society. To learn more about Maryknoll and Orbis Books, please visit our website at www.maryknollsociety.org.

Unless otherwise noted, scripture quotations are taken from the New Revised Standard Version.

Manufactured in the United States of America.
Manuscript editing and typesetting by Joan Weber Laflamme.

### Library of Congress Cataloging-in-Publication Data

Names: Beck, Robert R. (Robert Raymond), author.
Title: Jesus and his enemies : narrative conflict in the four Gospels / Robert R. Beck.
Description: Maryknoll : Orbis Books, 2017. | Includes bibliographical references and index.
Identifiers: LCCN 2017021205 (print) | LCCN 2017031622 (ebook) | ISBN 9781608337088 (e-book) | ISBN 9781626982437 (pbk.)
Subjects: LCSH: Conflict management—Biblical teaching. | Bible. Gospels—Criticism, Narrative. | Jesus Christ—Adversaries—Biblical teaching. | Jesus Christ—Conflicts—Biblical teaching. | Enemies—Religious aspects—Christianity.
Classification: LCC BS2545.C573 (ebook) | LCC BS2545.C573 B43 2017 (print) |
DDC 226/.066—dc23
LC record available at https://lccn.loc.gov/2017021205

# Contents

*Acknowledgments*        *vii*

*Prologue: In the Grip of a Narrative*        *ix*

**1. Reading the Gospels**        **1**
New Perspectives  2
Postcolonialism  5
Conflict in The Gospels  13
The Following Chapters  27

**2. Mark**        **31**
Mark's Project: The Resistance Campaign  31
Mark's Story: The People's Messiah  46
Conflict Resolution in Mark  66
Resistance as Nonviolent Action  73

**3. Matthew**        **77**
Matthew's Project: The Return of the Kingship  78
Matthew's Story: Reimagining the Messiah  88
Conflict Resolution in Matthew  103
Resistance as Non-retaliation  113

**4. Luke-Acts**        **119**
Luke's Project: A Path to the Gentiles  119
Luke's Story: Opening a Route to the God-fearers  135
Conflict Resolution in Luke-Acts  168
Resistance as Lifestyle  177

5. **John**                                                                    **181**
   John's Project: The Story of the Word    183
   John's Story: Jesus of Nazareth    193
   Conflict Resolution in John    208
   Resistance as Love    221


6. **Narrative Conflict in the Gospels**                                        **223**
   Counter-Narratives and the Accused Woman    223
   In the End . . .    227


*Index*                                                                         **229**

# Acknowledgments

Frank Cordaro asked for this book. Wally Helms and the priests of Davenport gave me a chance to make a first attempt. Robert Ellsberg advised a thorough rethinking of that version. Amy Lorenz and John Waldmeir read through everything, questioned everything, and made invaluable suggestions. Other discussion partners proving critical to the work included David Pitt; Deborah Fleming; Mona Wingert, OSF; Jean Beringer, OSF; and Ann Wertz. The One Mean Bean coffeehouse and River Lights 2nd Edition bookstore provided congenial venues for some lively and searching discussions. Loras College gave me an office and allowed me to make use of the secretarial skills of Carol Oberfoell and Colleen Fitzpatrick. Thanks to all.

# Prologue

# In the Grip of a Narrative

Part of the background noise in the lives of Americans is a torrent of mainline and social media reports concerning acts of violence. Mass killings, defined as shootings with four or more victims, seemingly occur almost daily. Those incidents dramatic enough to receive national media coverage are typically followed by an upsurge in gun sales. Yet none of this is news. That is a problem. We seem helpless to do anything about it. The greater the perceived danger, the greater is the impulse to defend ourselves and those near to us. And so we are susceptible to the warnings that the only protection against a bad guy with a gun is a good guy with a gun.

Good guys and bad guys. This is the language of stories. Life as we know it is actually filled with complex people, much like the complexity we recognize in ourselves. But stories divide everyone into two camps, the protagonist and the antagonist, the hero and the villain, the good guy and the bad guy. And the good guy is always on our side.

We recognize this story—it is the basis of every Western we've seen or read. It is the story in which right and truth prevail. But it is a myth, not only in the sense that it is not true, as experience shows, but also in the more technical sense of being a foundational story. It is the story that undergirds the sense of a common identity in a people, a culture. It is part of the American mythos, the narrative that has us in its grip, and right now it is getting in the way of a safe America.

Often our reliance on violence for our supposed security seeks religious support. One common approach is to cite a verse from the Gospels, for example, "They [the disciples] said, 'Lord, look, here are two swords.' He replied, 'It is enough'" (Luke 22:38), or draw support from citations of the early books of scripture, perhaps Deuteronomy or Joshua. But piling up biblical verses does little but apply "bumper stickers" to the story that already has us in its grip. It leaves the cultural drama intact and uses biblical garnishes to make it more palatable. But it is still the same national mythos. In the end, the only answer to the powerful sway of a story is another story. What this book tries to show is how that other story is the Gospel, told as an entire story. It is the anti-myth to our national myth.

There are four Gospels in the New Testament; that is, the good news comes to us in four versions. Each tells the story in its own way, with its own set of concerns. But what all have in common is their critical edge, their refusal to take the common cultural myth for granted. In the pages that follow this critical edge is examined in each of the four ways of telling the story.

We are not accustomed to attending to the Gospel story in its full account, let alone looking at the four versions in their distinctiveness. But it is here that we find the Gospel writers' sense of what the conflict is about and how they believe it could be resolved. An early clue is that the story, in all versions, ends with a crucifixion. But there are differences in what the different evangelists see in that, and that difference is frequently enough linked to the problems that they, and their communities, are facing in their own times and places. The assumption made here is that it is in examining those Gospel responses that we will find what we need to make our own Gospel responses to conflicts confronting us today.

# 1

## Reading the Gospels

How are we as Christians to act in situations of conflict? How are we to engage in necessary conflict without abandoning the demands of love? This is the real test of the command to love one another, which finds its most exacting demand when we are in firm opposition. Certainly the Gospels have much to say about this. But perhaps the most obvious place is to be found where we seldom look; in their stories of Jesus, the four Gospels have the qualities of dramatic narrative. In answer to the questions just asked, this book looks at the narrative conflicts in the Gospels and how those conflicts are resolved as ways to discover what the Bible, and the Gospels in particular, believe about issues of violence, force, and coercion.

In recent years biblical studies have taken a similar turn away from content toward context, from the message to the medium. Turning our attention toward the writer and the act of writing is a part of this change of direction. Without disregarding the message being delivered, the new question asks what this story meant for the person writing it. What events were happening at the time that made this Gospel seem important? How did the writer intend to address that moment? These are some of the questions asked in this book. Each Gospel is treated as an independent witness to Jesus's story, each showing him in a drama that confronts and resolves differences. Each shows in its own way how love behaves under conditions of conflict.

In taking this approach we are asking a different question from those who are looking for the historical record of Jesus, such as Reza Aslan in his popular book, *Zealot: The Life and Times of Jesus of Nazareth.* Instead of reconstructing the historical events of Jesus's life, we are seeking the views of those whose accounts we have—Mark, Matthew, Luke, and John. The object of our quest is the word of these witnesses.[1]

Many may not find this approach satisfying. They may want to know about Jesus, not about what the Gospel writers chose to say about him. Apart from noting that the only route we have to the story of Jesus is by way of these four evangelists, it needs to be said that this method delivers some good and useful results. It also allows us to see the four Gospels in their distinct individuality and appreciate them for it.

## NEW PERSPECTIVES

A new approach to these questions has been made possible by the emergence of new forms of biblical study. That most evident in this book is the new attention to literary qualities of the biblical writings. Where previous "literary" studies devoted most of their attention to the history of the writing process that resulted in the biblical books, with an eye to calculating their value as historical witness to events, some recent approaches are more convention-ally literary. They study the works in relation to their qualities as literature and observe the ways in which they achieve their effects in the manner in which other literature does.

This shift in focus amounts to a paradigm shift in biblical studies. Related to this literary turn is an entire set of analogous

---

[1] Reza Aslan, *Zealot: The Life and Times of Jesus of Nazareth* (New York: Random House, 2013; reprint paperback 2014). While these pages do not attempt to do so, if I were to recommend a book about the life and times of Jesus of Nazareth that I find most helpful, it would be Sean Freyne, *Jesus, a Jewish Galilean: A New Reading of the Jesus Story* (New York: T & T Clark, 2004).

developments. The short survey of such current studies given here indicates the kinds of work to which the present reading of the Gospels is indebted. These have in common the move from giving our primary attention to the content of the narratives, with their account of events, to the circumstances in which those accounts were written. We can ask new questions. In the case of the Gospels, what struggles were occurring in the life of the communities of the evangelists that convinced them that a narrative of Jesus's life would provide a proper response? For our purposes the narrative conflict that we examine in the Gospels can be imagined as a response to a social conflict in the world of the evangelist. In turn, the answer given by the Gospels can be seen as providing us with similar possible solutions.

This window onto the world of the New Testament is opened by the using the social sciences, archeology, and historical records as supplements to the scriptures. Each of these deserves a word of explanation.

**Historical Studies**

In recent years the longstanding search for the historical Jesus has taken a new turn. Focus has moved away from the pursuit of the authentic words of Jesus in the Gospel text. Having failed to achieve robust results there, the search moved its attention away from the text itself to the historical conditions that produced it. The question becomes: What do these writings mean for us in light of those circumstances? In those historical conditions we discover a situation that invited a response—a response that, in the case of the Gospels, takes the form of a narrative about Jesus. In our awareness of those historical times, already defined by conflict, we find in such social situations perspectives that assist us as Gospel readers. Perhaps it can be imagined as something like a new version of the *Imitation of Christ,* focusing for our benefit on the story of Jesus. We find lessons about how to enter into conflict and bring it to a satisfactory conclusion, ethically and sometimes even practically.

## Social Sciences

Historical anthropology has opened our eyes to the place that cultural categories have in framing the biblical texts. Two important examples for our purposes are the ritual categories of holy and unclean and the social categories of honor and shame.

The categories of holy and unclean are prominent in Jewish writings, shown especially in the book of Leviticus. But studies have revealed how these categories provide an illuminating way of organizing the Jewish world of the New Testament as well. Graduated categories that run from the most holy to the unclean include places, times, and persons, as well as the more commonly expected areas of meal gatherings and worship settings.[2] However, holy and unclean categories are also at work in most ancient societies, and in some ways in our own as well. The language provided by the ritual categories of holy and unclean especially help us understand the workings of Mark's narrative, for instance.

Honor and shame values defined Greco-Roman culture. This is conspicuously evident in the culturally foundational epic *The Iliad*. Homer's epic revolves around an impasse in the war effort caused by an insulted Achilles, who retires to his tent. It is not until the honor issues are resolved that they can lure him back into the arena, so they can finish the war and go home. Important to honor-and-shame societies are matters of saving face; competitive challenge and its response; distinct social levels of society, including well-defined gender roles; and so forth. While these have been explored exhaustively in classical studies, biblical studies have shown that these categories also permeated the ancient Mediterranean world, including the Jewish part of it. While there are distinctions between ancient group culture and today's individualistic version, some aspects remain alive today—for instance, in the sports world. For our purposes honor values are helpful in discerning the conflict situations in Luke's Gospel.

---

[2] For a fuller treatment and references, see Robert Beck, *Nonviolent Story: Narrative Conflict Resolution in the Gospel of Mark* (Eugene, OR: Wipf and Stock, 2009; Maryknoll, NY: Orbis Books, 1996), 65–70.

## Archeology

Excavation of ancient sites offers another example. In traditional biblical studies archeological evidence was brought to bear in support of conclusions about the Bible arrived at on other grounds. Insofar as contemporary practice allows archeological science to present an independent witness in its own right, with its own methodology and secure findings, unexpected information about biblical times has surfaced. A striking example is the existence of Sepphoris, a vibrant Jewish city in the Hellenist style, that is unmentioned in the Gospels, despite the fact that Nazareth was one of its satellite villages during the time of Jesus. Any work that was performed by a Nazareth "carpenter" was likely for citizens of Sepphoris.

The shift from a handmaiden science to independent witness represents a refocus of attention from the content of the scripture (from exploiting the evidence of archeology when it suited) to establishing a firmer sense of the social setting at the time these writings were produced. In this sense it is a partner of the historical sciences, which help to present an in-depth portrayal of circumstances of the writing, as well as the events depicted in the writing. It too can be called a shift from message to medium insofar as it places its attention on the conditions of the writing, and in that way moves us from the content to the expression.[3]

# POSTCOLONIALISM

## Empire Studies

These changes in the quality of attention have facilitated a number of new directions in biblical studies. Two of these, which might quite justifiably be called paradigm shifts, are important to what we are doing here: empire studies and Judaism studies. The first

---

[3] Jonathan Reed, *Archaeology and the Galilean Jesus* (Harrisburg, PA: Trinity Press International, 2002).

of these, *empire studies,* examines the influence of imperial power on the society, culture, and faith life of the biblical writers.[4]

The dearth of direct mention of the Roman Empire in the New Testament emerged as a problem once we learned about the issues that stirred the larger world of the New Testament. However, the contemporary field of *postcolonial criticism* has helped toward understanding this situation and will also assist us in our efforts here. Postcolonial criticism is a body of writings that consists of responses by members of the formerly colonized world to their experience of nineteenth-century European imperialism. One-time colonized peoples—from India, Palestine, Egypt and other African former colonies, the Caribbean Islands, Australia, Ireland, and elsewhere—have contributed to these critical writings. Franz Fanon's groundbreaking volume *The Wretched of the Earth* marked the beginning of a flood of pointed analyses. Edward Said's study *Orientalism* established the critical tradition firmly in the public eye. One Australian collection of essays captures the approach in a trenchant title: *The Empire Writes Back.*

## The Problem of National Identity

Certain common themes link postcolonial critics. One is the problem for the former colony of constructing a *national identity.* During the period of colonization its identity was typically determined by the colonizing power, always to the advantage of the latter. In the view of the imperialist, the natives were shiftless, unable to maintain a disciplined work schedule, emotional rather than rational, and so forth. Thus, the Orient was made to seem exotic and vaguely immoral, a lively fantasy land for the conventional European, but one that scarcely represented the self-image of the natives involved. Or, to pick an example that is closer to home and thus more vivid, the Irish were defined as mercurial, obstinate,

---

[4] Richard Horsley, *Jesus and the Spiral of Violence: Popular Jewish Resistance in Roman Palestine* (Minneapolis, MN: Augsburg Fortress Publishers, 1993); Warren Carter, *The Roman Empire and the New Testament: An Essential Guide* (Nashville, TN: Abingdon Press, 2006).

emotionally unreliable, and pugnacious, against a British image of itself as sober, adult, and responsible. A national character had to be retrieved, or devised, in order to counter the caricature that had been provided by the imperial conqueror. Retrieving an adequate cultural self-image would often take the form of inventing one, seen for instance in the example of the Irish poet W. B. Yeats exhuming ancient Celtic myths for the purpose of creating a national past and character.

The community of biblical scholars recognized in these efforts certain parallels with the situations and story of Israel. For much for its existence, and most of its time since the Babylonian exile, it persevered as a colonized people, under the sway of a series of foreign empires. Life under the Babylonian, Persian, and Greek world empires provided the occasion for assembling and shaping much of Hebrew scriptures. In the New Testament period that empire was Rome. And it was Roman power that was called upon to bring the story of Jesus, it was hoped, to a conclusion, through crucifixion.

*The Concessions of Hybridity*

*Hybridity* emerged as part of the postcolonial effort toward recovering communal identity. Hybridity teaches that recognizing and accepting one's culture as a mix of native and imperial, colony and colonizer, is a necessary step in recovery. Most postcolonial writers are vividly aware of the fact that they write in the language and critical categories of the cultures that had been imposed upon them by the colonizers. Irish writers, again, offer an illustration. In James Joyce's novel *A Portrait of the Artist as a Young Man*, Stephen Dedalus converses with a Jesuit teacher over the old English noun *tundish,* surprised that the British Jesuit is not more knowledgeable about his own language—a language that historically was not Stephen's, as he viewed the matter. In a similar way the biblical record represents a voice of the colonies of the empire writing back, though keeping it discreetly indirect. These patterns were fairly universal among the experiences of various colonies.

Having been exposed to postcolonial thinking, students of biblical study began to realize distinct implications for their own work. On the one hand, the use of the Bible by Christian countries to validate imperialist ventures needed to be exposed. On the other hand, similar features could be discovered in biblical writings, all of which, both Old and New Testaments, were written under conditions of imperial submission. The connection with the Gospels resides in the realization, given clarity by historical and archeological information, that both post-exilic Israel and New Testament Judea were colonized peoples. They experienced similar tensions and responded in similar ways. That is what interests us here. For the New Testament, of course, it was the Roman Empire that dominated the scene. Realizing this allows a fresh look at the texts and the claims they make. While the Roman authorities are not often mentioned explicitly, this is hardly surprising. It is expected from those who are habitually conscious of powers looking over their shoulder; they have learned to deflect surveillance. Common to the Gospel narratives, it must be noted, is their conclusion in the crucifixion of Jesus—a practice reserved to Roman authorities, representing one of the harshest moves the Roman Empire had conceived toward controlling subject peoples, with special attention to potential rebellion.

## Titles of Jesus

Empire studies have most often focused on claims made for Jesus shown to be in conflict with imperial claims. The titles given Jesus, such as Lord, Son of God, and Savior of the World, were reserved for Caesar Augustus. To posit them of Jesus of Nazareth would have been seen as confrontational.[5]

But the perspectives contrasting with imperial values pervade the very narratives themselves. For instance, the familiar

---

[5] For a comprehensive coverage of imperial titles and tropes that are attributed to Jesus in the Gospels, see Craig A. Evans, "Purpose of Mark," in *Word Biblical Commentary,* vol. 34b, *Mark 8:27–16:20* (Nashville, TN: Thomas Nelson, 2001), lxxx–xciii.

Christmas story of Luke 2:1–14, which tells of the Holy Family traveling south from Nazareth in Galilee to an inn at Bethlehem in Judea, involves the familiar census requirement of Caesar Augustus. The underlying reality is the *Pax Romana*, the universal peace, established by the Roman Empire and enforced through military occupation. The original audience would be aware of the purposes of such a census, namely, to provide bodies for military conscription, taxation, or unpaid labor. The demand to make a long trip under difficult conditions during the final term of a pregnancy would be considered typical hardship of the occupation.

But it is in the final moments of the story, when the angels appear to the shepherds, that we complete the picture. In the words, "on earth, peace," we find the authentic peace that counters the claims of the *Pax Romana*.

In this way perspectives akin to postcolonial studies allow us to understand the Gospel narratives in the major context of the Roman occupation of Judea. And this includes the destruction of the city of Jerusalem and its Temple, the removal of the hub of the Jewish world.

## Judaism Studies

The second kind of paradigm shift concerns the relationship of Judaism to the Gospels.[6] Contemporary biblical studies show a fresh appreciation of the Jewish character of the New Testament itself. Disastrous events of the twentieth century have made it imperative to pay fuller attention to the role of apparent anti-Jewish sentiments in the stories of the Gospels. This more complete awareness has also affected biblical studies. A reassessment of the anti-Semitic tendencies in the history of Christianity was made especially urgent as anti-Jewish Christians drew upon the New Testament to support their biases. In the wake of the Holocaust (or Shoah)—the systematic massacre of one-third of the world's Jews during the 1940s in Germany—Christian complicity prompted

---

[6] Jacob Nuesner and Bruce Chilton, *Judaism in the New Testament: Practices and Beliefs* (London: Routledge, 1995).

Christian writers, as well as ministers, to examine their tradition. This self-examination includes the role and use of scripture in the Christian churches. To what extent have Christians asked the biblical texts to support a bigotry that has turned out to be lethal on a massive scale?

In the case of the Gospels, such a shift in perspective enables us to reassess the profound and multifaceted images of Judaism in the New Testament. It prompts a reassessment of the role of Judaism in the narrative conflicts. The sad distortions are familiar. The role of the Pharisees and Jewish religious authorities in opposition to Jesus in Mark's Gospel had become an excuse to place blame on "recalcitrant" Jews. The Gospel of Matthew provided a text for making the claim that the Jews are cursed ("His blood be upon us and upon our children" [Matt 27:25]). Luke was read as favoring Rome over against the Jews. John's Gospel, while naming the opposition to Jesus as "Pharisees" some thirty times, has supplemented this term with the label "Jews" some sixty times, nearly all negative. In all of this there is ample material for an unexamined negative response based on the Gospel texts.

However, there seems to be a remedy for this. If we pay attention to the circumstances of the writing, we can make the adjustments demanded. At a general level it is important to note that the biblical narratives were written by Jews for Jews, and that the conflict depicted there is in this sense an in-house debate. Matters changed for the New Testament when Gentiles began to form the majority of Christians. It became possible to take a stand outside the Jewish horizon and mindset and to read the texts in a way that later became normative.

As regards the Jewish question more specifically, each Gospel narrative was composed under different circumstances, and the parties in conflict as described by each reflect those circumstances. Both Mark and Matthew reflect a crisis within Judaism brought about by the confrontation with Roman methods of retribution. Luke-Acts (considered here as a single project) rather dramatically reverses this, adopting a standpoint on the side of the Roman Empire, raising new questions. Meanwhile, John's Gospel makes "the Jews" a major collective participant in the struggle, which has generated considerable discussion as to whether this text takes a vantage point outside or inside the Jewish world. Each Gospel is slightly different, and each benefits from a closer look.

## Effects on Recent Biblical Studies

The two paradigm shifts of empire studies and Judaism studies are relatively recent in biblical study and will affect our reading of the text. On the one hand, our new knowledge argues for a more situated understanding of the Gospel texts, in particular the struggles that are enacted there. It is not enough to describe them in terms divorced from those circumstances, although an appreciation of the abstract qualities of narrative will be an immense help. On the other hand, this new information brings with it a fresh and compelling reading of those texts that allows an understanding of their relationship to us and our world today in important ways. If, in fact, life and art intersect, these plot lines have something to tell us about our own experience in entering into and resolving conflict, just as they did for the original readers.

## New Perspectives in Social-Conflict Theory: Beyond Just War and Pacifism[7]

Changes in biblical studies are not the only place in which a radical change of perspective has affected what we are doing here. In terms of the real world to which we try to relate these texts, another change has rearranged the circumstances. The long tradition of two stances toward Christian peacemaking, just war theory and pacifism, is faced with a new model. It is necessary to take stock of what has been called a profound shift in the ethics of war and conflict—changes in the emerging understanding of social conflict.

---

[7] Jonathan Schell, *The Unconquerable World: Power, Nonviolence, and the Will of the People* (New York: Holt Paperbacks, 2004); Gerald Schlabach, ed., *Just Policing: An Alternative Response to World Violence* (Collegeville, MN: Liturgical Press, 2007); Ivan Kaufmann, "If War Is Wrong, What Is Right? The New Paradigm," in Schlabach, *Just Policing.*

The traditional positions of just war and pacifism have dominated Christian thinking about conflict ethics. The first, attempting
to discern the moral condition of engaging in violent conflict, has
all too often been the rationalization for war. The second, equally
grounded in moral considerations, maintains a firm distance from
warmaking. But in its tendency to avoid conflict altogether, it may
come at the expense of threatening to permit injustices to have
their way, unresisted. A new vision appeared with the experiments
of Gandhi,[8] a possibility in the form of nonviolent resistance,
which can briefly be described as combining active resistance
with nonviolence.

Its viability has been demonstrated in its subsequent history. In
the US civil rights movement, under the guidance of Martin Lu-
ther King, Jr., who had schooled himself in Gandhi's techniques,
we relearned the Gospel witness to nonviolent action, something
Gandhi himself had mentioned. In rapid order following that,
liberation movements—in the Philippines, Korea, and Haiti; the
Solidarity Movement in Poland; the end of the Soviet occupation
of Eastern Europe; and the end of apartheid in South Africa—all
showed nonviolent methods to be effective.

Political theory affects any literary reading of the Gospels that
attempts to understand them in the light of narrative conflict development and resolution, as this book does. The paradigm shift
in conflict theory encounters that in biblical studies.

---

[8] Analysts have interpreted Gandhi's experiments in order to make them
available for use in studies like this one. Gene Sharp's theories of power and
nonviolent action have proven helpful in practical ways as well, most recently
in the Arab Spring. Ideas of political power as consent of the governed have
been elaborated by Elizabeth Janeway, while Joan Bondurant has provided
us with significant insights into Gandhi's method of Satyagraha—"truth
force"—the name he coined for nonviolent action. These theorists are especially useful in projects like this one, since they provide an interface between
life and narrative art. René Girard is known for his studies of the relationship
of literature and social conflict, which includes many writings about the role
of the Gospels in this area. His theories also offer certain insights upon which
we can draw.

## CONFLICT IN THE GOSPELS

Along with noting the helpful shifts in biblical studies and social-conflict theory that help to make this kind of reading possible, we need to pay attention to the character of literary study itself, because that is the route to the perspective we are taking.

Those advocating for social justice and peacemaking as part of their faith experience have customarily turned to the scriptures for support and enlightenment. In this cause the Gospels have been scrutinized for instruction, drained of every drop of implication. We are accustomed to relating to the Gospels in small pieces, in sayings, parables, and stories about Jesus, for example, Matthew 5:39 instructs us to turn the other cheek; Matthew 5:44 tells us to love our enemies.

But, as was mentioned earlier, there remains one kind of scriptural witness, right in front of our eyes, one that we tend to disregard. Where we might look for insight into this and similar questions is in the Gospel dramas themselves. We ask: How do these four accounts deal with the conflict at the center of their narratives?

### Adjusting Our Lenses

We are accustomed to direct our attention laser-like on the *content* of the writing. For what we are doing here we need to adjust our reading lenses and attend to the *medium* of writing as well as its content. This is not a move unknown to us. We have been known to lament the degree to which the "media" shape the news, as reflected in Marshall McLuhan's phrase, "The medium is the message."

In the Gospels we are typically interested in what is being taught, what is being said, what Jesus did. But here we are also interested in the *ways* of storytelling, *how* the stories are told. We read the Gospels passage by passage. We hear individual stories in church. We are accustomed to treating the individual incidents of the Gospels as standing alone, without paying much attention to their narrative context. However, the evangelists labored to place the individual stories in a larger story, and we can gain in understanding by honoring their efforts. The narrative plots of the Gospels offer lessons about conflict, as they tell the story of Jesus. They develop conflict situations and resolve them. But to see this, we need to recognize these writings as the complete, thoughtfully constructed works they are.

### What Kind of Writing Is It? The Problem of Genre

All writing, literary or not, fits into one or another convention for that kind of writing. These conventions are carried by the culture, and readers bring them to the task of reading. The name for such conventions is *genre*. Much of the meaning for the reader comes through the kind of writing he or she perceives it to be. This is as true of road signs and instruction manuals as it is of best-selling novels. We know the difference between a free-verse poem and, say, the clues for the crossword puzzle. We know that the simple instruction, "Eat," on a road sign is an invitation, not a command. We fill in the rest of the meaning: "You may be hungry, or even simply in need of a break, and if so we have a place for you to satisfy that need." In most cases where the reader and writer share a culture, the genre function is transparent and unconscious; the guidance it provides does not need our direct attention. But for any foreign visitors who do not share our culture, our genres can be confusing. When we read the New Testament, we are those visitors. We who are not a part of first-century Mediterranean culture may find ourselves making genre mistakes in reading the Gospels.

As for the question of the specific genre of the Gospels, this has long been argued without firm consensus. The current candidate for the most likely common genre (if there is a common genre) is from Greek culture—*Hellenistic biography*. While this may be an accurate identification of a genre within its original culture, and in that way solve a historical question, it does not help those of us who are reading these works in our very different culture, equipped with our own collection of possible genres. For this reason it seems plausible to turn to something more suitable, namely, the category of *narrative*. While this approach is broader in some ways, it does allow us to take a look at how the Gospels work as narratives. And in this we will be able to see their handling of conflict, and how they understand it to be resolved.

## How the Gospels Work as Narratives

We examine how the Gospels work as narratives under five headings.

1. *The Gospels Are Literature.* This may seem obvious, and yet it is something we need to think about. Literary qualities abound in the biblical writing, from figurative language to shaped plots, poetry to proverbs. For literature, attention to the quality and methods of the writing is at the heart of reading. It opens vistas not available otherwise.

So it is with the Gospels. The *individual authors* have left their imprint on the story they tell. The Gospel writers have distinctly different takes on the story of Jesus, and that is what interests us here. They are similar, but different. The relationship among three of the Gospels is undisputed, given that Mark, Matthew, and Luke share large stretches of text in verbatim agreement. Although verbal identity is almost entirely missing in John's Gospel, due to major similarities his Gospel is not excluded from this problem. We would prefer they were either entirely different, indicating that they were not aware of one another's work, or that they were less contradictory in their differences.

The similarity combined with dramatic differences creates a question about the extent of their creativity. The *boundary between fact and fiction* is at stake here. When we notice the liberties the Gospel writers take, amply illustrated in the following chapters, we are inclined to think of these as the methods used by fiction writers, and consequently assume the Gospels to be fiction. The tools we use to read fiction are indeed helpful for understanding the effects the evangelists are trying to achieve. But this does not mean these authors are writing fiction. Literary effects do not affect the quality of any writing as fact or fiction.

Most verbal or written accounts of events, including those we consider factual, use the tools of persuasive language, as "news stories" on television indicate. We have only to think of a common experience. Someone arrives late to a meeting and announces, "You'll never believe what happened to me on the way here!" Immediately everyone prepares for what is coming. They can expect to be at the receiving end of every tool of narrative art at the disposal of the storyteller, from suspense to diversionary delays to a calculated degree of exaggeration. We understand this. However, these strategies do not make the event fictional. Just the opposite, in fact. All the storytelling effects are brought into play precisely to support and emphasize the factual character of the event. It is a way of saying, "This really happened to me!"

In a somewhat similar way, the Gospel writers employ the rhetorical and narrative strategies available to them, precisely to bring out the remarkable truth of the story. One need only imagine asking them if they were writing fiction. They would be appalled at the idea. Even so, they felt obliged to interpret their story with considerable freedom.

So, while readers sometimes find it important to try to reconcile these differences, here we will try to make the most of them, with an eye to gaining an insight into the intent of each of these writers. For anyone seeking a factual report, these differences are sufficiently pronounced as to cause discomfort. But for literary studies they are the very life blood.

2. *The Gospels Are Narratives.* In itself, *narrative* simply means "something that is told." To identify stories as narratives is to highlight the fact that a narrator is involved. A storyteller is present. But as we know from our experience with gifted humorists telling a joke, the quality of storytelling makes a difference. In a similar way, a "voice" is telling the story, coloring how it is told. In a way, the narrator operates like a filter, allowing certain aspects of the story to be revealed, while causing other parts to be concealed. In a mystery story this activity of concealing and revealing serves to unfold the plot in ways that keep the readers' attention. In other cases ideological preferences may be at work.

While we are all aware of these factors, it is good to make them explicit as a part of our examination of the act of writing.

Earlier we considered the written word as a means of delivery for a story. The narrator is a central part of this delivery system. But once we start thinking about the means of delivering the story, we realize that the narrator is one part of a continuum that extends from the author to us, the readers. And first of all we need to be clear that *the narrator is not the same as the author.* The author is also part of the delivery system of the story. But the author lives (or lived) in real time, whereas the narrator lives inside a book, always there, telling the story. There are different kinds of narrators for an author to choose among. The narrator may be a central or peripheral character in the story. Or it may be an omniscient narrator telling the story from a privileged vantage point outside the action. The omniscient narrator knows the inner workings of the characters' minds, especially that of the main character, or protagonist.

The Gospel of Mark, for instance, has an omniscient narrator. The omniscient narrator knows things the normal observer could not. Consider, for instance, the prayer in the Garden of Gethsemane, which Mark quotes. None of the characters is present, and those nearest are asleep. This suggests that Mark did not get this from anyone present at the event. The simplest explanation is that the author is using the time-honored technique of the omniscient narrator. With a general idea of what happened, Mark fashions the prayer, possibly basing it on a version of the Lord's Prayer he had available to him.

But once we speak of the author, we think of the original audience. The author who lived in real time had readers who also lived in real time and were contemporaries. However, we today know nothing of them except what we can learn from the writing itself. The reader identified by way of the writing is technically called the *implied reader.* It is the reader implied by the written text. When Mark says, in a parenthetical comment, "Let the reader understand" (Mark 13:14), this would be, for us, his implied reader. The proposed identity of the implied reader is an important link to the historical setting of the writer, since it can be connected with historical aspects we know otherwise. It will prove to be of major importance in what we are doing here.

In Mark, again, the implied reader is indicated by features such as Aramaic words in the text. On the one hand, the Aramaic terms are included; on the other hand, they are translated. This suggests a diverse readership. For some, Aramaic is meaningful; for others, it requires translation. Another method for determining the implied reader would be to deduce what kind of person would have at hand the background necessary for understanding the world of this text. In this way scholars have determined, for instance, that the reader of Luke-Acts is a God-fearer (or God-worshiper), a Gentile ally and supporter of the Jewish synagogues. Only such a reader would be conversant with the range of situations required by Luke's project. Determining the implied reader is immensely helpful in situating the narrative in its message.

As just noted with the example of Luke, the narrative creates a virtual *world* in our imaginations, one that is a similar to but distinct from the real world. Selected and arranged to serve the storyteller's needs, *the world of the story* conveys a particular impression. It chooses from the real world those features that, while creating a rather complete world unto itself, still is colored through the lenses of the author's project. In the Gospels, for instance, this world contains two primary geographical settings. One is rural and called Galilee; the other is urban and called Jerusalem. These, of course, represent real places, but in the story they represent a certain set of contrasting values that shapes their meaning. For instance, it is notable that in the historical Galilee there were two major cities, Sepphoris and Tiberias. The Gospels do not mention them. Jesus is portrayed spending his time among the villages, as if that is all there is in Galilee. And this is despite the fact that Nazareth was for all practical purposes a suburb of Sepphoris and served as one of the city's support communities. But this is not the emphasis in the Gospel narratives.

3. *The Gospels Are Dramatic Narratives.* Where discussion of narrative pays attention to the delivery system of the story, the question of dramatic qualities turns attention elsewhere, to the

content that is related—the action and plot, the *content*, if you will. Strictly speaking, drama is acted out, not told by a story-teller. However, we can say that dramatic action is related by the storyteller, and that the characteristics of drama can be helpfully used to discuss the story.

To say that the Gospels have dramatic characteristics needs no defense. The proliferation of popular versions in novels, films and stage productions tell us as much. From *The Greatest Story Ever Told* of previous generations through *The Last Temptation of Christ*—both films from books—and *Godspell* and *Jesus Christ Superstar*—staged musicals, to Mel Gibson's *The Passion of the Christ*—a film—and more recent television dramas—such as *Son of God*—the Gospel story has provided the basis for compelling storytelling. All of these are testimony to the power of the narrative that is the Gospel story.

For some time now the literary aspects of the Gospel narratives have been an object of scrutiny.[9] The underlying assumption, borne out by these studies, is that the Gospels are carefully constructed accounts, arranged with deliberate art. What the studies have in common is a sensitivity to the literary qualities of the texts, including features such as narrative voice, settings, characters, and plot.

Like all stories, the Gospels involve *characters*. It must be emphasized that characters live on the page. Although they represent real people, they are selectively drawn. Characters' traits are chosen to serve the purposes of the storyteller, according to how they relate to the story and contrast with the opposing characters. For instance, the only information we have about the Gospel characters is what is needed to tell the story. We do not know what any of them, including Jesus, looked like. Whatever we know about Jesus is selected to dramatize his contrast with either his opponents or his disciples.

---

[9] A sensitivity toward the narrative quality of the Gospels is shown, for instance, in commentaries such as Luke Timothy Johnson, *Sacra Pagina: The Gospel of Luke,* vol. 3 (Collegeville, MN: Liturgical Press, 2006); and Mark W. G. Stibbe, *John's Gospel* (London: Routledge, 1994).

As we know, characters usually appear in two camps, one with which the reader sympathizes and one that the reader opposes. The main character usually belongs with the first group; that character is formally called the *protagonist*. The opposing side is that of the *antagonists*. In popular language, of course, these are known as the hero and the villain, or the good guys and the bad guys. We prefer the more neutral terms here.

Jesus is always the *protagonist*, although he is conceived differently in the different works. His *opponents* are usually members of the religious establishment. The scribes and Pharisees have this role in Mark. They are continued as such in Matthew's work, although he shifts the emphasis toward the Pharisees. Luke includes these, and adds other categories, with particular reference to lawyers (*nomikoi*). John's favorite word for the opposition is "Jews," which has given rise to no end of anguished explanations. Each of these presents special problems and needs to be viewed in terms of the individual Gospel projects.

The *disciples* take different positions in the story, sometimes as part of a subplot, as in Mark, and sometimes as a layered story, as in Matthew. These also will be discussed in their separate narratives, especially under the heading of links to the readers. The role of the disciples takes on particular interest for us, insofar as these figures in the narrative are generally presented as surrogates for the believing readers of the text. This is our piece of the action, as it were.

The characters interact in a pattern, which is the *plot*—famously described by Aristotle as having a beginning, middle, and end. One or more plot lines may be present in a single story. These plotted stories are most at home in drama, in theaters, where no narrator is present relating the action. But when a narrator is present, telling the story to us, we have dramatic narrative. Plots have some typical characteristics. In the rising action the tension builds to a turning point, after which, in the falling action, the story winds down with a certain inevitability to the conclusion, or dénouement.

The Gospels are conspicuously barren of description of persons and places, except where such information is necessary to make sense of the story. The story prevails, and the drama is the point.

Which is to say that the portrait we have of Jesus—the four portraits, actually—are not visual. They are instead the four stories themselves. The picture of Jesus is that of Jesus in action. It is this understanding that underlies the focus on dramatic narrative in this book.

What interests us for this project is the portrayal of *conflict* in the story. Central to the plot, if it is to engage us, is the development and resolution of dramatic conflict. Conflict comes in many shapes and sizes, but it is what creates the tension that keeps us interested. We want to know how it will be resolved. Or we have a suspicion as to how it will be resolved, and we want to find out if we have surmised correctly. Careful attention to the plot shows us how, when, and where the conflict develops in the rising action. It shows us where it peaks and turns the corner toward the falling action. And it allows us to perceive how it resolves the conflict, bringing the narrative to an end.

This *resolution of the conflict* is one of the main interests of this book. Our presumption concerning the conflict resolution of the narrative is that it reflects this author's image of how conflict and conflict resolution work in the real world. In each case the narrative presents a theory in action, playing it out for us. Mystery novels favor shrewd deduction as the answer to life's problems. Romance novels privilege true love. Westerns like to resolve matters with shootouts. In effect, every dramatic narrative implies a theory of how to resolve conflict.

But stories differ, as do storytellers. Just as every story implies a theory of conflict resolution, so does every storyteller favor a certain kind of conflict. Sherlock Holmes, Batman, and Miss Marple all find themselves in difficulties peculiar to their kind of story. And each has a characteristic way of dealing with it. The position taken here is that this is also true of Mark, Matthew, Luke, and John in their telling of the story of Jesus.

The *narrative contract* identifies the task that Jesus is assigned to complete in the course of the narrative. It is of interest because we may otherwise simply assume that God has sent Jesus to die a sacrificial death in order to satisfy a debt. However, the Gospels picture Jesus faced with a *specific task*. The narrative contract specifies what each particular Gospel has to say in this regard.

This term refers to an occurrence at the initial stages of a narrative. The protagonist is engaged to perform the action that unfolds in the coming story. In films, we typically witness this as the opening credits play. A particular example is found in the *Mission Impossible* series. Each episode begins with the main character, an intelligence agent, being directed to a recorded message with a voice intoning, "Your mission, if you choose to accept it, is . . ." The sentence concludes with a description of the task to be performed. The protagonist is contracted for the task. That is the narrative contract. It serves the audience by setting it up for the narrative. It explains what needs to be done. The members of the audience know what to expect, and they know when the task is achieved and the story is over.

All four of the Gospels have such moments, and they provide guidance in understanding the intent of the evangelist in telling the story of Jesus. For example, in Mark's Gospel the baptism of Jesus serves this purpose. The voice from heaven is shown citing two passages from the Old Testament, Psalm 2:7 and Isaiah 42:1. The first places Jesus in the role of Messiah; the second in the role of the Servant of Yahweh. These are contrasting roles, and Jesus is expected to work them out. The following narrative shows how that happens.

Understanding the nature of the narrative allows a clarification of its role in the Gospels. Instead of a pattern of action in which God for some mysterious reason requires Jesus to suffer, we now have a narrative contract in which God sets him on a task, and it is the task that includes risk and cost, and suffering. The suffering is a byproduct of the task, not the immediate imperative. All of the Gospel narratives share this pattern. Although liturgical or theological reasons may be given for God to be requiring crucifixion, the narratives of the Gospels do not share that outlook.

Each of the Gospels favors certain key terms to indicate the area of dispute in the conflicts in which they engage. They offer clues as to what the particular Gospel counts as the central struggle in the plot. These can be called the *terms of conflict*. These terms identify the issue at stake in the narrative conflict. They allow us to determine more precisely what each particular Gospel sees as the issue being disputed in the story. This varies from Gospel to Gospel, and it is a clue to the evangelist's center of interest.

In popular literature, for example, the terms of conflict vary depending on whether it is a romance novel, or a detective story, or some other genre. While the first may pivot on a competition between two lovers, the second more likely has to do with discovering a guilty party. An example in Mark's Gospel is his use of "holy" and "unclean." These terms are borrowed from Jewish ritual, though they had been expanded to cover most areas of life. In Mark, the terms "Holy Spirit" and "unclean spirits" become focal to his depiction of the primary conflict in the narrative. Jesus is the "holy one" who braves the risk of encountering the "unclean" in order to heal and restore. The "unclean spirits" oppose what he is doing.

4. ***The Gospels Are Counter-Narratives.*** The Gospels break the rules. They consistently refuse to follow the patterns set out by our cultural conventions for resolving conflict, whether story or in social custom. Most of the time our narratives reflect and express our social presumptions. When the Gospels deliberately depart from those conventions, we can identify areas of critical difference. We discover elements of social criticism in both the practice of Jesus and the interpretations of the Gospel writers.[10]

*A Reading Strategy*

In any program of interpreting a narrative text in terms of its contexts, both scriptural and political, a *reading strategy* is necessary.

---

[10] Pierre Maranda and Elli Köngäs-Maranda, *Structural Analysis of Oral Tradition,* University of Pennsylvania Publications in Folklore and Folklife, no. 3 (Philadelphia: University of Pennsylvania Press, 1971). See also, Beck, *Nonviolent Story*, chap. 7.

In the present instance, that strategy means reading the Gospel text against the presumptions of culture, whether ancient or modern. Typically, the manner in which a piece of writing breaks conventions is more instructive than the way that it follows them. In that sense the Gospels can be seen as *counter-narratives*, since they can be shown to break expected patterns. This is the reason for our attempt to identify key expected patterns of these narratives. In the following chapters we pay attention to how a Gospel narrative refuses certain expected moves in resolving its conflicts.

At certain moments, as a narrative moves toward closure, two changes are apt to happen. One concerns the "hero"; the other concerns the "villain." These are also the keys to the ways in which the Gospels diverge them from their expected course.

A common pattern is that of *poetic justice,* evident in social interactions as well as in popular forms of narrative. Villains are given a taste of the damage to which they have been subjecting others. The liar is deceived; the bully humiliated. In stories that feature violence, this means that the violent character experiences reciprocal violence and is often dispatched in that way.

This pattern involves the transformation of the hero. Up until this point this character was identified by a refusal to participate in the kind of wrongdoing that characterized the villain. This nonparticipation is the hero's main claim to virtue. But at a certain point in the story there comes a time, after a painful search of conscience, when the hero changes his or her approach and decides to give the villain a "taste of his own medicine." For this, the hero has to act like the villain, contradicting the hero's characteristic manner of being. In the case of violent stories, this means the violent villain is treated with violence. This so-called poetic justice, of course, needs to be distinguished from actual justice. Another name for it, in actual life and history, is retribution, or what we often call payback. This is the pattern that the just-war theory attempts to control, even while conceding the impossibility of eliminating it. In actual fact it usually sets the stage for another move in the cycle of violence, as the opposition now prepares to avenge its wounds.

*Purge: The Villain Depersonalized*

A second change likely to occur in conventional narrative affects the villain. Here another transformation occurs. Toward the end of the story, this character typically becomes thoroughly identified with the evil he has been causing, that is, completely *depersonalized.* It is as if the character and the character's set of traits reverse positions. Or as if a noun and an adjective switched places. The character becomes simply a face for the evil to be erased from the world of the story. This makes it possible to have a "happy" ending simply by disposing of the villain, the more permanently, the better. Thus, the contaminating evil is stemmed, the world of the story is cleansed. This purgation of evil from the story world is what "happily ever after" means. It can be called a purge, as a partner to payback. In the pages of history it is called ethnic cleansing or scorched earth. It attempts to control the future by eliminating any possibility of repeating the harm. Of course, it does nothing of the kind, and in fact ensures lasting and deep resentment and avowed retribution. This energy maintains feuds and other patterns of reciprocal violence.

This is the pattern that nonviolent action refuses, and this study tries to find where the Gospel narratives draw back from the common cultural expectations. Those expectations are typically shown in story forms and patterns that express the language and values of the culture. The procedure followed here is to present the Gospel narrative in contrast to a pertinent story pattern that is overturned or refused by the Gospel.

5. ***The Gospel Narratives in the Times They Were Written.*** There is one more move to be taken. It is here that we engage the recent studies in historical, archeological, and sociological disciplines, noted at the beginning of this chapter. In the case of the Gospels we can take advantage of the current renewed attention to the historical conditions that affect the writer. Whereas historical interest in previous eras of biblical study focused on the historical value of the Gospel accounts themselves, the more recent attention considers the surrounding conditions that serve as background to

the writing. It draws attention to the events of the time, especially in the ways that narrative and events can interact.

Viewing the Gospels as narratives invites us to look at each of them as a whole. Viewing them for their dramatic qualities allows us to see how they present and resolve conflict in the narrative. Viewing them in the historical context of their time of writing allows us to understand them as they relate to the historical struggles that serve as backdrop to their narratives, often presenting alternatives contrary to the prevailing impulses of the times.

So it is that the following chapters consider the conflicts contemporary to the writing as the background, both in the deep sense of long-range background and the more immediate influence of the near background. In this regard the historical record that has been invaluable for reconstructing the times is the work of Flavius Josephus, a contemporary of the evangelists, whose two volumes, *The Wars of the Jews* and *The Antiquities of the Jews,* chronicle these events. While Josephus's witness of the events is strongly slanted in favor of the established powers and his own self-interest, once his biases are taken into account his contribution is unparalleled.[11]

It must be clearly reasserted that the historical setting of the narrative differs from the world of the story. The world of the story is a projection of the narrative; the historical background is the world into which the narrative fits and comments upon. The world of the Gospel story shows Galilee as consisting of villages only. The historical world as revealed by witnesses such as Josephus and archeological findings shows Galilee as containing two significant cities that dominated the economy of the territory, including that of the villages. Looking at both together, we can understand how the Gospels present Jesus as revitalizing the villages, given the conditions that we need to recover, but that the original readers would already know.

The relationship between the story and the world in which that story is told is true of any narrative production. In the case of the Gospels it explains why there are four and not just one. Subsequent

---

[11] *The New Complete Works of Josephus*, trans. William Whiston, commentary Paul L. Maier (Grand Rapids, MI: Kregel Publications, 1999).

circumstances and different conditions called forth newer versions to fit subsequent and different needs. Why did Matthew and Luke find it necessary to write other Gospels, if there were not new conditions demanding a new reading of the story of Jesus? Add to that the fact that the Gospels include references to matters of concern to the writer and his time. This in itself indicates a relationship between the act of writing and the conditions in which the writing took place.

## THE FOLLOWING CHAPTERS

Each of the subsequent chapters will investigate a separate Gospel—Mark, Matthew, Luke-Acts, and John. In general, we consider three things: the narrative as narrative; the dramatic qualities of the story told; and the historical setting of the writer. The historical setting typically concerns a crisis of the time, which the writer addresses with his work. Each of the following chapters has four parts: a proposal for the evangelist's project, as situated in the crisis of the times; a description of the story's narrative conflict as told by the evangelist; the resolution of conflict as presented in this particular Gospel; plus a final assessment in terms of nonviolence theory.

Our assumption is that each of the Gospels tells the story of Jesus in its own way, with its own emphasis. The combined story with which we are familiar, in which the various Gospel accounts are called upon to contribute traits for a composite narrative of Jesus, is not given here. Instead, we understand that there are four stories of Jesus, each with its own integrity. These need to be described for the insights they offer.

We will take up the Gospels one by one, examining each through the features that we have named here, starting with Mark's Gospel. It is accepted that Mark initiated the Gospel narrative project, and Matthew and Luke borrowed his narrative as the foundation of their own. This conclusion, made from close philological study, is even more obvious when examined in terms of the narrative. Mark, then, appears in the following chapter as the birth of the Gospel narrative. This text sets the frame of the story and deserves attention to the terms that it sets for the rest, as well as for itself. Mark's Gospel is closest to a story of nonviolent confrontation. For this reason its moves and assumptions are worth noting.

The Gospel of Matthew is treated in Chapter 3. In many ways Matthew's Gospel text is closest to that of Mark. Like Mark, this Gospel can be seen as crisis literature. Written in the aftermath of the Temple destruction, it addresses the trauma of loss and the need for a new direction. As the most explicitly Jewish of the Gospels, it looks to the future of a seemingly demolished Judaism, making a case for the Jesus movement. Here the nonviolent conflict-resolution pattern of Mark is more narrowly focused on the moment of response, not on retaliation.

In Chapter 4, Luke's Gospel is considered in conjunction with the Acts of the Apostles, following current assessment that they form a unified project. Any consideration of the narrative as a whole by necessity must then take into consideration the full project. For Luke, the identification of the implied reader is especially important, as we trace the movement of the Jesus community into the public arena of the larger world. Luke's primary contribution is his insistence on challenging cultural values, whether those of Judaism or of the Roman Empire.

John's Gospel is different from the others. The approach taken in Chapter 5 understands this Gospel to present an image of God as affected by the story and ministry of Jesus. In effect, the Gospel is a "re-theologizing" of the divine image. The narrative of the Word becoming incarnate unfolds along with the political story of Jesus of Nazareth. The logic of violence and the logic of nonviolent love play out in their separate registers.

In each case we look at the way the Gospel narrative develops its central conflict, using the "tools" mentioned above. The narrative contract—or mandate of the protagonist, Jesus—is identified, along with the special language used by this particular Gospel to name that central conflict. The concept of the implied reader allows us to place the narrative in the social setting of the writing—the conflict faced by the writer and his community.

This study leads to an understanding of the manner in which the narrative conflict resolution of each Gospel operates and how this contributes to an understanding of engaging in conflict without abandoning the demands that love makes upon Christians.

Throughout this book the Gospels are viewed as examples of a *literature of resistance.* What do we mean by *resistance,* a pervasive and somewhat slippery word? Here Thomas Merton's definition is relevant: "the defense of the dignity and rights of man against the encroachments and brutality of massive power structures which threaten either to enslave him or to destroy him, while exploiting him in their conflicts with one another."[12]

With the Gospels the political is not "politics as usual." Rather, it is a revision of the notion of social power in light of the Suffering Servant. It is not a flight from political activity, but rather a reworking of it. The consistent view taken here is that each Gospel narrative refuses something that is a constant in the cultural narrative it edits; it rejects something in the conventions of the culture. Insofar as the cultural solution to differences is force and violence, the cultural narratives reinforce this solution. But the Gospel narratives refuse it. It begins with Mark, and the others pick up on it, sending it in different directions.

The Gospel narrative is also a witness of the Divine moving into history. Religion in this sense is not separate from politics but both supports and judges it.

---

[12] Thomas Merton, "Toward a Theology of Resistance," in *Faith and Violence: Christian Teaching and Christian Practice* (Notre Dame, IN: University of Notre Dame Press, 1964), 4.

# 2

## Mark

### MARK'S PROJECT:
### THE RESISTANCE CAMPAIGN

Mark's Gospel is the first. We do not know who "Mark" was, only that this Gospel is attributed to him. There are more than forty early documents to which we give the title gospel. Four of them, however, are complete narratives and part of the New Testament. Mark's is the first. The Gospel tradition of narrative begins here, and for us the name Mark designates the inventor of the narrative gospel.[1]

What are we to make of this work? Christians have traditionally used this Gospel for devotional purposes, and it rewards that effort. That would suggest that Mark wrote for just this purpose. But in

---

[1] Earlier explorations in the narrative conflict of Mark are Robert R. Beck, *Nonviolent Story: Narrative Conflict Resolution in the Gospel of Mark,* chap. 7 (Eugene, OR: Wipf and Stock, 2009; Maryknoll, NY: Orbis Books, 1996); idem, *Banished Messiah: Violence and Nonviolence in Matthew's Story of Jesus* (Eugene, OR: Wipf and Stock, 2010), chap. 2. A benchmark study is that of Ched Myers, *Binding the Strong Man: A Political Reading of Mark's Story of Jesus* (Maryknoll, NY: Orbis Books, 1988). For a book useful in sorting out Mark issues from a theological viewpoint, see Eugene Boring, *Mark: A Commentary* (Nashville, TN: Westminster/John Knox Press, 2006). And for a groundbreaking narrative study, see David Rhoads, Joanna Dewey, and Donald Michie, *Mark as Story: An Introduction to the Narrative of a Gospel* (Minneapolis, MN: Fortress Press, 2012).

a similar way, fruitful liturgical use suggests a liturgical purpose for the work. Scholars also find success with theological readings. They study certain specifics, perhaps the sayings of Jesus, or maybe his titles. And yet, what is left unaccounted for is the arc of the entire narrative, its larger contours and trajectory. What happens when we look at the whole in its dramatic movement?

One effect that Mark has achieved by putting Jesus in a dramatic narrative is to suggest a purpose for Jesus's mission. We do not encounter a God who sent him to suffer and die, as if to balance some arbitrary ledger of debt and pain. Rather, we follow the story of one called to a difficult task that risks serious danger from hardened opponents. Mark has constructed a narrative with conflict development and resolution. The response to violent opposition is nonviolent resistance. Jesus of Nazareth, the protagonist in this narrative, assumes the initiative, responding to what he perceives as violation. Taking the well-known Messianic Secret of Mark not as a theological datum, but as a narrative strategy of unfolding his identity, *Jesus is shown to be a non-royal, people's messiah*, acting in marked contrast to the violent options favored at the time.

## Questions of Mark's Genre, His Time, and His Readers

What kind of writing is this? The question of Mark's genre of writing continues to elude scholars, as does the location from which he writes. Following certain recent studies, the position taken here is that this Gospel was written for circulation among the early churches. It can best be described as a resistance tract based on the example of Jesus. Written during the events known as the Great Revolt, 66–70 CE, it positions itself both in terms of the resistance movements in Galilee, with its signs prophets, social bandits, and popular messiahs (Mark 1—8), and in terms of the final revolt in Jerusalem (Mark 9—16).

Mark's story covers a time period of less than a year. It moves from the early work in the villages of Galilee toward Jerusalem, where it ends. Instead of regular visits to the city suggested by

Luke and John, and as we would realistically expect of pious Jews, we have a single movement toward the city that gives shape to the whole story. Mark is in control of his material, and this abbreviated narrative is intentional, presenting a problem to be solved. Its narrow focus needs to be accounted for, and this raises the question of genre.

Most recently, the question of genre has tended toward that of Hellenistic biography.[2] But the shape of this story is a problem. This Gospel is written in Koine, the common Greek of the street, rather than literary Greek. This suggests that Mark is not an example of high culture but rather exists at the level of popular works.

If the Gospel is a portrait of Jesus of Nazareth, it is not a visual portrait. The picture of Jesus is given in the action of the narrative, in its movement from villages to city, from edge to center. Read as a continuous narrative, the Gospel has the shape of a *campaign* rather than a life story. It evokes, in fact, certain campaigns of conquest, such as that of Herod the Great, who secured the outposts of unrest in Galilee before he moved on to Jerusalem to claim his kingship. It reflects the pattern of certain rebellions, such as that of John of Gischala, who moved from uprisings in Galilee to being a leader of the Great Revolt in Jerusalem.[3]

Unrest was characteristic of the time of Mark's writing and in the lives of his intended readers. Indications of an awareness of the final days of Jerusalem and its Temple, in Mark 13, suggests the Gospel was written during the times of the Great Revolt and last days of Jerusalem. A consensus among biblical scholars, working with certain written collections of stories and sayings of Jesus, dates Mark's writing at approximately 65–70 CE. This view of his

---

[2] See, for instance, David E. Aune, *The New Testament in Its Literary Environment* (Nashville, TN: Westminster/John Knox Press, 1985), 46.

[3] The story of John of Gischala is found in David M. Rhoads, *Israel in Revolution, 6–74 CE: A Political History Based on the Writings of Josephus* (Minneapolis, MN: Fortress Press, 1976), 122–35. The story of Herod's rise to power is contained in Books 14–15 of *The New Complete Works of Josephus*, trans. William Whiston, commentary Paul L. Maier (Grand Rapids, MI: Kregel Publications, 1999).

authorship sees Matthew and Luke making subsequent use of copies of Mark's written text, repurposed for their different situations. While more precise dating is debated, we know enough to realize the question of how Mark's narrative relates to those tumultuous events cannot be evaded.

*A Resistance Tract*

Efforts to identify the site of Mark's writing continue to be as elusive as the genre. Theories of implied readership have vacillated among possible communities; Rome, Syria, and Galilee all have adherents. The text presents problems in this regard. The remarkable aside in 13:14—"let the reader understand"—which is the only place in which the implied reader is explicitly addressed, comes in the context of the final struggle of Jerusalem. This argues a location nearby. And yet, the frequent translations of Aramaic terms into Greek implies a location away from Palestine, such as Rome.[4]

Other recent studies have questioned the assumption that a single church community was the provenance of the Gospel.[5] Making the assumption that the early communities were in touch with one another, this view explains how Mark's Gospel could have been available for use by Matthew and Luke. It also answers the problem of mixed signals in the text about the reader, since it would have been designed for readers in different locations. In

---

[4] Proposed locations include not only Rome (Winn), the site that tradition has assigned, but also Galilee (Roskam), or most recently, Syria (Marcus). See Adam Winn, "Resisting Honor: The Markan Secrecy Motif and Roman Political Ideology," *Journal of Biblical Literature* 133, no. 3 (Fall 2014): 594; Hendrika N. Roskam, *The Purpose of the Gospel of Mark in Its Historical and Social Context* (Boston: Brill, 2004); Joel Marcus, *Mark 1—8: A New Translation with Introduction and Commentary*, Anchor Yale Bible Commentaries (New York: Doubleday, 2002).

[5] Boring, *Mark,* 15. This is based on Richard Bauckham, "For Whom Were Gospels Written?" in *The Gospel for All Christians: Rethinking the Gospel Audiences,* ed. Richard Bauckham (Grand Rapids, MI: Eerdmans, 1998), 12.

fact, the intended reader would be anyone in a position of resistance. This could be Palestine, Rome, or elsewhere.

Current considerations include the possibility that the Gospel was written to be circulated. Apparently it was, since Matthew and Luke used it. Internal indications also include signals to both native Aramaic readers and non-Aramaic readers. Palestinian Jewish customs are explained, and yet the reader is warned about events in Jerusalem. From this and the previous arguments it can be considered a tract for resistance, written for Jesus-followers, wherever they find the model pertinent.

A distinct feature of this Gospel is the call for disciples to follow Jesus. Following him means reenacting his narrative. It means to follow him through his work, all the way to Jerusalem, in the manner of blind Bartimaeus of Jericho: "He received his sight and followed him on the way" (10:52). We can conclude that the genre of Mark's Gospel is that of a resistance tract, dramatizing the pattern of nonviolent resistance for Jesus's disciples.

*A Constructed Literary Whole*

Although written in the common language of the people, Mark's Gospel is artfully constructed. We need to elaborate this point, to show that the evangelist's control extends to the entire narrative. First, we go behind the scenes, in a sense, to watch Mark putting his work together. Later, we look at the dramatic shape of the written result.

We tend to read the Gospel as if it were a candid report of an eyewitness to the events. But if we are to realize the extent of his deliberate effort, it is important to show that this is not the case. Mark's Gospel is a carefully considered, artful narrative construction; it is shaped to make a statement. As a narrative, it was sufficiently powerful to persuade both Matthew and Luke to borrow it for the underlying narrative of their own accounts.

But what did Mark use for his sources? This first Gospel narrative was constructed from written collections of stories and available sayings. Scraps of oral memories were eventually written down in collections, where they were available to Mark.

Like a quilter making something new and engaging from those pieces, something carefully planned and beautifully executed, Mark constructed his Gospel. He is the inventor of the form. His method was to juxtapose episodes and teachings in a sequence that tells a story of Jesus's work up to his death. While the narrative is constructed by means of pairing units to build up sequences, Mark himself provided the overall plan. That plan is both simple and dramatic. In its simplest terms, it tells of a mission in Galilee followed by a turn toward Jerusalem to confront the authorities in the Temple. In the first part Jesus is shown addressing the travails of his day; in the second, he turns from symptoms to causes, challenging the source of the malaise.

A brief examination shows the artistry and inventiveness of Mark's narrative. A fundamental feature is the use of dual features. These characterize the text from the smallest level, as in the call of the four disciples, given in pairs (1:16–20), to the largest, as in the twice-told account of the multiplication of the loaves and fishes. The consistency of such duality throughout Mark's text argues for its integrity and originality, showing a wholeness and a consistent concept behind the writing.

*Double Features*

Parallel passages can be used to provide similar beginnings or endings. For example, the call of Peter and Andrew, James and John (1:16–20)—a doubled account in itself—introduces a set of stories showing the work of Jesus, while the call of Levi (2:13–14), using the same language and form, introduces some reactions against that work. Alternatively, binary forms can be used as a bracket for part of the text. The four apostles named in the call at 1:16–20 appear together as a foursome at only one other time. In Mark 13:3 they are present at the farewell discourse of Jesus to his disciples. This takes us from call to farewell, hello to goodbye. Similar patterning can be shown in every part of the Gospel. The entire work of Mark is skillfully constructed, with each part linked to other parts, making a coherent whole.

*Chiastic Patterns*

Mark's method was to set up similar episodes in contrast, placed inside other similar episodes. These can used to build mirror constructions that have been called chiastic forms, from the term *chiasmus.* In cursive, the Greek letter *Chi* looks like an "X," which describes the form visually. The basic pattern is *a-b-b'-a'*; there can be variations on the pattern. Thus, Mark 2:27:

> "The sabbath (a) was made for humanity (b),
> not humanity (b') for the sabbath (a').

But this technique is also used to construct the larger arrangements, seen already in the opening fifteen verses.

A  Gospel (1:1)
  B  Wilderness (1:2–4)
    C  Jordan (1:5–7)
      D  Baptism (1:8a)
      D' Baptism (1:8b)      - "Holy Spirit (1:8b)
    C' Jordan (1:9–11)      - "Spirit" (1:10)
  B' Wilderness (1:12–13)     - "Spirit" (1:12)
A' Gospel (1:14–15)

The theme of the Gospel (Mark 1:1, 14–15) brackets a set of mirrored verses. They turn on verse 8, where John contrasts his baptism (with water) with the one to come, baptizing in fire and Spirit. In verses 2–7 John is featured, first in the desert (2–4) and then at the Jordan River (5–7). After the turning point we learn about Jesus, reversing the pattern—first at the Jordan (9–11) and then in the desert (12–13). Furthermore, closer examination reveals that the individual parts of this passage also repeat the same pattern.

This kind of patterning shapes Mark's entire Gospel text. Another example, to our possible surprise, is the crucifixion scene, again constructed according to balanced chiastic principles. We are accustomed to viewing this event as akin to a bystander report, even though the account itself says that none of the disciples was present. But consider instead what Mark has achieved here. Five scenes form a mirror sequence. It resembles an artistic altarpiece. At the edges of the picture, beginning and ending the account, we have faithful followers: Simon of Cyrene (15:21) and the women (15:40–41), all parents of persons known to Mark's readers. In the center we have a scene that takes place about noon: the mockery of the passers-by (29–30) and the chief priests and scribes (31–32a) is enclosed by the notice of the two thieves (27, 32b), who join in the mockery. Articulated by the outer frame of Simon and the women and the central scene of mockery are two major scenes: the crucifixion at nine o'clock (22—26) and the death of Jesus at three o'clock (33—39). Each follows the same pattern, also a mirror form: text/symbol/symbol/text. The first text is an Aramaicism (*Golgotha / Eloi, Eloi lama sabachthani*). The first symbol is a drink of wine; the second is a cloth, untorn (cloak) and torn (Temple veil). These symbols echo the sayings on cloaks and wineskins in 2:21–22. The final text is a title for Jesus: "King of the Jews" (26) and "Son of God" (39).

Similar formatting is seen on a larger scale, and could be demonstrated at length, in each part.[6] The Gospel commonly has been discussed as divided neatly into two parts, distinct from each other but with many similar features. Galilee is the site of Mark 1—8, while Jerusalem becomes the center in Mark 9—16. And though the two have many parallel or contrasting features, each retains a solid identity of its own.[7]

The effort Mark put into his writing is evident in these patterns. They deserve to be taken seriously. They will guide us in interpreting Mark's work.

---

[6] See Beck, *Nonviolent Story*, 43–56.

[7] Ched Myers identifies "constitutive elements" in the two parts. He states that these do not represent the sequence of the unfolding narrative, but rather represent a structural model (Myers, *Binding the Strong Man*, 112). Eugene Boring offers a similar but different set of parallels (*Mark*, 4).

A  Simon of Cyrene (father of Alexander and Rufus)  (15:21)

B  Crucifixion (3rd hour—15:22–26)

a  (Aramaic) Title translated (*Golgotha*)

b  Drink (wine with myrrh)

b'  Cloth (divided
garments)                              - "crucified him (v. 24)

a'  (Roman) Title for Jesus
(Pilate: King of Jews)        - "crucified him (v. 25)

C  Mocking (to the 6th hour—15:26–32)

a  Two bandits crucified with him

b  Mockery of passers-by: destroy the Temple; save
yourself

b'  Mockery of priests and scribes: Messiah, cannot
save yourself

a'  Mockery of two bandits

B'  Death (9th hour—15:31–39)

a  (Aramaic) Title translated (*Eloi, eloi* . . .)

b  Drink (sour wine)

b'  Cloth (Temple veil)       - "breathed his last" (v. 37)

a'  (Roman) Title for Jesus (Centurion:
Son of God)                      - "breathed his last" (v. 39)

A'  Women observing (incl. mother of James the Less, Joses)

## Mark's Gospel in Its Historical Context

If we recognize the deliberate artistry of Mark's work, we may well ask what prompted him to put such effort into this textual witness to Jesus's story. Part of the answer can be found in the events taking place during Mark's time. In recent years efforts in the realms of archeology and history have revealed to us riches of background information that would have been common knowledge in the days the Gospels were being written. For perhaps the first time since then, we can get a sense of how the Gospels confront the assumptions of their times.

*Archeology in Galilee*

Archeology has revealed some of the causes of unrest during these times of political, cultural, and religious tensions. In Galilee, the importance of the cities of Sepphoris and Tiberias, unmentioned in the Gospel, emerges with greater clarity. These cities were projects of Herod Antipas during the time of Jesus. He rebuilt Sepphoris after Rome destroyed it in retribution for an uprising upon the death of Herod the Great. The younger Herod also founded Tiberias on the shore of the lake, in imitation of his father's founding of Caesarea Maritime on the shore of the Mediterranean. Sepphoris and Tiberius, like Herod's Caesarea and Jerusalem Temple, participated in the pattern of establishing building projects in the imperial style. They were blatant advertisements for the glory of Rome. Land was requisitioned to feed the cities, with peasant holdings turned into large agricultural estates. Peasants found themselves reduced from owners to tenant farmers, at best, or hired hands on the lands they formerly owned. Some lost everything, and with that the rise of social banditry appeared in an attempt to recoup losses. Taxation dictated the need for coinage, converting value into a form that could cross distances without spoilage. The method of paying in kind, the familiar reciprocity of barter, wouldn't do for sending tribute off to Rome. And furthermore, coins could carry the image of the emperor as a constant reminder of the imperial occupation.[8]

Biblical testimony also appears in the form of another Gospel source, shared by Matthew and Luke. This is the Q document, which, is typically dated earlier than Mark and believed to have originated in Galilee. While it is not used by Mark, it can still help us understand what is occurring in the background of Mark's story. Its presentations of the teachings of Jesus imply dire economic conditions, with people in need unable to repay debts and with divisions among neighbors that are intensifying.[9] The parables of

---

[8] Jonathan L. Reed, *Archaeology and the Galilean Jesus* (Harrisburg, PA: Trinity Press International, 2002), gives a detailed picture of first-century Galilee as discovered through archeology. For the significance of the Q Source (or Sayings Source) and its Galilean origins, see Reed, 170–96.

[9] Sean Freyne, *The Jesus Movement and Its Expansion: Meaning and Mission* (Grand Rapids, MI: Eerdmans, 2014), chap. 6.

Jesus imply a similar situation, evoking the experiences of hired laborers who no longer work their own land. Jesus's beatitudes and woes, his teachings of love of neighbor, of settling disputes, of forgiveness—all these imply a beleaguered village life.

Historians, particularly Flavius Josephus, confirm this picture with names and incidents. The Jewish historian Josephus, as he is generally called, has proved indispensable for our understanding of these times. A Pharisee, scholar, and Judean of some political importance, he lived from 37 CE to approximately 100 CE, making him a contemporary of the Gospel writers. Josephus wrote about the history of the Jews and devoted a special volume to the Jewish-Roman wars of his time. He was ambitious and pro-Roman, and he used his writing to argue his case. Once we account for his biases, we can make use of his reports.

*Brigands*. Following the lead of Horsley,[10] it is common to discuss the resistance described by Josephus under three headings: bandits, prophets, and messiahs. The bandits (or brigands) were peasants from the countryside who had lost their land. They turned to reprisals. As such, they are frequently referred to as *social* bandits. The better known were in Galilee. In the time of Herod the Great, the Galilean cave brigands famously resisted central control. Josephus claims Herod tamed them, but doubts remain about this. Others of note were Eleazar ben Dinai in Transjordan, who was active in the 30s–50s CE, and Tholomaus in the early 40s CE, in Idumea. During the Great Revolt the Sicarii and the Zealots were drawn from these ranks. A notable example is the Galilean John of Gischala.

*Prophets*. The so-called signs prophets were individuals from among the common people.[11] They represented a nonviolent witness to the social unrest. Announcing a looming turn of events,

---

[10] Richard A. Horsley, *Bandits, Prophets, and Messiahs: Popular Movements at the Time of Jesus* (New York: Bloomsbury T & T Clark, 1999). See also Rhoads, *Israel in Revolution, 6–74 CE*, 160–62.

[11] Rebecca Gray, *Prophetic Figures in Late Second Temple Jewish Palestine: The Evidence from Josephus* (New York: Oxford University Press, 1993), 112–44. Also P. W. Barnett, "The Jewish Sign Prophets—AD 40–70 Their Intentions and Origin," *New Testament Studies* 27, no. 5 (October 1981): 679–97.

they typically called followers out to the desert, the Jordan River, or some other suggestive locale, evoking Moses or Joshua, and symbolizing a need for a new beginning. Typically, the Roman army, which allowed no hint of dissent, would follow and slaughter them.

Examples of such figures span the times. Theudas (ca. 45 CE), promised the waters of the Jordan would part as they did for Joshua. His followers were imprisoned, and he was beheaded. He is mentioned in Acts 5:36. Another, the "Egyptian" (ca. 56 CE), apparently came to Jerusalem, gathered followers, and led them to the Mount of Olives to watch the walls of Jerusalem fall, like ancient Jericho. He is mentioned in Acts 21:38. Others include "the Samaritan" (ca. 25–36 CE); and Jesus, son of Hannah (62–69 CE), who went to the Temple. Josephus also mentions a few he does not name during the time of the Roman governors Felix (52–60 CE) and Festus (60–62 CE), as well as during the Great Revolt in 70 CE. Josephus cites John the Baptist as a prominent example of this type. He reports that John was executed by Herod Antipas, who feared he might inspire an uprising.[12]

*Messiahs.* The messiahs, like the prophets, were popular figures from humble origins.[13] But they differed from the prophets in that they made political claims and favored the use of force. Popular messiahs were more likely to appear in times of explicit uprising. Some examples of popular kingship include Judas, son of Hezekiah (ca. 4 BCE) in Galilee (Sepphoris); Simon (ca. 4 BCE) in Judea; Athronges (ca. 4–27 BCE) in Judea; Menahem, son of Judas the Galilean (ca. 66 CE), in Masada; and Simon bar Giora (68–70 CE) in Jerusalem.

## Brigands, Prophets, and Messiahs in Mark

Mark is aware of this aspect of life in the countryside of Galilee and Judea. He places Jesus in direct comparison with the social bandits by his use of the term *lestes*. As Josephus uses it, this

---

[12] Josephus, *Antiquities* 18.5.2, 116–19.
[13] Horsley, *Bandits, Prophets, and Messiahs*, 88–111.

word carries an undercurrent of violence. *Lestes* appears three times in Mark's Gospel, twice as an accusatory label for Jesus, and a third time when he is crucified between two bandits (11:17; 14:48; 15:27).

We can add to this picture the appearance on the scene of Barabbas, the condemned person traded for Jesus in his trial before Pilate, a figure who is identified as an "insurrectionist" *(sustasias-tés)*. This is a term Josephus reserves for insurgents from the city who joined in the revolt of 66–70 CE. Mark makes it clear that the comparison of Jesus with Barabbas is misguided, but he also demonstrates that the comparison can be made, and probably was.

Mark also aligns Jesus with the prophets, at least in the beginning. He shows him with John in the desert at the time of his baptism. But Jesus makes his crucial move from the desert to the villages of Galilee, with its critical shift in emphasis from sign to restorative action. The entire first half of the Gospel shows him active in works of healing and renewal among the villages. It is also significant that after the account of John's death, Mark shows Jesus leading people into the desert, where they are fed through marvelous means.

Jesus is explicitly identified as a messiah by Peter, and he dies with the title "King of the Jews" posted on the cross.

Mark's presentation of Jesus during his time in Galilee puts emphasis on his miraculous deeds, with a primary emphasis on healing. These are shown as acts restoring the community, an interpretation reinforced by his use of biblical quotations.

### The First Rebellion (66–68 CE)

Tension would build and wane, but eventually it blew wide open in the Great Revolt of 66–70 CE.[14] The revolt came in two waves. The first came with the original uprising. Unrest was already in the air. The revolt began when the Romans ruthlessly put down

---

[14] This description follows the account of Myers in *Binding the Strongman*, 64–69. A more detailed report is that of Rhoads in *Israel in Revolution 6–74 CE,* esp. chaps. 3–5.

protests against Gessius Florus, the Roman procurator in Jerusalem (64–66 CE), who had attempted, on orders from Nero, to extract funds from the Temple treasury. The priests were radicalized, and all Gentile offerings were refused, including those offered for the Roman Empire and emperor. This amounted to a declaration of war. The point of no return was reached when a provisional government was formed.

An unstable coalition formed when factions with different agendas joined the revolt. A rapid and volatile series of events followed. Under Eleazar, son of Ananias, Temple captain, the lower-class priests expelled the traditional priestly elite, sparking civil war. The Sicarii ("Daggers") arrived in support of Eleazar, further radicalizing matters by bringing into the mix the uncompromising ideology of the Zealots, which Josephus referred to as the "fourth philosophy": "No Lord but God." At this point they dislodged the priest leaders and burned the debt records. A Sicarius leader, Menahem, took control of the revolt and presented himself as king. He was rejected, and the Sicarii escaped to Masada. Eleazar regained control. The Roman garrison was given safe passage to leave but was treacherously slaughtered as it departed.

The Roman army's attempt to put the uprising down somehow failed, and the Romans retired. The traditional elite leadership, previously dislodged, now returned and managed to take control again. Another Eleazar, son of Simon, assumed leadership for the traditional priests and attempted to manage the situation and channel the rebellious energies, with an eye to negotiating a peace with Rome. It was at this time that Josephus, one of the elite, was sent to organize the uneasy situation in Galilee. The first wave ebbed.

*The Second Rebellion (69–70 CE)*

Although the revolt was in a holding pattern, things were not at rest. Brigand groups in the countryside continued their sporadic efforts. The Roman army aggressively rooted out opposition in the land, sparing only those in full collaboration with Rome. This, in turn, generated stronger and more extreme resistance. Many of the brigands involved escaped to Jerusalem, where the second wave was building.

The second overt rebellion was brutal and largely chaotic. In the winter of 67–68 CE, it erupted with the forming of a Zealot coalition under Eleazar ben Simon. Paying off old debts, the coalition began a violent purge of the aristocracy, prompting a wholesale departure. This reign of terror revealed that the revolt was in part a class war, with the commoners against the aristocracy, the rural against the urban. The Zealots rejected the priests and named a peasant with no qualifications or heritage as the high priest. A second civil war forced the Zealots back into the Temple area. The Zealots called for help from the Idumeans, who helped reestablish Zealot control for a time. But more purges, this time of the former leaders of the provisional government, resulted in the Idumeans pulling out.

Struggle for control broke the rebel forces into three groups— the Zealots in the Temple area; John of Gischala, a brigand chief from Galilee, leading a force in the city but outside the Temple area; and a certain Simon bar Giora, outside the city, with large forces and the support of what was left of the old guard. The Temple stood as the symbol of control.

The second wave ended with the siege of Jerusalem under the Roman general Titus. The warring factions were forced to cooperate, but the Romans sealed off the city. The lack of supplies, and the resulting starvation, brought about the end. The Temple was burned to the ground and the city plundered, the rebel leaders were executed, and the population was enslaved. The Roman army continued on to the Essene community at Qumran and the barricaded Sicarii at Masada to complete the conquest. In commemoration of the victory, the Triumphal Arch of Titus was erected in Rome by Domitian in 81 CE.

Just as Mark's account of the Galilee ministry of Jesus reflects the activity of the brigands, prophets, and messiahs of Galilee, so the Jerusalem section of the Gospel seems to resonate with themes and events of the Great Revolt in that city. Most commentators date the writing of the Gospel sometime during that time. Again, as with the Galilee events, the action of Jesus stands in dramatic contrast to the political events of the time.

## MARK'S STORY:
## THE PEOPLE'S MESSIAH

Once we have seen the craft of Mark's composition and the background of his historical setting, we can turn to a description of the narrative itself. In reading Mark's Gospel we should be conscious of his intent to present an argument on two fronts.

1. *Jesus's program stands in contrast to the violent revolutionaries, on the one hand.* It is in this regard that the background given above is useful for the reader today. Here the contrast is one of methods, violent and nonviolent.

2. *On the other hand, his efforts contrast with another form of resistance, namely, that presented by the purity rules of the Pharisees.* Modeled after the holiness regulations of the priests, the Pharisees expanded them to cover all Israel in response to the presence of the Gentile invasion in their midst. In this case the ritual language of "holy" and "unclean" provides Mark with a set of conflict terms that bring the narrative to a dramatic climax.

The first set distinguishes Jesus's nonviolent method from violent alternatives; the second contrasts his inclusion of outsiders—in contrast to policies of exclusion—as a path to social healing. Both enter the description that follows, but they have different impacts on Mark's narrative.

### Mark's Drama

A simplified version of a common outline of the Gospel gives us an initial image of the work as a whole, with its two main parts.

**Introduction: John the Baptist (1:1–15)**

I. Galilee
> A. The first week (1:16—3:6)
> B. The new family (3:7—6:6)
> C. The widening circle (6:7—8:30)

II. Jerusalem
> A. The road to the city (8:31—10:52)
> B. Confrontation (11—13)
> C. Passion, death, empty tomb (14—16)

While such an outline helps to orient us in navigating our way around the work, we should remember that a topic outline is more properly used to describe the organization of an essay. It does not so readily represent the dynamic of a story. For that we can turn to diagrams designed for describing dramatic works.

In dramatic narrative, the notion of *rising and falling action* is useful. This is frequently diagramed as a pyramid shape, rising and descending. In the rising action the conflict intensifies through a series of crises, finally reaching a turning point. The topic outline above reflects the rising action in the sense that each of the three parts in the Galilee section concludes with a crisis that requires a decision that, in turn, takes the story into the next part. The major turning point, however, is reached in the confrontation in Jerusalem, which then leads to the falling action of the passion account.

It is worth noting that again Mark has defined these two major parts of the drama with typically dual features. The first part, the rising action, moves from "cleansing" to "cleansing."

Capernaum Synagogue (Mk 1) → Jerusalem Temple (Mk 11)

The action begins with Jesus making the first move. In the synagogue of Capernaum he expels an "unclean spirit" from the holy place (1:23, 26, 27). Through a series of crises and responses, the action builds in intensity, culminating with the "cleansing" of the Temple (11:15–19). Mark surrounds the latter event with symbolic and scriptural commentary, emphasizing its crucial importance in the dramatic action. This completes the rising action.

The falling action is framed by two anointing events, in Bethany and at the empty tomb.

Bethany (Mk 14) → Tomb (Mk 16)

Together, the rising and falling events describe a dramatic arc that unites the whole. However, in Mark, as is the case in some dramas, the falling action doesn't follow immediately upon the climax of the rising action. The decision to remove Jesus, taken at the Temple cleansing, is delayed due to the favor Jesus enjoys with the crowds. We can imagine a pyramid with a flattened top. In time, however, with the assistance of the "betrayer," the narrative moves into its falling movement.

## Two Agendas in Conflict

The contrasting geographical sites of Galilee and Jerusalem are not only two territories in Mark's world. They also represent two agendas in dramatic conflict: Jesus's movement centered in Galilee; his opposition centered in Jerusalem. Jesus and his followers speak from the villages of Galilee. Theirs is an agenda of resistance and renewal. The scribes, on the other hand, represent the central authorities of Jerusalem. They represent the agenda that Jesus and his people oppose. We might characterize them as two camps that define the struggle at the center of the drama. While the scribes from Jerusalem visit Galilee to observe Jesus's movement in the first chapters (3:22), the turn toward Jerusalem in the last chapters brings Jesus to the city, and the story to its climactic events.

In the rising action, appropriately framed by the two "cleansings," the ritual language of "holy" and "unclean" dominates the disputes. Mark chooses the term "unclean spirits" to characterize the demons, deliberately putting them in contrast to the Holy Spirit. Jesus is shown doing works of power that consistently violate laws of purity or cleanliness. Typically, the healings of Jesus involve returning excluded members to the community.

The criterion of holiness is maintained by the opponents of Jesus, who preside over a system of discriminations of holy and unclean practices, places, persons, and times. For instance, in the story of the man with the withered hand, Jesus replaces holiness viewed as purity with its system of avoidances with another image for holiness, that of compassion. Rather than maintaining a "hands off" posture, this model reaches out and touches, as with the unclean leper.

The cleansing of the Temple represents a culmination of this move to reintegrate "disposable" members, so that "my house shall be a house of prayer *for all peoples*" (Mark 11:17; Isa 56:7). The cleansing of the Temple, which represents the holy center—the holy place, in the holy city, in the holy land—amounts to a judgment on the very *criterion* of holiness in this narrative.

In contrast to the purity regulations used by the Pharisees to resist contamination by the Gentile invaders, Mark's Jesus presents a program of holiness as compassion, overruling the purity regulations. In this conflict of practices, holy versus unclean, Jesus is shown criticizing the prevailing structures of his day, a critique that culminates in a prophetic challenge to the Temple itself. In this, he is shown to agree with the popular resistance figures and movements of his day. But when we contrast his mode of resistance to that which prevailed at the time, we find another contrast and conflict in the unfolding story.

## The Messianic Secret—A Narrative Strategy

One of the better-known aspects of Mark's Gospel is the so-called Messianic Secret. This refers to the repeated reticence of Jesus about his role, along with other features that seem to hide his identity. Almost no one in the Gospel recognizes or understands Jesus's identity and teaching. Those who experience his miraculous help are instructed to keep silent. Only those outside the unfolding narrative—angels, demons, and God (and the reader)—know who Jesus really is. Outsiders remain in ignorance, while insiders are given further instruction, as in the parables.

The Messianic Secret has been explored theologically, but its narrative value has been overlooked. It should be noted, first of all, that it reflects certain literary strategies. Selective disclosure is a primary feature of narrative, providing it with suspense building toward a climax. Hints of fuller information tease the reader forward. The common technique of dramatic irony has the narrator share information with the reader, who then watches the characters in the story learn what the reader already knows.

Mark uses dramatic irony to dramatize the difference between Jesus's actions and the other movements during that time. First, the messianic role of Jesus is hidden. But this is merely the beginning, for what this designation means for Mark is revealed gradually as false expectations are peeled away, layer by layer. Jesus, the Messiah, is not a king of dominating power. Rather, this is a *people's* Messiah. The methods of cruelly dominating authority are not endorsed, for Jesus is a servant Messiah. Confronted by the kingdom of God, the rule of empire is not inevitable, not impervious to resistance. But the manner of that resistance is shown in the dynamic of conflict and its resolution as dramatized in Mark's story.

## Titles of Jesus: Mark's Narrative Contract

The main parts of the Markan narrative structure involve those features that generate the theory of the Messianic Secret. It is seen in the baptism event, when the voice from heaven quotes scripture regarding Jesus. He is to be Messiah, but also Servant. A double allusion cites both the messianic text of Psalm 2:7 and the Servant passage of Isaiah 42:1.

This is the *narrative contract* that establishes the call of Jesus, the task of the protagonist of the story. This narrative contract takes its message from the combination of the quoted texts. The two passages both address a person who is given an assignment, a role. Yet they are different. Psalm 2:7—"You are my son"—cites a messianic psalm promising a reign of the most unforgiving imperial style. "I will give the nations as your inheritance. . . . With an iron rod you will shepherd them; like a potter's vessel you will shatter them." In this Gospel this image is attached to the promise of a messiah in the style of the "son of David." The image reflects their experience of imperial powers, for which such methods were a matter of course.

But this image is modified by another from the first verse of the first Song of the Servant, from Isaiah 42: "In whom I am well pleased." The contrast is stark. We move from severe king to oppressed slave, from shattering rod to gentleness: "He will not cry out, nor shout, nor make his voice heard in the street. A bruised reed he will not break, and a dimly burning wick he will not quench." The imagery reverses.

The tension between these two as it unfolds in Mark's story shows Jesus's mission to be both like and unlike other examples of popular messiah. If we take it as a narrative strategy for unfolding his identity, rather than a theological datum, we see Jesus shown to be a people's messiah, acting in dramatic contrast to the violent options favored at the time. Unlike the signs prophets, he works among the villages; unlike the social bandits, he nurtures their social units; unlike the false messiahs, he proposes a nonviolent approach to waging conflict.

In Mark's telling of the story, different voices in the narrative offer different ideas about the identity of Jesus. Those outside the human community—angels and demons, and the voice from heaven—have clear opinions. The human characters are not so sure. The first label given Jesus by others in the Gospel is that of carpenter (6:3). The second, provided by Peter, is Messiah (8:29). These titles are the beginning of a series of such tentative identifications. On the road to Jerusalem, Jesus will teach his disciples the meaning of servant discipleship, culminating in another title, Servant—as in the Servant of Yahweh in Second Isaiah. At their arrival at Jerusalem, with Jesus's challenge and subsequent debates about his actions, the title "Son of David" takes precedence, with its conclusion in the question raised by Jesus concerning the Messiah and David: "How can the scribes say that the Messiah is the son of David?" (12:35). In the farewell speech and final days a new title, "Son of Man coming on the clouds," from Daniel, takes over the narrative. This series provides us with a thread through the narrative.

Mark does not mention the early life of Jesus. His Gospel begins with John the Baptist proclaiming repentance in the desert and baptizing in the Jordan. Mark paints John with the colors of the signs prophets. In the sixth chapter we are told of John's death at the hands of Herod Antipas. The story is told as a flashback, while the Twelve are out on mission and we are waiting for them to return. Mark's account has legendary touches, such as the offer of half the kingdom. In this case it is almost a direct quote from Esther 5:3—"The king said to her, 'What is it, Queen Esther? What is your request? It shall be given you, even to the half of my kingdom.'" The story of John is set in classic terms of stories of uneven powers in conflict. Josephus informs us that Herod had John killed for fear he would inspire an uprising.[15] While Josephus reports the beheading of Theudas, he doesn't mention that of John. Mark groups John with the other signs prophets, in fact, the most famous of them.

After John opens the story, the protagonist is quickly introduced: Jesus came from Nazareth of Galilee and was baptized by John in the Jordan. In the later story of his rejection, in Mark 6:1–6, we hear only of his "native place." There he is also identified as "the carpenter, the son of Mary, and the brother of James and Joses and Judas and Simon." However we account for these relationships, the message from Mark is clear: Jesus is a villager and derives from the village. He is a peasant and shares the villagers' common predicament.

We see Jesus attracted to the mission of John, persuaded by his preaching of a new era. But after his baptism and the arrest of John, Jesus returns to Galilee, proclaiming the good news of God, announcing that the time of fulfillment had arrived, that the kingdom of God was at hand, and calling for repentance.

Already a note of tension enters the account, for any talk of a kingdom is blatantly political; it will inevitably be viewed as a threat by the Roman occupiers. The confirmation of this will be the title placed on the cross: "King of the Jews." That title was

---

[15] Josephus, Antiquities, 18.5.2, *The New Complete Works of Josephus*, William Whiston, trans. (Grand Rapids, MI: Kregel Pub., 1999).

placed in mockery, of course, but mockery that takes its sting from the sensitivity of Rome toward any who would think to make such a claim.

In Mark's presentation, Jesus began his ministry among the desert prophets like John, but he shifted back toward society, redirecting his efforts. The return to Galilee is a change of perception about what is to be done. Having begun among the signs prophets, Jesus turns toward the communities that are suffering. This change in focus should not be passed over without notice. It moves from a posture of waiting to one of direct action. To see this, it is crucial to keep the social predicaments of Galilee in view. Rather than wait upon a sign, Jesus begins to facilitate changes among those in the villages. Mark depicts him working among the villages and rural people of the area.

Jesus begins by calling followers. Four are named—Peter and Andrew, James and John—and will represent the followers of Jesus in the narrative. And then he begins his real work, in the synagogue in Capernaum, a town on the upper shore of Galilee that Jesus makes his center of operations.

In the synagogue he engages a number of parties as opponents. At the political level, the scribes here represent the religious establishment that will oppose him. At a deeper level, they represent the "unclean spirits," Mark's favored term for demons. Mark, here borrowing language from Jewish ritual, establishes basic terms for his presentation of the conflict in this story. Jesus is identified with the Holy Spirit (1:8, 10, 12), while his opposition is identified with the unclean spirits (1:23, 26, 27). The synagogue is the social as well as religious center of the community. The implication is that something is terribly wrong, that it has become a place infested by unclean spirits.

This begins a week bracketed by two synagogue stories on two Sabbaths (1:21–28; 3:1–6). The first shows Jesus healing and bringing the marginalized back into society, including an account of how he rather provocatively ignored the purity rules by touching the untouchable leper. Quickly, opposition shows up, questioning Jesus's practice as well as his claims. In announcing a new authority—to forgive, to make exceptions to the Sabbath—he sets out a program of placing human need above claims of religious orthodoxy.

The week concludes with a paradigmatic moment concerning Jesus's engagement with the purity laws. The Sabbath synagogue story of the man with a withered hand (3:1–6) demonstrates two attitudes toward holiness. For the Pharisees present, holiness meant preserving the holiness of the place and occasion by refraining from certain activities. Exceptions were allowed for emergencies, of course, but this was a withered hand, not an emergency situation. For Jesus, holiness meant exercising compassion, revealing on this particular day and in this place God's own mercy. It brings on the decision by the opposition, in the form of both Pharisees and Herodians, religious and political authorities, to have him destroyed. He is clearly recognized as a threat.

Soon this developing conflict is sharply defined, as scribes from Jerusalem appear on the scene and accuse Jesus of being possessed by demons (3:22). Mark uses this to show Jesus, the one unaffiliated with official religion, to be the one actually endorsed by God. "How can Satan cast out Satan?" (3:23). The sides are drawn between the one with the Holy Spirit and those who sin against the Holy Spirit by opposing him, who accuse him of having an unclean spirit. The latter are disclosed, by default, to be the ones actually in league with unclean spirits.

In response to the conspiracy against him, Jesus consolidates his own people, in part so that they can continue should something happen to him. He names the Twelve, "to be with him, and to be sent out to proclaim the message" (3:14), those who will receive special instruction. The Twelve and other disciples form a new family (3:34–35), contrasted with Jesus's natural family (3:21, 31–33), to whom the story will return at the end (6:1–6), where he experiences another rejection. During this period Jesus delivers the parables, followed by a lake crossing during which he stills a storm. He expels demons from a man in Gerasa, and heals two "daughters," one a twelve-year-old girl and the other who had been ill for twelve years.

A repeated theme in this part of the story is that of faith versus fear (4:40; 5:15, 33–34, 36; 6:6). This shows the difference between Jesus's program and the resistance programs of the time.

The social bandits who attempted to redress the losses by violent reprisals, or the messianic movements that attempted to regain control of their lives and land by military force, demonstrate a distinctly different approach to restoration. For anyone who thinks in terms of doing violence in service of Jesus, his actions show him to be endorsing just the opposite.

After the rejection in 6:6, Mark shows Jesus's mission expanding to the very edges of Galilee. With the door closed at Nazareth, Jesus sends the Twelve out in pairs to knock on other doors. While they are gone, Mark tells about the death of John the Baptist. The story is introduced by a question asked by Herod Antipas, king of Galilee, concerning the identity of Jesus. The answer he receives (the Baptist, or Elijah, or one of the prophets, 6:15–16) states a motif that returns to end this section (8:28). Upon their return from mission, Jesus invites the disciples to a secluded place for rest and restoration, but the crowds follow. Having just heard about the death of the Baptist, we now see Jesus returning to the desert, performing signs like the signs prophets. A second crossing by boat shows Jesus coming on the water. The frightened disciples fail to recognize him.

At this point the Pharisees, along with the Jerusalem scribes, show concern about the disciples' lack of observance of the purity rules at meals. Jesus now quite explicitly challenges the purity laws as human traditions overruling divine law and preventing response to human need. This unequivocally opens the way to a mission to the Gentiles, demonstrated directly by a trip to the territory of Tyre. There he responds to the plea of a Gentile, a Syro-Phoenician woman with a possessed daughter. Following that, a deaf-mute is healed in Decapolis, also outside the borders of Galilee.

A second miracle of the loaves features different numbers— seven loaves, seven baskets of fragments—presumably Gentile rather than Jewish numbers. A brief note of another crossing brings us again to the Pharisees, demanding a sign, as if in response to the earlier disagreement. Another boat crossing with the disciples, who have thus far not shown the least comprehension, gives Jesus an opportunity to test them on the meaning of the signs. A blind man from Bethsaida, Peter's hometown, sets up a comparison with Peter. The section concludes with a final exchange concerning Jesus's identity and Peter's recognition. In answer to a question from Jesus, Peter declares: "You are the Messiah" (8:29). But like the blind man, he sees only partially and will need further attention.

## The Secret Messiah

A strange exchange occurs here at the midpoint of Mark's Gospel. When Peter finally recognizes Jesus as the Messiah, he is silenced: "And he sternly ordered them not to tell anyone about him" (8:30). Immediately following this exchange, Jesus is shown announcing the first of three predictions of the events to be encountered in Jerusalem: "He began to teach them that the Son of Man must undergo great suffering and be rejected by the elders, the chief priests, and the scribes, and be killed, and after three days rise again. He said all this quite openly" (8:31–32). This is in contrast to his reaction to Peter's declaration.

At this point the Messianic Secret becomes explicit. When Jesus responds to Peter's announcement by enjoining silence about the messianic title, and then immediately follows this by speaking openly about suffering and dying in Jerusalem, Peter objects. He rebukes Jesus. In his view this is not what the Messiah is called to. He shares the common perception that the Messiah will be a dominating figure, restoring Israel to its rightful place in history and the world, something like a Jewish Caesar Augustus. In Peter's opinion, not only is Jesus's way of talking hopelessly defeatist, but it neglects the scriptural promises. And beyond that, Jesus no doubt expects them to continue following him, which is sounding more and more dubious.

In response, Jesus rebukes Peter: "Get behind me, Satan! For you are setting your mind not on divine things but on human things" (8:33). So now we have a full-blown argument unfolding in front of everyone. In Peter's defense, Mark relates his initial call, along with that of Andrew, James, and John, only after the baptism of Jesus had taken place. That was when the voice from heaven announced God's way of thinking. Peter, in Mark's story, was not present to hear it, so of course he does not know it. And he especially does not know its explosive content—that the role of Messiah will be undertaken in the image of the Servant of Second-Isaiah.

Jesus clarifies further. "If any want to become my followers, let them deny themselves and take up their cross and follow me" (8:34). First of all, this in effect renegotiates the earlier call by the lake. Then it was, "Come, follow me." And they left everything and followed. But now there are new demands to discipleship—deny yourself, take up your cross. Furthermore, this further demand has special reference to Peter, who will later find himself in the high priest's courtyard, beginning to take up his cross. It is then time for Peter to act. But he gets it backward, denying that he knows the one taking up the cross.

The dispute between Jesus and Peter is to be resolved shortly, on the Mount of Transfiguration, when the voice from heaven makes a second appearance in the story. Now it is not speaking to Jesus, but rather to those with him: "This is my Son, the Beloved; listen to him" (9:7). Dispute resolved. Jesus will instruct them on the way.

The coming journey to Jerusalem answers the visits of the scribes from Jerusalem to Galilee. It is presented as a long linear journey, from the northernmost site of Caesarea Philippi, at the headwaters of the Jordan, down through Galilee, to Jerusalem, where the Messiah belongs. These are three distantly placed locations on the map.

**The Suffering Servant**

After Peter makes his bold assertion and has it corrected, the lessons on the road continue. And so does the lack of comprehension. This part of the Gospel rehearses attitudes opposed to the revealed role of the Messiah—love of power, ambition, status seeking. Jesus responds with teachings on marriage and family (divorce issue), economics (the rich man), and politics (James and John). We find the actions of Jesus in Galilee grounded in his teachings.

The road narrative follows three "passion predictions" with a common format (8:31; 9:30; 10:32–33). First, Jesus announces he is going to Jerusalem, where he will die and then rise. This is followed by one or more disciples failing to grasp his point. This, in turn, allows Jesus a teaching moment. Despite this, they do not achieve real understanding in the entire course of the journey.

Peter's interaction with Jesus is the first of the three moments. The second involves all the apostles. They are arguing over their relative importance. Upon learning of their problem, Jesus lays out a principle: the first shall be last and servant of all (9:35). The principle is repeated at 10:31, forming a bracket for the teachings that come between. In this group of lessons the Pharisees make a return appearance, asking a question about divorce. Also, a rich man asks about eternal life, in what turns out to be a failed-call story.

The third and final exchange involves an ambitious request of James and John, which occasions a response that brings the symposium on the road to a close. In answer to their request to be given the primary seats in the coming kingdom, Jesus speaks of sharing in his cup and baptism. These clearly refer to his coming trials, with the cup reappearing at the last supper and in the garden prayer. The earlier baptism account was followed by his testing in the desert (1:9–11, 10–12). This is reprised in the garden temptation (14:32–42). To complete the parallels, the baptism sequence concludes with the arrest of John (1:14), while the cup sequence concludes with the arrest of Jesus (14:43–46). Looking at the larger narrative, the meaning of the baptism and the cup is evident.

The Twelve are upset at the presumption, or maybe the canniness, of the two brothers. That brings this stretch of narrative, and the Servant theme, to a clarifying moment. Jesus delivers a lesson on authority and discipleship of the Messiah as Servant: "So Jesus called them and said to them, 'You know that among the Gentiles those whom they recognize as their rulers lord it over them, and their great ones are tyrants over them'" (10:42).

We are asked to remember the portrait of kingship presented by Psalm 2, with its images of smashing with rods and crushing subservient populations, cited by the voice from heaven at Jesus's baptism. This is power as it is practiced in the wider world. But not here. "But it is not so among you; but whoever wishes to become great among you must be your servant, and whoever wishes to be first among you must be slave of all. For the Son of Man came not to be served but to serve, and to give his life a ransom for many" (10:43–45).

Again, the first shall be last, a servant. We have a new reading of the messianic role. It began with the baptism voice modifying the traditional image of power with a reference to the first verse of the first Servant Song (Isa 42:1). Now the lessons conclude with Jesus modifying the image of Gentile abuse of authority with reference to the final verses of the last Servant Song (Isa 53:11–12). The disciples are servants because they follow the Servant himself.

Another blind-man story, that of Bartimaeus of Jericho, completes the account of the journey to the city. The scene offers a contrast to the "blindness" of James and John, just as the blind man of Bethsaida did with Peter earlier. But it also introduces the next part of the story, for we are now at the last station before entering Jerusalem. The reader notes the party of Jesus enters the city with knowledge of the crucial revision of the messianic role, but also remembering the lack of comprehension on the part of Jesus followers. The contrast between the no-longer-blind son of Timaeus, who understands, and the sons of Zebedee, who remain blind, is telling.

The carpenter has been recognized as the Messiah. And the false interpretation has been corrected, because on the way to the city Jesus redefines *messiah* in terms of *servant*. But now further clarifications are needed. With the entry into the city, we come to the climax of the rising action of the dramatic plot—the Temple cleansing. What began in the synagogue of Capernaum comes to fullest expression in the Temple.

At this point Mark's narrative introduces a new title for Jesus: Son of David. Twice in the previous scene we heard Bartimaeus call out: "Son of David, have mercy on me!" (10:47, 48). Now, as Jesus enters into the city in a procession rich with scriptural overtones, we hear the onlookers cry out: "Blessed is the coming kingdom of our ancestor David! Hosanna in the highest heaven!" (11:10) The outcry anticipates powerful, direct action. And yet some readers have noted that Jesus ignores this new title, very unlike his response to others.

## Jesus Enters Jerusalem

With the entry into Jerusalem we come to the final week of Jesus's life. Mark counts it out with numbered days. On the first day he enters the city, stops in momentarily at the Temple, then retires to the village where he will stay during his time here. The village is Bethany, across the Mount of Olives to the east of the city. The next day he returns to perform the dramatic action we have come to call the Temple cleansing. It is a deliberate, calculated move.

With Josephus's accounts of the Great Revolt in Jerusalem, we gain an understanding of the role of the Temple in any major protest of conditions at that time. The Temple is the center of Jewish consciousness as a people. It is the place where a statement about religious compromise, class injustice, corrupted leadership, or any kind of social injustice must be aired.

Nowhere in Mark's text is this prophetic action called a cleansing. But to call it so is not a misnomer—at least not in this Gospel. All along, Mark has shown Jesus deliberately ignoring, even subverting, purity laws, valuing them less than the need for healing and restoration of excluded persons. As Mark has contrived to tell the stories, the purity regulations consistently impede Jesus's works of compassion. But the purity system is known to be centered in the Temple of Jerusalem, the holy center of the holy city. Jewish writings have shown how a concentric series of zones, like circles in a target, move out from the holy place toward areas of lesser purity until we arrive at the "unclean" territory of the Gentiles. Similar circles relate to persons in their proximity to the Temple worship, times, and seasons. Jesus's action signifies that the Temple no longer serves its proper function. It is significant that the verb used to describe his expulsion of the merchants is the same verb used elsewhere for exorcising demons.[16]

Mark has underlined the importance of this scene with a cluster of biblical allusions providing commentary. At the center is the quotation in the cleansing passage itself. Not unlike some other places in Mark, two quotes are combined—Jeremiah 7:11 and Isaiah 56:7. The first is taken from Jeremiah's famous temple sermon, which serves as a precedent for Jesus's own performance. The second alludes to Isaiah 56:1–8, the introductory passage to Third Isaiah, which foresees in the day to come that those banished from the holy place will now be included. For "my house shall be a house of prayer for all peoples." It clearly refers back to Jesus's efforts to return the leper and others to active life in the kingdom of God. Its invocation in the Temple action implies a failure in a system that would achieve success by banishing some of its members.[17]

The week that begins with this event has many resonances with the initial week of Jesus's campaign. Similar motifs abound—a prophetic cleansing of a holy place, questions about Jesus's authority, and subsequent debates. This moment stands at the end of the long rising action that began in the synagogue of Capernaum; it now comes to a climax in the Temple itself. The series of crises and regroupings in the mounting plot end here, with this singular moment. Most important, the decision made at the end of that first week, that Jesus should be destroyed (3:6), is now revived in response to the Temple action (11:18). This initiates the efforts by the authorities that will result in Jesus's death on a cross.

Their effort is stalled, however. Tension builds again as the opponents of Jesus, frustrated in their attempts to stop him, seek an advantage. Jesus proves effective in debating those who try to trap him in his speech. A pertinent example of their efforts is seen

---

[16] For a fuller account see Beck, *Nonviolent Story*, 65–70 and 159–65.

[17] Other passages surround the action. For instance, the citations from Zechariah 14 announce the arrival of "that day." The three references are to crossing the Mount of Olives (Zec 14:4); feast/time of "ingathering" (Zec 14:3); clearing the merchants from the Temple (Zec 14:21).

in the attempt to trip him up on the question of paying taxes to Caesar. They hope to present him with a dilemma that will force a choice against either the people, who oppose the tax, or the Roman authorities, who do not forgive opposition easily. Already we find the recourse of turning to Roman solutions being suggested. While Jesus's answer neatly parries their thrust, his request for a coin is equally devastating. His opponents are shown to be carrying into the sacred precincts a coin with the image of the emperor, who styles himself a god. They reveal themselves to be compromised.

## Son of David

At the end of the Temple debates Jesus finally turns his attention to the title "Son of David." In a speech that might otherwise seem obscure, but which turns out to be pivotal for the narrative, he cites Psalm 110 to question the royal pedigree of the Messiah:

> "How can the scribes say that the Messiah is the son of David? David himself, inspired by the holy Spirit, declared:
>
>> 'The Lord said to my Lord,
>> "Sit at my right hand
>>     until I put your enemies under your feet."'
>
> David himself call him Lord; so how can he be his son?" (Mark 12:35–37; see Ps 110:1–2)

Here we see Jesus's answer to the acclamations of blind Bartimaeus and the throng on the road to the city, which went unremarked at the time. For Mark, this little speech separating the role of the Messiah from its royal expectations is crucial. Downplaying royal status makes room for the possibility of a popular messiah drawn from the ranks of the village populace. In the next chapter Jesus is seen warning against false messiahs and false prophets, implying that they are similar enough to cause confusion (13:22). By suggesting that Jesus is not a messiah in the royal manner, the question about the Son of David establishes the basis for the concern about popular messiahs. Like the false messiahs, he is mounting a resistance; unlike them, his methods reject violence.[18]

Psalm 110 is messianic, and it partners with Psalm 2 in its depiction of the royal messiah to come. Its language of "shattering kings," "filling [the nations] with corpses," and "shattering heads" (Ps 110:5–6) recalls Psalm 2, which Mark cited at the baptism. This royal strand of tradition depicted the messianic regime as imitating the imperial examples that had oppressed the children of Israel in the past. But now comes a further clarification. Just as the messianic promise of Psalm 2 was corrected by the Servant passage of Isaiah 42, and the messianic declaration of Peter was clarified by the teaching about the Servant delivered on the road to the city, now the image of the royal entry into the city, suggesting a conquering hero, is adjusted by questioning the royal claims.

The role as the harsh despot is rejected. And in that rejection we understand that Mark's Temple cleansing does not depict an act of violence. The cloud of scriptural quotations assign it the status of a prophetic act. If we are to understand violence as harm directed at persons, then there is no violence here. John's account may have a whip of cords, but John also speaks of driving out animals (John 2:15). For Mark, destruction, or something similar, is limited to the prophetic tipping over of tables (Zec 14:21). As for the effect on persons, it would seem to be liberating in its judgment on the obstacles that separate people from God.

---

[18] For the rejection of "Son of David" in Mark, see Boring, *Mark*, 316, 348; and especially Elizabeth Struthers Malbon, "The Jesus of Mark and the 'Son of David,'" in *Between Author and Audience in Mark: Narration, Characterization, Interpretation*, ed. E. S. Malbon (Sheffield, UK: Sheffield Phoenix Press, 2009). Malbon argues that "in Mark's Gospel, the title 'Son of David' is ignored by Jesus when offered by Bartimaeus and argued against by Jesus as linked to 'the Christ,' a view he attributes to the scribes. In addition, neither the Markan narrator nor the Markan voice of God picks up the title. Since these three voices—the Markan voice of God, the Markan Jesus, and the Markan narrator—are the three most valued by the Markan implied author and implied audience, it is inappropriate to go against them when interpreting Markan christology, especially Markan narrative christology, which is the larger project in which I am engaged" (177–78).

## Son of Man

No sooner has Jesus dispelled the title "Son of David" but another appears, and this of his own choice—the "Son of Man" coming on the clouds (13:26–27). Formally, Mark 13 is a farewell speech—a biblical convention in which a famous person, usually near death, delivers his parting words. Examples include Jacob (Gen 49:1–29), Moses (Deut 1:1ff.), and Paul (Acts 20:17–35). Jesus addresses the same four disciples who were called at the start, Peter and Andrew, James and John (1:16–20). One phase of the narrative is closing; another is beginning. We are moving into the final chapters of the Gospel.

This chapter is also sometimes called an apocalyptic discourse, as it employs the traditions of *apocalyptic writing*. It presents a picture of someone in the past predicting a future that coincides with the present time of the writer. In Daniel 9—11, Daniel, a figure from the Babylonian exile in 587–39 BCE, is portrayed predicting events of the author's own time, the persecution under the Seleucids, 168–64 BCE. Similarly, Mark, writing during the time of the Great Revolt in Jerusalem, shows Jesus anticipating it. Reference to the apocalyptic book of Daniel is not coincidental, of course, since the figure of the Son of Man coming on the clouds is taken from Daniel 7:13–14.

The apocalyptic tone has prompted some to see the entire Gospel under the sign of the end times. Certainly with the Great Revolt, a certain time of Judaism was indeed coming to an end. But an imminent conclusion of all things would seem to make Mark's decision to write a Gospel pointless. In addition, it has been noted that for first-century believers, Jesus included, apocalyptic visions were not so much a promise of the future as an alternative vision of the present. It was a vision drawing on Israel's biblical ideals "to challenge the existing unjust social structures, not by the traditional means of a militant resistance, but by a new and creative interpretation of the kingdom of God."[19] It provided a point of comparison.

---

[19] Sean Freyne, *Jesus, A Jewish Galilean: A New Reading of the Jesus-Story* (New York: T & T Clark, 2004), 140.

In that respect it is appropriate for Mark to bring the apocalyptic "Son of Man" into his narrative at this time. In the approaching passion account, the Roman presence, in the person of Pilate, is the primary opponent that takes Jesus to his death. However, the apocalyptic vision of the Son of Man gives Mark's Jesus two kinds of leverage.

First of all, it claims an *authority* that transcends the Roman empire and its world-dominating reach. The kingdom of God that Jesus preached is grounded in the rule of God, one greater than the Roman gods. We see here the convergence of Jesus's campaign with other campaigns of the day, although contrasting in method. As in the drama of the Great Revolt, Jesus acts out of allegiance to a greater power. Second, in its vision of a future that includes *resurrection,* it dismisses fear of death. It promises a resistance that cannot be deterred by any imperial methods designed to intimidate and humiliate, such as crucifixion. The One who gives life will not be subject to the power that takes life.

The claim of authority reminds us of the earlier non-apocalyptic use of the Son of Man title in Mark 2:28. There the Son of Man is said to have authority to forgive and have mastery over the Sabbath. This is a principle of priorities: "The sabbath was made for humankind, not humankind for the sabbath" (2:27). The power of forgiveness and discretion over the Sabbath privileges human need over religious observance. In that first week the Son of Man theme incorporates the rights of the common person. Once again, we see Jesus as a people's messiah, representing human needs against a dismissive, contemptuous leadership.

The gradual revelation of Jesus as the people's messiah places his story in contrast to the violent and futile efforts at resistance in his day. His story is by no means one of flight from resistance to destructive powers. Rather, he takes an alternative, nonviolent approach.

## The Falling Action

With that we come to the falling action of Mark's story. Throughout the early chapters in Galilee, the rising action, the struggle was represented by a language of purity concerns, pitting the Holy Spirit against the "unclean spirits." Consistently, Jesus's attention to the health of various Israelites who were excluded from active participation in life and worship was presented as disregard of the purity rules, by which they would be separated from the rest. This strand of the narrative culminated in the cleansing of the Temple, the central reference point of the purity system, in an act that in effect denied its function.

That was the rising action of the story. Now we move into the falling action, which virtually coincides with the passion account. The falling action is marked off in the text by the framing device of two burial anointings—neither truly complete—at Bethany (14:3–9) and at the tomb (16:1). But the falling action can be more adequately discussed in a separate section about the narrative conflict resolution in the Gospel.

## CONFLICT RESOLUTION IN MARK

Mark's story concludes in the classic pattern of nonviolent confrontation, unfolding along lines formally described by Gene Sharp in his analysis of Gandhi's campaigns.[20] In a final week, spent commuting between the Temple in Jerusalem's Mount Zion during the days and Bethany on the Mount of Olives at night, we discern a pattern that expresses itself in Jesus's challenge in the Temple and the opponents' arrest of Jesus in the Garden of Olives, which concludes with the nonresistance that results in the crucifixion on a third site. Despite its brevity, Mark's resurrection account assures the reader that Jesus's nonviolent response is successful immediately, even while indicating its social remains unfinished.

Mark's Gospel is poised in a struggle between two territorial centers, Galilee and Jerusalem, which in turn represent two agendas. One is that of Jesus, situated in the villages of Galilee. Jesus is opening a new vista seen in festive, inclusive meals and healing

---

[20] Gene Sharp, *The Politics of Nonviolent Action,* 3 vols. (Boston: Porter Sargent Publishers, 1973).

actions. The opposing vision is that of the authorities of Jerusalem, committed to a purity system that honors God by excluding persons who embody the blemished world. Just as the scribes from Jerusalem visited Galilee to check on the activity of Jesus (3:22), so Jesus later turns toward Jerusalem, where the final moves of the narrative play out. In the concluding moves of the narrative, these two religious positions take on a new symbolic shape, etched in the very terrain of Jerusalem.

The final week of Jesus's story is stepped out between two hills, the Mount of Olives and Mount Zion (the Temple mount). The two face each other across the Kidron valley. At night Jesus stays in the village of Bethany, over the crest of the Mount of Olives. This more rustic location recalls his commitment to the villages of Galilee. During the day he travels to the Temple mount, where he instructs the crowds and engages his opponents.

This daily commute between the Mount of Olives and Mount Zion establishes a pattern, one that provides the basis for the conflict activity during the final week. Overlaid upon the pattern of Jesus's daily commute is a dynamic of mutual confrontation, marked by the key word *lestes*, the word previously identifying the "social bandits" of Jesus's time. It carries a rich cluster of meanings, but all of them imply a sense of violence, a forceful incursion of some kind. In the Gospels it is given various translations. Its use in Josephus indicates a "brigand." In Mark's closing chapters the word appears three times, variously translated, and the three define a schema in the narrative.

The first occurs at the *Temple cleansing* (11:17). "Is it not written, 'My house shall be called a house of prayer for all the nations'? But you have made it a den of robbers [*lestes*]." This concludes the rising action, throughout which Jesus has been on the offensive, from the cleansing of the Capernaum synagogue (1:21–28) to the cleansing of the Temple in Jerusalem (11:15–19). This moment now generates the second.

The second use of the word is at *Jesus's arrest in the Garden* (14:48). "Then Jesus said to them, 'Have you come out with swords and clubs to arrest me as though I were a bandit [*lestes*]?'" The Jerusalem officials have already begun discussing eliminating

Jesus. But their moment is deferred, due to Jesus's popularity with the crowds (Mark 11:18). Eventually, they enlist Judas in their cause, and Jesus is arrested (14:46–48). This initiates the falling action of the piece.

The third time the word is used is recounting the crucifixion: "And with him they crucified two bandits [*lestoi*], one on his right and one on his left" (15:27). The crucifixion of Jesus between two bandits concludes the story of Jesus in the narrative.

The crucifixion account introduces a third site: "They brought Jesus to the place called Golgotha (which means the place of a skull)" (15:22).[21]

## The Dynamics of Nonviolent Conflict Resolution

The workings of this system are illuminated by the theory of nonviolent action analyzed by Gene Sharp. His descriptions of nonviolent action are known worldwide, employed most recently in the Arab Spring, when he was in Internet communication with the leaders of that resistance movement. He sets out his ideas in *The Politics of Nonviolent Action*. Sharp's theory of power underlies his idea of nonviolent action.[22] He sees political power as deriving from the consent of the governed. This is true of all forms of government, democratic or not. When public consent is withdrawn, authority evaporates, and consequently it can no longer be assumed that commands once given will be obeyed. Consequently, they must now be enforced.

In his third volume, *The Dynamics of Nonviolent Actions*,[23] Sharp analyses Gandhi's campaigns. His schema can be broken

---

[21] Though we may think of the place of crucifixion as a hill, neither Mark nor the other Gospel writers identify it as such.

[22] Gene Sharp, *The Politics of Nonviolent Action: Part 1, Power and Struggle* (Boston: Porter Sargent Publishers, 1973). His ideas on social power have been usefully elaborated in Elizabeth Janeway, *Powers of the Weak* (New York: Random House, 1988).

[23] Gene Sharp, *The Politics of Nonviolent Action: Part 3, Dynamics of Nonviolent Action* (Boston: Porter Sargent Pubishers, 1985).

into three basic stages, although in actual practice the first two may be repeated many times. The first stage is a disciplined *nonviolent confrontation* on the behalf of the protesting party, typically designed to expose and resist overtly an oppressive social process. Discipline is required to maintain nonviolence in the protest, consciously refusing instruments of force. In Mark, this is the work of Jesus that culminates in the very public cleansing of the Temple. His deliberation is shown in the way he surveys the area on one day and returns for his action on the next (11:11–12, 15). It stands as a culmination of a program building throughout the rising action of the narrative plot.

Sharp's second stage is a *repressive response* against this initiative and prompted by it. In this second stage the dominating party reacts to the protest with instruments of force that it has traditionally used to suppress resistance. Typically, this takes the form of threat, a show of force rather than actual violence. Lethal instruments may in fact be used, but doing so removes their value as threats, and in fact may win public sympathy for the protesting party. In Mark's narrative we see this in the Jerusalem officials' response to Jesus's Temple action: the decision to destroy him (11:18). However, due to the favor that he enjoys among the people, they are unable to make their move—until they come to him at night, in the Garden.

The third stage in Sharp's analysis is a deliberate act of *non-retaliation* in response to the repressive action of the dominating party. While this may look like surrender, it is not. The classic image of "going limp" shows protestors not resisting arrest, but likewise not cooperating, not surrendering. Non-retaliation is a way of continuing the resistance without a violent reaction. In this sense the move is as much an initiative on the part of the nonviolent resister as the original protest. In Mark's Gospel non-retaliation governs Jesus's response to his arrest. In this first Gospel the sword wielder is not identified as a disciple. While one of the bystanders chooses a violent action, lopping off the ear of one of the arresting guards, Jesus publicly and purposefully refuses this response.

With Sharp's help we can see how the narrative conflict resolution of Mark's Gospel takes shape. It also helps us understand
what Mahatma Gandhi meant when he said, "Jesus was the most
active resister known perhaps to history. This was nonviolence
*par excellence.*"[24]

The rising action builds tension through a series of crises and
responses, leading to the culminating crisis which is the turning
point in the plot. The falling movement of the narrative that follows unwinds with a feeling of inevitability. This falling action
is traced through the narrative by moments of "handing over," in
Mark's account, *paradidomi.* However, when the word involves
Judas, it is typically rendered as "betray."

Initially appearing in the passion predictions on the way to
Jerusalem, handing over assumes its dramatic place in the falling
action, where it describes the increasing distance of Jesus from
his own people. Judas, described at this point as a member of
the Twelve (14:10, 43), hands Jesus over to the council (14:42,
44). Its members, in turn, hand him over to Pilate (15:1). After
the episode featuring Barabbas, Pilate hands him over to the soldiers (15:15). At each transfer Jesus moves farther from his own
people and closer to actual crucifixion. On the cross, Psalm 22:2
articulates his abandonment: "My God, my God, why have you
forsaken me?" (15:34).

The account of Jesus's abandonment underscores the complete
absence of coercive power in Jesus's nonviolent conflict resolution. It demonstrates failure of the opponents' effort to dominate;
it also shows a refusal to adopt the power of domination. It stands
as an affront to those who believe that the only effective form of
resistance is through the use of force or coercion.

After his death, Joseph of Arimathea, a member of the council,
works to retrieve Jesus's body (15:42–46). Mark's account retraces
each step of the alienating distance, alerting us to its importance.
Joseph goes to Pilate, who turns to the centurion, who reports to
Pilate, who permits Joseph to take the body of Jesus.

---

[24] Quoted in Thomas Merton, *Gandhi on Non-Violence* (New York: New
Directions, 2007 <1965>), 55.

## The Empty Tomb

The women come to anoint Jesus's body, but there is a problem. They do not know how they will enter the tomb. This suggests that the story is not to be taken literally. When they reach the tomb, they not only find the stone rolled away, but they also discover someone is already there. A young man "dressed in a white robe" is waiting for them, as if they were expected (16:5). Events have moved on, and this young man has been assigned the task of explaining things to them. His message is twofold. *First, Jesus is risen.* The anointing is now called off. It was premature. From the viewpoint of the narrative, sealing the tomb would threaten to end the narrative, bring the story to a finish. In a similar way, anointing Jesus's body would have been an ominously final touch. It is the ritual that would end the story of Jesus. But it is not to be; the story is not finished.

The unfinished character of the story is seen in the narrative itself, in its abrupt ending, if it can be called an ending. Unlike the other Gospels, Mark tells of no resurrection appearances of Jesus. If we exclude the longer and shorter endings, Mark "concludes" at 16:8. The text-critical evidence indicates that the endings that follow were added later by others.

Resurrection appearance stories arise in the Gospel tradition when the story of Jesus has been relegated to the past, as something that happened one time. This occurs in Luke, for instance, where the ascension signals the end of the appearances, which happened for a time and then stopped. But Mark is not ready to close it off, unwilling to assign the story to the past. It is not a past story but a present one.

The man dressed in white adds a *second part to his message.* In addition to stopping the moves that would end the story of Jesus—the sealed stone and the anointed body—he opens it in a new direction: "But go, tell his disciples and Peter that he is going ahead of you to Galilee; there you will see him, just as he told you" (16:7).

He seems to be promising a personal meeting with Jesus, and this might be what Mark intends. But what will happen at that meeting? Here we might consider Matthew an authoritative inter-preter. In his account they do meet, and Jesus commissions them to go to the nations. That amounts to a new narrative contract, as a new story begins.

But what about Mark's interpretation? The message of the man dressed in white does this. The phrase "just as he told you" refers back to 14:28. There Jesus predicted Peter's denial. But this is not to be considered in isolation. It is part of a larger plot line in the story, one that concerns the meaning of discipleship as following. A brief sketch shows them.

Peter is emblematic of the disciples here. His, and their, story begins with his call (1:16–18), when he and his brother left ev-erything to follow Jesus. But this strand of the story arrives at a second and more serious juncture when Peter identifies Jesus as the Messiah (8:27). As we've seen, he is correct about the identi-fication of Jesus as Messiah, but woefully incorrect about what it means for Jesus, and consequently for his followers. Immediately, Jesus announces his move toward Jerusalem, the proper destina-tion for a messiah. But it is framed in terms of the Suffering Ser-vant, who will suffer and die, and in three days rise. As we have seen, Peter demurs, and an argument ensues (8:32–33).

At this point that original call by the lake was renegotiated in a sobering new direction. "If any want to become my followers, let them deny themselves and take up their cross and follow me" (8:34). There was no talk about a cross back in Galilee. And while this applies to all his followers, Peter is the paradigm, as will be seen in the narrative to come. In the courtyard of the high priest Peter gets it backward. Instead of denying himself and taking up his cross, he denies he knows Jesus, who is engaged at that time in taking up the cross.

It is this moment of denial, referred to by the man dressed in white, that is foreseen in Jesus's words at the last supper:

"And Jesus said to them, 'You will all become deserters; for it is written,

"I will strike the shepherd,
    and the sheep will be scattered.""

But after I am raised up, *I will go before you to Galilee.*'"
(14:27–28, emphasis added)

The story of the empty tomb points to a reenactment of the story of Jesus in the lives of the disciples. Mark portrays Jesus in action. Mark's portrait is a narrative, not a visual description. To follow Jesus means to adopt his storyline as Mark has set it out. His followers have not managed to do this so far. But the man dressed in white points them to a new beginning.

## RESISTANCE AS NONVIOLENT ACTION

The example of Gene Sharp and other contemporary theorists helps us to see how Mark's narrative conflict resolution speaks to social action today. Certain implications can be spelled out at this point.

In the narrative Mark has given us we find a narrative pattern that conforms to what today is called nonviolent action and conflict resolution. It is a pattern modern analysts derive from the practice of Gandhi and call *nonviolent resistance*.

*Nonviolent action* should be distinguished from other patterns of behavior with which it might be confused. Reinhold Niebuhr insists that the Gospel narrative is one of pure *nonresistance* and not nonviolent resistance—something we will examine more closely in response to Matthew's story of Jesus. Niebuhr denied the possibility of nonviolent resistance; he saw Gandhi's actions as a surreptitious form of coercion. But the Gospel narrative shows Jesus actively resisting, though nonviolently. This is not a case of *pure nonresistance.*

Nor is it *pacifism*, if that is understood as avoiding conflict, since the Gospel shows a determined and active resistance to oppressive social practices. It does not depict a flight from conflict, as would be suggested by Mark 13:14 ("those in Judea must flee to the mountains").

Nor is it *passive resistance*, which surreptitiously coerces by closing the options open to the opposing party, thus ensuring the result the protestors want.

Nor is it *sabotage*, if that is understood as a refusal to take responsibility for disruptive actions by operating incognito. This violates the final move of the action, that of non-retaliation, which consists of standing forth as accountable, though not violently.

*Nonviolent action,* on the other hand, actively resists unjust social structures without invoking violent means. This assertion typically evokes arguments about the meaning of violence. Does it include the harm of persons only, or also damage to property? Is spiritual violence included as well as physical destruction? Generally it is positioned between two extremes. At one end is violence narrowly defined, as in the work of Gene Sharp, used here. For him, only actions directly harmful to persons can be called violent, leaving room for a wide range of behaviors to be called nonviolent. Destruction of property and psychological injury are not included in his understanding of violence.

Gandhian theorist Joan Bondurant warns against using nonviolent methods to coerce, arguing that they do not reach the nonviolent level of Satyagraha—Gandhi's name for his practice of nonviolent action—but rather Duragraha, which employs nonviolent techniques in a subversive and psychologically coercive manner.[25] In light of that we might adjust our reading of Mark, inasmuch as the final abandonment of Jesus argues against any sense of coercive power.

Mark's Gospel story has been laid out in some detail, with the realization that the narrative that he has given us is also that which Matthew and Luke adopted for their own purposes. An appreciation of the shape and dynamics of Mark's narrative plot serves us well in seeing what the other two evangelists were doing in their own right.

Mark's carefully constructed narrative of Jesus takes the form of a nonviolent resistance campaign. Jesus is presented as a people's messiah, sprung from the peasant villages of Galilee.

---

[25] Joan V. Bondurant, *Conquest of Violence: The Gandhian Philosophy of Conflict,* rev. ed. (Princeton, NJ: Princeton University Press, 1988 <1958>); also Joan V. Bondurant and Margaret Welpley Fishcr, *Conflict: Violence and Nonviolence,* repr. ed. (New York: Aldine Transaction, 2008).

Initially identified with John the Baptist, and the signs prophets of the early resistance, he leaves the desert to work in the villages of Galilee, which have been devastated by invasion and economic disruption. In works of healing and teachings in parables he strives to reknit the frayed fabric of the village communities. In this, he stands in stark contrast to the brigands and false messiahs, who respond with violence, to futile effect.

This alternative pattern of resistance favored by Jesus is shown to reach a climax in the final part of the Gospel, which dramatically contrasts with the events taking place in the Great Revolt in Jerusalem, occurring during Mark's time, and serving as the event he disputes with his story. In a pattern of action that can be accurately defined today as nonviolent conflict resolution, Jesus confronts the powers without resorting to violent methods. In this, Mark's Gospel still serves as a model for today.

# 3

---

# Matthew

Some fifteen to twenty years after Mark's Gospel was written and circulated among the communities of Jesus's followers, the person we call Matthew wrote another, based upon the narrative produced by Mark. Matthew was a Jewish scholar, a scribe in the wisdom tradition. He belonged to a community of Jews who were followers of Jesus. Whether or not his community was expelled from the synagogue or was in danger of being so—a disputed issue—Judaism defined his perspective. *His concern is the Jesus movement in its Jewish setting.*

This Jewish Christian, writing after the fall of the city and destruction of the Temple at the hands of the Romans, adapted Mark's narrative to the conditions that prevailed in his time. The catastrophe brought about the eclipse of many of the Jewish institutions and parties, including the priestly party, the Essenes of Qumran, and the Zealots at Masada. The Pharisees based in the villages largely remained, and the neo-rabbinic movement that succeeded it provided Matthew's church with its greatest competition. The future of Judaism lay at stake. Meanwhile, rancor against Rome increased, inflamed by the Fiscus Judaicus—a punitive tax on all Jews throughout the empire—which resulting in the scattered uprisings of the Kitos (Jewish-Roman) wars. Competition with the post-Pharisaic movement prompted Matthew to pitch his Gospel narrative as a *struggle for authentic religion*, the "hypocrites" versus the "impostor."

Matthew presents Jesus as the authentic heir of the tradition. His use of a story pattern of the banished, then forgotten, and unexpectedly returning prince allows Matthew to show why Jesus, the royal descendant of David, was not recognized as such.

## MATTHEW'S PROJECT:
## THE RETURN OF THE KINGSHIP

If Mark was the first to write a Gospel, Matthew was the first to decide we needed another. This decision is not without its surprises. It is worth asking why this author felt it necessary to produce another version of Mark's work. What made the original no longer satisfactory? How had circumstances changed to prompt him to produce an update of Mark? And especially, what new directions are taken in this narrative? These are the questions that direct the comments in this chapter.[1]

### Genealogies and Conflict

Matthew's Gospel begins with a genealogy, a list of fathers who "begat" sons. For years we have mined this passage as a thematic introduction containing theological signals for the narrative to come. But in this approach we are ignoring the primary function of genealogies and why Matthew might want to begin with one.

Genealogies have an important function for times of transfer of power or property. They reduce the possibility of successional feuds or civil war when a lord departs the scene. If a clear plan for succession is in place, the transition is smoother. In other words,

---

[1] For a fuller treatment, see Robert R. Beck, *Banished Messiah: Violence and Nonviolence in Matthew's Story of Jesus* (Eugene, OR: Wipf and Stock, 2010). For an empire studies reading, see Warren Carter, *Matthew and the Margins: A Sociopolitical and Religious Reading* (Maryknoll, NY: Orbis Books, 2001). For a helpful standard commentary, see Daniel J. Harrington, SJ, *Sacra Pagina: The Gospel of Matthew* (Collegeville, MN: Liturgical Press, 2007).

there is a clear link between genealogies and issues of conflict and potential violence.

Genealogies come in two kinds, branched and linear, and both are important. Branched genealogies, such as we find at the beginning of books on the history plays of Shakespeare or commentaries on King David or King Herod show the relative position of everyone in the family. Linear genealogies trace a line through the branched genealogies to arrive at a person at the end of the list who is identified as the proper receiver of the property or power in question. Matthew's genealogy is linear.[2]

Linear genealogies exist to reduce bloodshed during times of transition. These genealogies systematically reduce a field of claimants (technically, "dynastic shedding") by automatically eliminating entire categories of descendants—typically all the females and all males peripheral to the main line.[3] In the end, the two names that remain are those of the eldest son and the second son, the latter standing in reserve. The second son is an ambiguous figure, celebrated when required to fill in, but condemned should he force a transition, as in the stories of usurping the throne. It is when a claim is contested that linear genealogies come into play. Instead of civil war, we have a dispute about lists.

Linear lists demonstrate *continuity* and *legitimacy*. The genealogy makes an assertion about the last person on the list: this one is the legitimate heir. But the argument for legitimacy is accomplished by showing continuity with the founder, situated at the beginning of the list. And while linear genealogies are intended to reduce bloodshed during times of transition, they have their own ironic, unintended effect, insofar as they identify for the benefit of any ambitious usurper the individual to be eliminated to clear

---

[2] Robert McLachlan Wilson, *Genealogy and History in the Biblical World* (New Haven, CT: Yale University Press, 1977), Marshall D. Johnson, *The Purpose of the Biblical Genealogies with Special Reference to the Setting of the Genealogies of Jesus* (Eugene, OR: Wipf and Stock, 2002).

[3] James Flanagan, "Succession and Genealogy in the Davidic Dynasty," in *Quest for the Kingdom of God: Studies in Honor of George E. Mendenhall*, ed. H. B. Huffmon (Warsaw, IN: Eisenbrauns, 1983).

a path to the throne. It places, in effect, a target on the back of the primary claimant.

The branched version also has advantages for those who are ruthlessly ambitious. It provides a map for the usurper who wishes to be thorough, a precaution often thought necessary. Examples are many. In the story of Herod usurping the Hasmonean rule, we see his rather systematic elimination of the roster of claimants. And then, through Mariam, he marries into the family so that he stands as the sole male in line.

A similar pattern can be seen in the rise of King David to power by piecing together the different stories of the demise of Saul's family. We learn in 1 Samuel 31 about the death of Saul and his sons Jonathan, Malchishua, and Aminadab. Then, in 2 Samuel, the moves consolidating accession to power are decisive. In chapter 3, Saul's strongman, Abner, is removed; in chapter 4, Ishbaal is murdered; in chapter 9, Meribaal and Micah are contained. The rest of the clan is eliminated in 2 Samuel 21. David also married into the family, taking Saul's daughter Michal as his wife. Throughout, David is presented as an unwilling recipient of overzealous followers, such as his nephew Joab, who does the dirty work for him. David protested, but he did not refuse the result (2 Sam 3:22–39).[4] Other biblical examples exist, notably the revolution of Jehu and his zealous extermination of the Omride dynasty (2 Kgs 9:14—10:28). The pattern was not unknown to readers of scripture.

## Matthew's Genealogy and Conflict in the Gospel

Matthew's awareness of this potential for bloodshed can be seen in his story of Herod's massacre of the Bethlehem boys, a comprehensive elimination of any threat from the Bethlehem family of David. So while it has the many functions explored in commentaries, we should realize that Matthew's genealogy is no exception to this world of contested claims.

---

[4] For an unvarnished account of David's accession to the throne of Judah and Israel, see Steven L. McKenzie, *King David: A Biography* (New York: Oxford University Press, 2002).

In fact, it sets the terms for the narrative conflict in the story to follow, prominently separated into three sections, with the stated aim of showing how fourteen generations are to be found in each section. The divisions serve to highlight the names of Abraham and David. Unlike Herod the Great, shortly to appear in Matthew's story, Jesus is shown to be both a Jewish son of Abraham and a royal son of David. We have the historian Josephus's word that Herod was considered neither Jewish nor royal. Antigonus, the last king Herod deposed, pointedly called him "a commoner and an Idumean."[5] We might assume this assessment was more widespread. So this establishes a first line of argument—Jesus, as Son of David, more properly deserves the throne that Herod occupies than does Herod.

With this we have a major departure from Mark's account. Matthew insists on the royal status of Jesus, as Son of David, whereas Mark's Gospel proclaimed a people's messiah, sprung from humble roots and not tainted by royal hubris. But Matthew has different needs and pursues different objectives. The Son of David promises to restore the lost kingdom. Furthermore, the vision of restoration expands beyond the particular reign of Herod to include overcoming the imperial power that he represents as Rome's client-king. Beyond that, it brings into play the entire history of imperial control that from the time of the end of the Davidic rule has prevented Judea from enjoying its true place in the world.

In 1:12–16, Matthew's genealogy spans the elapsed time from the end of the Babylonian exile to the arrival of Joseph, husband of Mary, with Jesus named as his heir. We generally read this to be making the simple point that Jesus belonged to the clan of David. But as we have seen, the function of genealogies, through dynastic shedding, is to trace the proper heir to the throne. If a claim of heritage is made, the genealogy is designed to show it. It would seem, then, that Matthew is proposing that Jesus is more than simply a member of the family. He is the coming "son of David," the

---

[5] Josephus, Antiquities, 14.404, *The New Complete Works of Josephus,* William Whiston, trans. (Grand Rapids, MI: Kregel Pub., 1999),

legitimate royal messiah. If this is the case, then the third part of Matthew's list—that tracing from the Babylonian exile to Joseph, the legal father of Jesus—evokes images of a succession of royal figures in their own form of exile. One is reminded of certain European royal families in exile, meticulously keeping track of the line of succession, waiting out the current modern interval, ready to resume command when the time arrives.

It is at this point that Joseph's dream enters the story with its prophecies concerning the son to be born (1:18–25). For Matthew's narrative, this is the mandate, the narrative contract establishing the task for the protagonist, Jesus. He is to "save his people from their sins." As we know from its insistence in this Gospel, "his people" means "the lost sheep of the house of Israel" (10:6; 15:24). But mention of "their sins" brings to mind the long return from exile, for this is the price of retrieving the kingdom (Isa 40:2).

The return is not always easy. For example, Tom, a Vietnam vet, has spent much of his energy since the early 1970s assisting war-scarred veterans upon their return to the United States. Most of the time he is deliberately calm and quietly persuasive. But at times he becomes strident, suppressed rage surfacing abruptly. When called out on it, he offers an embarrassed apology: "I am not home yet. I am not completely home, but I am almost home." After five decades he is not yet "completely home." Returning home is not always easy; it is often elusive and sometimes impossible.

This is the problem that besets Naomi in the book of Ruth. Ruth is important to Matthew. He names her in his genealogy (Matt 1:5); he borrows the genealogical form he uses from the ending of Ruth (Ruth 4:18–22); and he appropriates the striking scene of Naomi's return home for use in his Gospel. Naomi's story can be read as a parable of Israel's delayed return from its exile in Babylon. Naomi arrives back in Bethlehem after a decade-long absence (Ruth 1). She is barren and bereft, unable to have her affairs settled until the end of the book. Until then she is not yet entirely home.

Biblical passages view the exile as a result of sin, Israel's unfaithfulness to the Covenant. Release from that debt is a condition of return from exile (Isa 40:1–2; Dan 9; Ezra 9). In 539 CE, with the edict of Cyrus, the exiles were allowed to return, and with that the promise to Abraham (Gen 12; 15; Matt 1:12, 17) was fulfilled. But the return was not complete, because they were unable to achieve self-governance; the kingdom was not restored, and thus the promise to David (2 Sam 7:11–16; Matt 1: 6–7, 17) was left unfinished. It would not be until the Messiah arrived that the exile would be entirely over. Only with the end of the imperial occupation would Israel be entirely home.[6]

Framed in this way, Matthew's theme of the Son of David hails back to the loss of the kingdom at the beginning of the Babylonian captivity. For him, the return of the Son of David as Messiah means the end of the exile and the fullness of the return. It is as the Son of David that Jesus can be counted as the Messiah who brings God's kingdom. It is in these circumstances that the story of Jesus unfolds for Matthew.

## The New Historical Situation

Matthew brings his story of an unfinished exile to a world changed from that of Mark. The Great Revolt had failed. The Roman army had taken the city and the Temple at great cost to the Jews. Judaism was in disarray. The center of its world, the Temple that symbolized the one God, was now a burned scar in the earth, a constant reminder of the new predicament. With the destruction of Jerusalem, the Sanhedrin, the Jewish council, was gone, and with it the Sadducee party. The Essenes at Qumran, at the north end of the Dead Sea, were routed and destroyed (though not before they hid their library in the caves in the cliffs, now called the Dead Sea scrolls). Finally, the Zealots (Sicarii) who had taken refuge in the fortress of Masada in the south were conquered after a two-year siege, but only after they had committed mass suicide and destroyed all their own property. It was a defiant gesture against the Roman army, which lived off the spoils of defeated enemies.

---

[6] The expectation of the exile ending with the coming of the Messiah is given, for instance, in N. T. Wright, *The New Testament and the People of God* (Minneapolis, MN: Fortress Press, 1992), 381.

What vestiges remained included the Pharisee movement. The Pharisees responded creatively to the devastation by shifting their attention to the Torah, acclaiming it the new "temple" at the center of their faith life. By Matthew's time the neo-rabbinic movement established by Gamaliel was already evolving. The rabbis rose to prominence, replacing the priests in the vacuum left by the absence of the Temple, with the synagogue becoming the focus for religious gathering. This movement toward rabbinic Judaism would prove the primary competitor for the soul of Judaism for Matthew's community. His gospel argues his case for Jesus and his followers as the future of the faith.

The Roman destruction of the Temple was more than a military victory over a difficult and stubborn people. It was also a theological statement meant to demonstrate the superiority of the Roman gods over the God of the Jews. This point was further driven home by the Fiscus Judaicus, a tax imposed by the Emperor Vespasian upon all Jews. Previously, the Temple tax levied for the upkeep of the Jerusalem Temple was imposed only upon men aged 20 to 50 years. But the new tax was required of every Jew, not only the adult men. Women, children, the elderly, and slaves were now also taxed. Even more infuriating, the new tax was to be collected in support of the Temple of Capitoline Jupiter in Rome, the central temple of Rome and symbolic of its imperial sway, underlining the theological implications of the destroyed Temple of Yahweh in Jerusalem.

## The Jewish-Roman Wars

The humiliation that resulted from the Temple destruction and the new tax expressed itself in an era of intense and sometimes alarmingly violent rebellions. The unrest of this era was occasionally called the Jewish-Roman wars or the Kitos rebellion. Beginning with the Great Revolt in Jerusalem in 66–70 CE, and concluding with the Bar Kochba Rebellion in 135 CE, Jewish nationalism boiled over periodically into full revolt. The resistance was not limited to Judea. In 115–117 CE, the entire region experienced rebellion. Seeing an opportunity, Judean forces throughout the diaspora rose in revolt. Uprisings occurred on the island of Cyprus and across North Africa, in Cyrene, Libya, and Egypt. While the bulk of the Roman army was occupied with Trajan's Parthian War on the eastern perimeter of the empire, other outposts of the empire were maintained by smaller peacekeeping garrisons. Overwhelmed Roman garrisons along with Roman citizens were slaughtered. Eventually, the Roman general Lusius Quietus (who gives his name to the Kitos wars) brought things under control.

The culmination of this period of rebellion was the Bar Kochba revolt in the years 132–136 CE. This time situated in Judea itself, the revolt was led by Simon bar Kochba, hailed as the Messiah. The rebels maintained an independent state of Israel for over two years, but an army of six legions utterly crushed it. With this comprehensive Roman victory the era of Jewish resistance decisively ended. To a greater extent than even the Great Revolt of Judea of 70 CE, the Bar Kochba revolt brought about an extensive depopulation of Jewish communities. Jews were effectively barred from Jerusalem.

## The Jewish Christians

Although they were included in the repressive measures that followed, Jewish Christians did not participate in the rebellion. The noninvolvement of Jewish Christians in all of the nationalist fervor of the times is widely noted, and it raises the question of why. Rather than distaste for military violence or cowardice, it seems the Christian community of Jews operated by a distinct set of values grounded in the discipleship of Jesus of Nazareth. Matthew, writing his Gospel in the time of mounting nationalist intensity, presents a principled opposition to violence. Christians were acting on principle, not simply moved by expedience.

Given the messianic hopes aired during the Bar Kochba rebellion, it is likely that Jewish nationalism was fueled by the memories of the past and a desire to restore the lost kingdom, the full return from the losses of exile. We see, in any case, that Matthew makes this connection, and his picture of Jesus announcing that the kingdom of heaven is at hand gives expression to this desperate yearning.

*Matthew's Task: Retrieving the Authentic Identity of Israel*

We can appreciate the new situation of Matthew's faith community by comparing it with Mark's. In Mark, we find oppression confronted through nonviolent conflict engagement and resolution. Our theorist for this manner of action was Gene Sharp and his analysis of nonviolent confrontation, so instrumental during the Arab Spring (see Chapter 2). However, after the failure of the Great Revolt during Mark's time, with Judaism now in shambles, we find Matthew in a situation dramatically heightened. Think in terms of the Syrian revolt now, not the Arab Spring. The turn toward violence has escalated, and new solutions are needed.

*The Contribution of Postcolonial Criticism*

Postcolonial criticism, a body of thought that arose in the twentieth century, offers a framework for understanding the work of Matthew in its time. Postcolonial criticism became a possibility after the rise of the intellectual elite in the former colonies of the great European nineteenth-century imperialist expansion, such as India, African nations, Middle Eastern lands, and the Caribbean. It offers certain categories useful for perceiving aspects of Matthew's project. This is true even though the biblical situation was one of absolute conquest by an empire, rather than an empire's withdrawal, as in the twentieth century.

The postcolonial predicament for the former colonies was to retrieve an identity for themselves, even if they had to invent it in part. Trying to heal the breach between what they were before the invasion of foreign elements and the place they now were, independent again, they appealed to a "return to the sources." A concern for authentic cultural identity came from the sense that another culture had been imposed upon their own. A term created to explain this blend of old and new identities was *hybridity.*[7] But it became important to clarify what was being borrowed and what

---

[7] For example, see Leela Gandhi, *Postcolonial Theory: A Critical Introduction* (New York: Columbia University Press, 1998), 123–40.

was not. Similar patterns are evident in the biblical writings—for instance, in the use of Greek, the language of the empire. In this regard much effort went into the task of unmasking the false consciousness of the empire in the service of demonstrating the authenticity of the native culture.

For the Jews, colonialism ended otherwise, not with the withdrawal of the empire, but rather the complete reduction and eventual removal of the colony. However, the people endured. And from this different kind of location, the loss of Jerusalem and its Temple precipitated them into a similar effort of retrieval. The narrative of Matthew's Gospel can be read in such a light. His return to sources for suitable precedents fits this conception of the task. Examples abound. Abraham is the father of them all. Joseph, son of Jacob and the dreamer who led Israel into to Egypt, prefigures Joseph from Nazareth. Moses, the founder and lawgiver who brought them back and authored the five books of the Torah, is reflected in the five major discourses of Matthew's text. And, most pertinently, King David would be the father of the Messiah destined to restore their lost kingdom. With the return of the House of David, the exile would finally come to an end.

Consequently, we are not to read Matthew's Gospel, the work of a Jewish author in a Jewish community of Jesus-followers, as being anti-Jewish. While it offers a prophetic criticism of Jewish leadership, it does not dismiss Jews from the coming future. In proper context Matthew's text is situated alongside other expressions of Judaism against the common enemy, the empire that has so ruthlessly diminished it. Other forms of Judaism stand as rivals to Matthew and his community, vying for the authentic identity and the destiny of Judaism. This is the role of the Pharisees in Matthew's narrative—a group that can be seen from a modern point of view as unfairly maligned in Christian history. What we have in Matthew's Gospel instead is the story of a rivalry of siblings facing a common enemy.

As for the Roman Empire, it does not receive overt criticism in Matthew's text, a fact that has caused its role to be overlooked in the past and discounted by many today. But the imperial presence emerges vividly enough once we are alerted to its influence.

Colonized peoples work "under the radar," avoiding the volatile moods of empire. The vignette of the Magi leaving Judea (Matt 2:12) speaks volumes. They are warned in a dream—a warning, we are to understand, given by the God of Matthew and his readers, the true God of Judaism, who teaches his people how to survive or to evade encounters with the lords of force. It stands in sharp contrast to Herod, vassal of Rome, slaughtering the innocents of Bethlehem. At work here was another kind of divinity entirely.

Thus the fierce nationalism that exploded periodically into unproductive violence in the final years of Jerusalem finds a contrast in Matthew's insistence on non-retaliation. For, if the rivalry with the neo-rabbinic movement enters Matthew's narrative in the form of an unflattering portrayal of the Pharisees, the uncompromising differences with the nationalists appears in this Gospel's unyielding opposition to violent methods of settling disputes.

## MATTHEW'S STORY:
## REIMAGINING THE MESSIAH

Unlike Mark, Matthew insists on the royal status of the Messiah. But he transforms the messianic hope from its anticipated theme of domination to one of service. His sustained attention to the Servant of Yahweh, in Isaiah 40—55, alters the role of David kingship in the post-exilic era.

Competition with the post-Pharisaic movement prompted Matthew to pitch his Gospel narrative as a struggle for authentic religion, the Pharisaic "hypocrites" vs. Jesus, the so-called impostor.[8] Matthew presents Jesus as the authentic heir of the tradition, tracing his heritage back to Moses and David. Matthew's use of a traditional story pattern of the banished, forgotten, and then returning prince enables him to show why Jesus, the royal descendant of David, was not recognized as such. Banished from Bethlehem, Jesus grows to

---

[8] The charges of imposture and hypocrisy are explained in "The Empire Refused," below, as pivotal for the narrative conflict.

maturity in distant Nazareth, only to return to Judea and its capital, Jerusalem, as an adult. As the claimant to the throne of David, Jesus stands in opposition to the history of foreign imperial usurpation of Israel's kingdom of Yahweh, for the return of the Messiah signals an end to the history of exile and foreign occupation.

Matthew chose to address the situation facing him and his community of believers with a story. The story he had at hand was the Gospel of Mark, with its drama of resistance. However, he needed to make adjustments. The situation had changed, and initiating a challenge was no longer the suitable message; they were, instead, rebuilding from the shambles.

## The Banished Prince

Matthew borrowed Mark's account but then reworked it by way of a remarkable alteration. He placed Mark's narrative inside another story—the ancient formula story of the banished prince. The outlines of the story we know well: a palace coup ousts and kills the king and his family at the hand of the king's younger brother. However, the infant prince escapes the usurpation, being spirited away by faithful family retainers and sent into the countryside, where he grows up unaware (usually) of his true heritage. At some point he shows his true heritage by a sign, such as pulling a sword from a stone. Then, prepared by a mentor, he returns with an army and successfully regains the kingdom, restoring the rightful dynasty and thoroughly purging the kingdom of its usurper.

Ancient examples include the stories of Oedipus, Theseus, Siegfried, and also Moses, a story important to Matthew. Literary examples include the *Odyssey* and *Hamlet,* each famous for ending with grim, comprehensive killing. This story formula is still alive and active. One modern example, among others, is the *Lion King,* with its account of the young lion king, Simba, against the usurper, Scar.

Just as a musical figure such as a fugue or jazz improvisation can be recognized despite undergoing transformations, so a story formula such as this survives intact despite changes in its format. *Hamlet* takes the story of the banished prince straight. The

*Odyssey* makes one variation: the father leaves home rather than the son. But it is the same story. The Moses story tells it from the side of the usurpation, now seen as a rebellion, and turns a conservative story about preserving the old regime into a revolutionary story overturning it. But it is the same story, told from different sides. And so is the case of Matthew's treatment of the banished prince.

When a stock scene is repeated in literature, it has come to be known as a *type-scene*. We see it in genre literature today. In the old westerns, there were standard scenes—the stagecoach robbery, the gunfight on the main street, the bar fight. The fun was in seeing how the typical scene played out in this particular movie. This happens in the Bible as well. A striking instance is the story pattern of the patriarch meeting his future wife at the community well. It happens time and again, and the interest lies in seeing how it is done this time around.

An instance pertinent to our story is the type-scene of the public entry into town. When Naomi, with her daughter-in-law Ruth, returns to her hometown of Bethlehem after years away, she encounters wonder and consternation. Questions are asked:

> And when they came to Bethlehem,
> the whole town was stirred because of them.
> And the women said, "Is this Naomi?" (Ruth
>     1:19)

Matthew introduced to his Gospel two scenes similar to Naomi's arrival. In Matthew we also find someone of note entering the city, provoking a citywide stir, raising questions about identity. The first scene is the entry of the Magi:

> Wise men from the east came to Jerusalem,
> saying, "Where is the child who has been born
>     king of the Jews?" . . .
> When King Herod heard this, he was frightened,
> and all Jerusalem with him. (Matt 2:1–3)

This was early in the Gospel. But there is another, similar scene toward the end of the Gospel, when Jesus enters Jerusalem in the triumphal entry:

> And when he entered into Jerusalem,
> the whole city was in turmoil,
>     asking, "Who is this?" (Matt 21:10)

These two scenes echo each other, both highlighting an arrival at Jerusalem. But there is more to it. Together they mark the beginning and end of a chain of events that follow one another like falling dominoes.

The arrival of the Magi starts the action of Matthew's narrative. Once Herod is alerted, the family of Jesus needs to leave town, going to Egypt. After Herod dies, they can return, it would seem, but Herod's replacement by his son Archelaus is scant improvement. So the family settles instead in an obscure northern town called Nazareth, in the sufficiently distant location of Galilee. In Matthew's Gospel, Nazareth is unknown territory. We are told little about it, and with the family moving there, the story fades out. We hear nothing of the time spent in Nazareth. The narrative only comes back to life when Jesus is an adult. A sign at his baptism indicates he is the awaited one. He leaves Nazareth for Capernaum, which will serve as his center of activity during the first part of his mission. An allusion to Isaiah's passage about the loss of the northern tribal territories of Zebulon and Naphthali suggests that the retrieval of the kingdom will begin where its lands first were lost, in Galilee of the nations. And so begins the long return to Judea and its capital, the city of Jerusalem.

## The Homecoming of the Hero

The circle in the text is also the story of the hero's homecoming. It is the traditional story of the banished prince, now returning home to the lost kingdom. The many variations of the story pattern have

one thing in common—again, think of *Odysseus* and *Hamlet*—
they end in a moment of comprehensive revenge. No trace of the
corrupting influence is spared the cleansing bloodshed. As with
*Hamlet,* Matthew's interest is primarily in the time of the return,
the struggle to regain the territory from which Jesus was banished
in the past. This also is the part of the narrative based on Mark,
but now it is transformed. Mark relates a prophetic initiative to
protest an unjust social situation; Matthew frames it as a response
to an past injustice.[9]

To make doubly sure his audience is getting the picture, Matthew accents each of the stages of the story with quotations from
scripture. The first of these is representative, with its formulaic
introduction leading to the quoted passage. In respect to Joseph's
dream, we read:

> Now all this happened in order that what was spoken by the
> Lord through the prophet would be fulfilled, saying, "Look,
> the virgin shall conceive and bear a son, and they shall name
> him Emmanuel." (Matt 1:22–23)

Tracing the cycle of places in the story of homecoming, we find
consecutive references to Bethlehem (2:6), Egypt (2:15), Nazareth
(2:23), Galilee (4:15), and Jerusalem (21:5). But we should note
that Matthew's story misses the final stage about ruthlessly regain-
ing the kingdom. And here we find the crucial difference between
the traditional story of the banished prince and Matthew's use of
it. In Matthew we find no slaughter of enemies, no resettlement
and restoration of the lost dynasty. Rather than a military assault,
the return of Jesus to Judea is characterized by a prophetic judgment. Those who see themselves accused by his prophetic action
retaliate, however, and the story appears to end with his death.
However, the tomb is discovered to be empty, and the risen Christ
appears to the women visiting the tomb, and then to the Twelve
on a mountain in Galilee.

---

[9] For a fuller account of this pattern, see Beck, *Banished Messiah,* 57–79.

## Another Version of the Messianic Secret

The homecoming pattern shapes Matthew's story in a number of ways useful to him. One of these is his version of the so-called Messianic Secret associated with Mark. In Mark, the messianic role of Jesus is hidden because of the traditional misconception of its royal Davidic character. Despite lacking royal pedigree, Jesus unexpectedly is found to be the people's messiah. But in sharp contrast to Mark, Matthew insists on the royal heritage of Jesus; that royal dimension is precisely what was hidden and is now to be revealed. In Matthew's recounting, few know what the reader knows—that Jesus is actually a native of Bethlehem rather than Nazareth. His royal connections, shown in the genealogy, are presented to the reader, not those within the narrative. So one of the purposes of the formula story of the banished prince is to justify the appearance of an unanticipated royal who is legitimized not only by his abilities, but even more by his credentials as the heir of the lost kingship.

Thus Jesus, as Son of David, is important for Matthew. The title authorizes his claim for representing the true identity of Israel over the rival strains of Judaism. Jesus's authentication is found in the scripture—not only in reenacting of the story of Moses, but also through the ties to David, reconnecting to the lost lineage.

## The Long Return: The Mission of Jesus

Matthew also applies his series of scripture quotations to the return journey, defining the character of that return. His strategy is to contrast the Emmanuel passages of Isaiah 7—12 with those of the Servant of Yahweh from Isaiah 40—55. The first, in today's understanding, date back to the original Isaiah, while the second are from the anonymous Second Isaiah, the prophet of the exile.

Matthew begins with the image of Emmanuel, the royal figure of the king found in the early chapters of Isaiah. In addition to the citation of Isaiah 7:14 in Joseph's dream (Matt 1:23), another appears at the beginning of Jesus's mission (Matt 4:14–16). These

Emmanuel passages evoke the images that have given the season of Advent its particular flavor. In Matthew's usage they picture the Davidic kingship in its full splendor.

But as Jesus enters into his work in Galilee, another part of the book of Isaiah is favored, reinterpreting the meaning of the Messiah as the story unfolds. In Matthew 8:17 and 12:18–21, the fourth and first songs of the Servant of Yahweh are cited (Isa 53:4; 42:1–4), with the first of these quoted in its entirety. With this, the identity of the Messiah is realigned from the archetypical royal to the image of the servant. And with that, the new interpretation of the meaning of "son of David" is announced. Matthew revises Mark's narrative to counter false expectations prevalent in his own day. These expectations are anticipated in the narratives proposed by the voices in the desert setting out rival programs for the Messiah.

Once Jesus is ready to begin his adult mission, many signs indicate his special place in the coming task. First of all, there is the voice from heaven, quoting scripture: "This is my Son, the Beloved, with whom I am well pleased" (Matt 3:17). Matthew changes Mark's second person "you" to the third person "this." For Matthew, unlike Mark, the voice does not address Jesus in the manner of a narrative contract establishing a task for the main character. Instead, it addresses those others within earshot, which includes the reader. It is not a moment of revelation for Jesus, but rather for those around him. It is the moment in which the true king is identified, before he begins his return. The shift from Emmanuel to Servant is anticipated in the voice from heaven.

But another voice presents us with an important precursor. John the Baptist also is identified by prophetic indication as "the voice of one crying out in the wilderness: 'Prepare the way of the Lord, make his paths straight'" (3:2). When Matthew frames his version of the Gospel with the formula story of the banished prince, the role of John the Baptist changes. He becomes the mentor preparing the hero for the return journey to reclaim the kingdom and restore the authentic rule. And here, too, we find a quotation from scripture: Isaiah 40:3. It confirms the servant identification of the

Promised One. But John the Baptist also represents a partial vision of the task ahead, and this is part of the unfolding drama.

## The Empire Refused

There is still another voice in the desert, also quoting scripture. It is identified as the voice of Satan, the adversary. The visions of Jesus in the desert (4:1–11) are temptations concerning the possible but false ways of conducting the work of the Messiah. That is, in the context of a return to reclaim the lost kingdom, they propose alternatives, common misconceptions of how authority is to be exercised. The three temptations conclude with Satan offering the kingdoms of the world. This is the imperial model explicitly stated. There is one condition: Satan asks that he be worshiped as emperor. There is no clearer statement of the Gospel's understanding of empire than this requirement: following empire is akin to worshiping Satan, and the decision to worship Satan is equated with choices that make him like an emperor.[10]

Later, of course, God and Caesar will be placed in competitive positions, when during Jesus's debates in the Temple he is confronted with Caesar's coin. For the present, we learn what is at stake. In effect, this desert temptation would recreate the kingdom of God in the image of empire. Jesus flatly refuses this proposal, identifying it as blatant idolatry: "Worship the Lord your God, and serve only him." When Peter later recognizes Jesus as Messiah, he seems to embrace this false vision of the coming kingdom. Jesus's words inevitably follow: "Get behind me, Satan! You are a stumbling block to me; for you are setting your mind not on divine things but on human things" (16:23).

When discussing Mark's Gospel, we noted that current understanding of apocalyptic writing would see it as less a prediction of the future than as an alternative vision of the present. It offered a critical view of existing social injustice by way of its alternative view. Building upon that, some New Testament scholars distin-

---

[10] Ibid., 146.

guish among three utopian visions of that time—the *triumphalist,* the *deferred,* and the *revolutionary.*

> These are the triumphalism of imperial power regarded as the fulfillment of history; the deferred eschatology of those hoping for an eventual utopia, but who are prepared to accept the current status quo; and thirdly, the revolutionary expectation of an imminent and radical change.[11]

The imperial vision, especially as realized in the reign of Caesar Augustus, represented the first of these, the triumphalist. It was the utopia fully realized, according to its adherents. Believers of the third kind, the revolutionary, included both the messianic figures who adopted military methods and the nonviolent prophets who anticipated an imminent intervention of God. They represented contrasting approaches to reordering an unjust society. But both groups anticipated a period of radical change, total and imminent. The second vision was most prominently represented by the party of the Pharisees. This group was seen as particularly associated with the deferred promise, hoping for an eventual transformation of society, but willing to endure the present conditions for the time being. One feature of Matthew's story of Jesus is the shift from immanent to deferred promise, from revolutionary to that akin to the Pharisees. That also contributed to their competition for the future of Judaism.

In the desert encounter with Satan, Jesus is presented with one option for being the messiah—he can be part of the imperial model, utopia realized, in the fullness of the good life. We know that the utopia thus envisioned means fullness of life only for a few; for those outside its gates, desperation and discontent urge

---

[11] Sean Freyne, *Jesus, a Jewish Galilean: A New Reading of the Jesus Story* (New York: T and T Clark, 2004), 127. See further John J. Collins, "Temporality and Politics in Jewish Apocalyptic Literature," in *Apocalyptic in History and Tradition,* ed. Christopher Rowland and John Barton, JSP Supplement Series 43, 26–43 (Sheffield, UK: Sheffield Academic Press, 2002), 29.

many toward revolution, as in Judea. Jesus categorically refuses Satan's offer.

In John the Baptist another utopian model stakes a claim in Matthew's Gospel. Here the revolutionary impulse enters the story. John does not represent the militant impulse that drove some to take up arms and force history to make its changes. Rather, in John we see an example of the "signs prophets" who anticipated the heavenly visitation to be happening at any moment, upending the injustices that control their lives and bringing the kingdom of God into being. These are the prophetic figures who went into the desert or to the Jordan evoking images from the stories of Moses and Joshua as a way of calling for a new beginning.

Matthew shows John using the harsh imagery of rupture, evoking a sense of urgency. "Repent, for the kingdom of heaven has come near"—the time is ripe. "Even now the ax is lying at the root of the trees. . . . His winnowing fork is in his hand" (3:2, 10, 12). In contrast to the direct refusal he gives to Satan's offer, Jesus accepts the call of John. In this regard he sides with the resistance to the imperial vision. Matthew brings it home to us by showing John's message being repeated verbatim by Jesus in his first public statement in this Gospel: "Repent, for the kingdom of heaven has come near" (3:2; 4:17).

After this initial proclamation we see Jesus continuing the urgent language and imagery of John: The tree shall be known by its fruits. Every tree not bearing fruit will be cut down and cast into the furnace of fire. You brood of vipers (see Matt 7:15–20; 12:33–34; 13:39–43, 49–50; 23:33). Jesus borrows, and extends, the vocabulary of the Baptist.

But this convergence is not the entire message. Before long we see Jesus performing healing acts not anticipated in John's program. Two themes begin to emerge together—"proclaiming the good news of the kingdom" (4:23; 9:35; 24:14), and healing (4:23; 9:35; 10:7). This shift, from John's message to new thinking, is neatly shown in a set of images—deserts and gardens. At the beginning, John is preaching a judgment that is about to occur. He calls for a decision, a cutting off of all false options. We witness the prophet of deforestation, imagining the impending judgment as an axe at the root, reducing the unruly foliage to a desert.

After he is arrested, John sends messengers from his prison cell to Jesus: "Are you the one who is to come, or are we to wait for another?" (11:3). It seems that the program is not developing as he expected. What is the delay? And where is the metaphorical axe? Jesus's response is critical to Matthew's account: "Go and tell John what you hear and see: the blind receive their sight, the lame walk, the lepers are cleansed, the deaf hear, the dead are raised, and the poor have good news brought to them" (Matt 11:2–6).

With this response Jesus announces that healing will be the theme that distinguishes the preaching about the kingdom. Jesus alludes to biblical passages from Isaiah that depict the restoration of the people as a greening of the desert:

> The wilderness and the dry land shall be glad,
> the desert shall rejoice and blossom; . . .
> The glory of Lebanon shall be given to it,
> the majesty of Carmel and Sharon. . . .
>
> Then the eyes of the blind shall be opened,
> and the ears of the unstopped;
> then the lame shall leap like a deer,
> and the tongue of the speechless sing for joy.
> For waters shall break forth in the wilderness,
> and streams in the desert. (Isa 35:1–6)

John's axe is replaced by a program of reseeding the barren land. It too is a language of renewal, but it brings another vision of what that is to be.

Along with shifting the focus of the messianic mission from judgment to healing, Matthew shows Jesus discarding John's insistence on a nearing, even immediate, judgment, and moving his vision to something in a more distant future. This is seen particularly with the parables. In particular, the parable of the Weeds and the Wheat advises leaving judgment up to the landowner at the time of harvest. But that harvest is "at the end of the age" (13:40, 49).

Again, according to the typology of utopian visions, Matthew's program of deferral would align Jesus with the Pharisees, the most prominent example of those who espouse a deferred realization of the promise. This alignment may help explain why Matthew's vision positions Jesus and the Pharisees as such strong antagonists, with their two visions of deferral. Which will secure the future?

Once we see that Matthew wishes to claim that the true soul of Israel is to be found in the Jesus movement, we can appreciate how authenticity is a primary theme in his Gospel. Typically, Matthew frames it in terms of inside versus outside, insisting that the two be consistent. The lack of such consistency is what Matthew calls hypocrisy. Examples include the teachings about almsgiving, prayer, and fasting (6:1–18), and the woes against the scribes and Pharisees (23:1–36). Whereas the emerging neo-rabbinic movement adapted to the new era by promoting the Torah as the center of Judaism, replacing the lost Temple, the Jesus movement, as Matthew presents it, reached back further into the time of Israelite origins to anchor its claim fully in the tradition on the way to suggesting a new beginning.

Two passages in Matthew's Gospel have a kind of uncanny resonance. In the scene after the crucifixion and preceding the resurrection, the Pharisees approach Pilate with a proposal that he put a guard at the tomb of Jesus. Their reason, like their action, is surprising:

> "Sir, we remember what that *impostor* said while he was still alive, 'After three days I will rise again.' Therefore command the tomb to be made secure until the third day; otherwise his disciples may go and steal him away, and tell the people, 'He has been raised from the dead,' and the last deception would be worse than the first." (27:63–64, emphasis added)

This language of an impostor, claiming that his promise of resurrection is inauthentic, finds its contrast and partner in Matthew 23:

"Woe to you, scribes and Pharisees, *hypocrites*! For you are like whitewashed tombs, which on the outside look beautiful, but inside they are full of the bones of the dead and of all kinds of filth" (23:27–28, emphasis added)

In this line Jesus accuses the Pharisees of a similar inauthenticity. They are the real impostors and hypocrites. The matter at issue is the ability of the speaker to represent authentically the true identity of Israel in the post-Temple era. Matthew's narrative makes it clear that the tomb empty due to resurrection has a better claim on the future than tombs full of dead men's bones.

The charges of hypocrisy and being an impostor are essentially equivalent in their accusation of inauthenticity in portraying a role. This set of terms is the conflict language at the center of the struggle between the antagonists in the primary plot of the Matthean narrative. Each implies an adopted role, adding an undertone of inauthenticity. Each could easily be translated as "fraud." We tend to think of hypocrites as lacking personal integrity. The term began in the theater, referring to playing a part. Matthew uses the term *hypocrite* much more than the other Gospels, almost always in reference to the Pharisees. Similarly, an impostor pretends to a position or status that is undeserved, assuming the identity or character of another, commonly as regards a royal office.

The dispute about the authenticity of the Messiah continues into the closing chapters of the Gospel. Matthew's answer to the first charge against Jesus as an "impostor" (27:64) is found in the formula story of the banished prince, now returned to his kingdom. In Jesus's return, the kingdom returns—and the exile is ended. Jesus's return in this Gospel story, banished and now back as legal royal heir, evokes that larger expectation, now presented as completed.

And yet, the fulfillment of the promise is frustrated. We noted that the kingdom of Israel was not revived as anticipated by the promise. The family of David did not return to power. Matthew writes as the frustration of defeated Judea overflows into the Jewish-Roman wars around the Mediterranean rim. What is Matthew saying about Jesus as messiah? He has certainly made a strong case for Jesus being the Son of David, the proper claimant to the throne.

What then is Matthew doing? The return from exile was supposed to find a completion when the messiah came. So why does it not? Is it because the Messiah was rejected, and therefore, so was Judaism? Is that what the line that traces through a certain series of verses means? Three crucial moments define the theme. First, we see the promise that Jesus will save his people from their sins (1:21). This has the character of a programmatic statement regarding Matthew's narrative. A second moment occurs with the cry of the crowd at the crucifixion, "His blood be upon us and on our children" (27:25). At this point the narrative program has apparently come up empty, a failure. A third moment is the final commissioning, in which the disciples are sent out into the world (28:16–20). This line of argument has been invoked to argue Matthew sees Christianity replacing Judaism. And yet, did Matthew really abandon the promise to Israel?

## The Meaning of Kingship Language

Eventually we have to decide whether Matthew's language of kingship is metaphorical or literal. Is it poetry or politics? If he is not affirming the political kingship of Jesus, it is presumably metaphorical. This could be. But what does the metaphor signify? Is it a theological claim of salvation history, as often stated, and not meant literally at all? Perhaps Matthew is replacing political realities, which seem to have failed, with eternal values to come. Perhaps he is saying that there is another world that is more important and that political reality is little more than an illusion.

Or is it a metaphor directed toward political power? Is it not so much denying the reality and value of the political as it is framing the political in terms of eternal values that should guide it? Maybe it is a metaphorical critique of realpolitik.

And if it is *not* a metaphor, then what is Matthew saying? He has devoted considerable energy to presenting Jesus as the Son of David: the genealogy, the promises, the story of the exile and return. Maybe he wants to be taken literally. If Matthew is intending Jesus to be the factual royal messiah, then we must conclude that the very nature of the messiah's kingship is being reconfigured. And that political repercussions will follow.

Following this train of thought leads to the realization that Matthew's strategy is not simply a matter of yoking the title of Messiah to that of Servant, as we saw happening in Mark 1:11, in order to revise the messianic expectation. Matthew takes it further. By setting the story in the context of exile, both in the genealogy and the formula story of the banished and returning prince, he rewords the messianic tradition itself. The return from exile turns out to be something different from the resumption of the status quo ante. What has intervened between the loss of the kingship and its recovery is the exile itself. And any return brings with it something of the exile, with its new understandings.

During the time in Babylon the concept of God was purified, and the self-concept of Israel was changed along with it. So, the new understanding of the messiah king also needed to be adjusted. Matthew is making the case that the very idea of messiah was transformed during Israel's exile experience. Any royal messiah that emerged would be required to represent the experience of the servant Israel. Jesus is Messiah as Servant because by this time the messiah had to be such. Matthew is bringing this truth to post-Temple Judaism, and to any others who read his Gospel. Matthew presents a viable and tradition-authenticated view of the messiah as representing a post-exile Israel, one that performs a witness function to the nations. It is a witness function that serves as an act of resistance to the popular forms of exerting power. It is a corrective on politics as usual. This is not a Christian answer to Judaism, but rather a clarified expression of a strand of Jewish thinking that emerges in Matthew's Gospel. It is a conclusion drawn from the message of the Servant.

In the fourth of the Servant Songs, God is presented as in dialogue with the kings of the nations, stunned to discover that God favors this apparently abandoned and disfavored Servant, Israel, and all it stands for (Isa 52:13—53:12). The Emmanuel/Servant contrast mentioned earlier traces the shift from power figure to servant figure for Jesus. Matthew heightens the contrast of king and slave, with the pre-exilic Emmanuel passages giving way to the post-exilic passages introduced by Matthew in 8:17 (Isa 53:4) and the entire first Servant Song:

> "Here is my servant, whom I have chosen,
>> my beloved, with whom my soul is well
>>> pleased.
> I will put my Spirit upon him,
>> and he will proclaim justice to the Gentiles.
> He will not wrangle or cry aloud,
>> nor will anyone hear his voice in the streets.
> He will not break a bruised reed
>> or quench a smoldering wick
> until he brings justice to victory.
>> And in his name the Gentiles will hope."
>> (Matt 12:18–21)

The end of the exile, then, is not innocent of the memory and lessons of the exile. The return of the messiah signals the end of waiting for the end of the exile as resumption of the time before. Here the postcolonial idea of hybridity might be remembered; the one returning home is not the same as the one who left.


## CONFLICT RESOLUTION IN MATTHEW

Just as the head of the Holy Family was not the first dreamer named Joseph to go into Egypt, so the family was not the first to return from Egypt to the land of Israel. Along with the David story, the story of Moses is one of the Old Testament precedents important to Matthew in his presentation of Jesus. The Exodus provides an important type for his Gospel. The Moses story, however, is also a prominent instance of the formula story of the banished and returning prince. In fact, it serves to illustrate one of the features of that formula pattern echoed in Matthew's Gospel narrative.

As shown in the first chapter, the Gospels are counter-narratives. At the heart of the Gospel narratives there is a moment of refusal of the ways stories have been told. In particular, the satisfaction in stories is typically derived from two impulses found at the conclusion of stories: paying back the villain for the harm that person has been doing to others, and purging the world of the evil that has contaminated it.

## Payback and Purge

Moses's story begins with the massacre of the Hebrew children, just as Matthew's story of Jesus begins with the slaughter of the boys of Bethlehem. In the Moses story this disaster is answered by the death of the oldest boys among the Egyptians at the first Passover. Here slaying answers slaying—the law of retribution. Payback. In contrast, when Jesus returns to Judea, no slaughter occurs. The Gospel refuses to answer calamity with calamity.

Furthermore, the flight of the Hebrews is finally achieved with the devastation of the Egyptian forces in the floods of the Red Sea. In this, the threat is finally, and completely, overcome. Here we see the other stratagem of purgation from evil, or purge, this time rather literally portrayed. The Moses story thus illustrates another strategy common among narratives for bringing a story to a satisfactory conclusion. But it also is one that the Gospel refuses to adopt. Matthew's story concludes with neither of these moves favored by narrative tradition—neither payback nor purge.

Probably the most quoted passage in the Bible concerning nonviolence is in the Sermon on the Mount, Matthew 5:39—"But I say to you, Do not resist an evildoer. But if anyone strikes you on the right cheek, turn the other also." It is followed by the injunction to love one's enemies (5:43–48). The refusal to retaliate in kind is central to another theme of Jesus's teaching in Matthew, namely, the need to forgive one another. Much of the discourse of Matthew 18 is devoted to an examination of this need. It also involves the refusal to pay back in kind, a refusal made in the spirit of deliberate, unsentimental love.

Matthew dramatizes the teachings in his narrative. Of the three moments we saw concluding Mark's narrative conflict, Matthew selects two for emphasis: Jesus's prophetic action in the Temple and his arrest in the garden. In the first he joins the story of the Temple cleansing with that of Jesus's triumphal entry, which he elaborates considerably. In the second he develops Mark's account of Jesus's arrest in the garden with some significant touches. Together with these two we see the refusal of purge and the refusal of payback.

Matthew has orchestrated a grand scene for Jesus's entry into Jerusalem. Where Mark sets the Temple cleansing on the following day, underlining its deliberate nature, Matthew has merged the accounts of both the entry and the cleansing into a single, sweeping event (Matt 21:1–11, 12–17). With Matthew, the chanting of "Hosanna" continues into the Temple area (21:9, 15), for the cleansing is an integral part of the return itself. Once in the Temple, Jesus continues healing people, and we recall his activity in Galilee. And the introduction of the type-scene in 21:10–11, showing the entire city disturbed and asking questions about the new entry, completes the circle of events begun with the Magi entry in 2:1–3.

But, as noted earlier, that circle ends here. The homecoming of the banished prince does not include the final purgation of the story formula. This typically would eliminate with extreme prejudice the entire usurping party, as in the story of Moses, or the *Odyssey*, or *Hamlet,* or the *Lion King.* Or any example you wish to invoke. In refusing the impulse to return harm for harm, as signaled earlier with Herod's slaughter of the innocents in Bethlehem, the return and action in the Temple dramatizes more than simply non-retaliation. In its deliberate confrontation it also shows Jesus's move as one of resistance. It is prophetic but not militant.

What is Matthew telling his readers? In the context of the post-Temple anger at the time of his writing, he shows Jesus presenting an alternative to the prevailing mood. But there is also a judgment on the Roman tendency to favor total solutions to social problems. Matthew is signaling the bankruptcy of such efforts.

In the garden arrest scene in Matthew we come to the most explicit rejection of retaliatory action to be found in the Gospels.

Matthew retains the main elements of Mark's account, including Jesus's charge they are treating him like a *lestes* (insurrectionist). But Matthew elaborates the scene with many changes, the most famous likely being the sword saying: "All who take the sword will perish by the sword" (Matt 26:52). This saying of Jesus appears only in Matthew's Gospel. By itself, apart from its context here, it would simply be a statement of a principle derived from experience in the ways of the world. It states a karma-like law of social interaction. Those who make violence their business tend eventually to succumb to it. It is worthwhile taking a moment to notice this more general meaning, apart from any application to the disciples.

But in context, in Matthew's Gospel, it is properly seen as a nonviolent saying. Uttered at the precise moment when the option for violent resistance offers itself, it becomes a protest against that form of resistance. In the action of the story, when a sword is raised to retaliate against those arresting Jesus, it is a rebuke to those who would resist with swords. In Matthew's Gospel the one with the sword is said to be among those accompanying Jesus, unlike in Mark, where the one wielding the sword is a bystander. Thus the force of the saying is directed toward disciples; the followers of Jesus do not act out their resistance in this way.

And yet, more than the disciples are present, hearing this statement of principle. Two parties are involved in the arrest. In addition to the disciples, there are those making the arrest. The principle clearly applies to those who regularly employ violence in addition to those who are directly instructed not to. If this is the case, as it surely seems to be, then we might have a way of understanding what Matthew is doing when he not only recasts Mark's call for nonviolence but also addressees the theme of exile in his narrative.

### The Meaning of Jesus's Rejection

One way of reading the Gospel would place everything upon the person of Jesus, his divine sonship, his universal salvation, his crucial place in salvation history. A version of this holds that Matthew charges the Jews with the death of the Christ, as testified to by the king in the parable of the Wedding Feast, who burned the city of those who murdered his servants (Matt 22:7). We've seen that a case is sometimes made that the rejection of the Messiah by the Jewish leaders has resulted in the punishment of Judea.

But is not something else happening here? When we realize that the person of Jesus is presented in the Gospel as a narrative, a way of acting, the rejection of the person becomes a rejection of the meaning of his life, the lesson it dramatizes. In such a case the rejection of the Messiah is a rejection of what the Messiah has to offer. The crucifixion of Jesus is disclosed as a rejection of the principle of nonviolence that Jesus announces and enacts. The cry of the people, "his blood be upon us and on our children" (12:18–21), becomes another expression of the principle of the sword saying—"all who take the sword will perish by the sword." Jesus offers the Servant option that rejects the use of payback, of violence for violence. Payback is, of course, the option chosen by the nationalists who take on the Roman army, and lose. And it is conspicuously not the option chosen by the community of Christian Jews, for which Matthew might be viewed as spokesperson.

Matthew puts his own stamp on the narrative procedures of payback and purge, drawing upon Jewish tradition of bloodguilt. Bloodguilt traditionally attaches to the slayer and his family; for example, when David places the bloodguilt of Abner's death upon Joab and all his family (2 Sam 3:28–30). Bloodguilt can last for generations in families (2 Kgs 9:26). It can affect cities (Jer 26:5) and nations (Deut 21:8), and lands (Deut 24:4).

A main concern in the biblical deliberation over innocent blood is the need to bring to justice cases of murder—the spilling of "innocent blood." The shed blood of Abel cries out for vengeance against Cain (Gen 4:10). This biblical theme joins with that we have already seen as the principle of the sword saying. Insofar as the aim of the biblical theme is to exact retribution by executing the murderer (Deut 19:10, 13), we again encounter the narrative category of payback, returning harm for harm.

But beyond this, it adds a social dimension in its attention to the effect upon the community in which the deed occurs. The blight of contamination reflects a distinct aspect of injustice, the degrading social effect that unaddressed injustices can impose upon a society. It is easily imagined as a blight needing purging:

> You shall not pollute the land in which you live; for blood pollutes the land, and no expiation can be made for the land, for the blood that is shed in it, except by the blood of the one who shed it. You shall not defile the land in which you live, in which I also dwell; for I the Lord dwell among the Israelites. (Num 35:33–34)

We come again to the imagery of contamination, like that of the holy and unclean so prominent in Mark's Gospel. And we also return to the notion of purgation, or the narrative ploy of purge. As in narrative examples, purging is typically a cover for comprehensive violence.

### A Parody of Payback and Purge: Judas and Pilate

In two related passages unique to Matthew's resolution of conflict in the Gospel, these themes reappear in ironic form.[12] Judas and Pilate are shown to feel the guilt of shedding innocent blood. Common features include the response, "Look to it yourself," as well as the appeal to being absolved of shedding "innocent blood."

In chapter 27 we read about the death of Judas, which involves the attempt to return the thirty pieces of silver introduced earlier by Matthew (26:15).

> When Judas, his betrayer, saw that Jesus was condemned, he repented and brought back the thirty pieces of silver to the chief priests and the elders. He said, "I have sinned by betraying innocent blood." But they said, "What is that to

---

[12] Beck, *Banished Messiah,* 178. See also Raymond Brown, *The Death of the Messiah,* vol. 1 (New York: Doubleday, 1994), 659, on Jacques Escande, "Judas et Pilate prisonniers d'une meme structure (Mt 27,1–26," *Foi et Vie* 78 (June 3, 1979): 92–100.

us? See to it yourself." Throwing down the pieces of silver
in the Temple, he departed; and he went and hanged himself.
But the chief priests, taking the pieces of silver, said, "It is
not lawful to put them into the treasury, since they are blood
money." After conferring together, they used them to buy the
potter's field as a place to bury foreigners. (27:3–7)

This futile attempt to "pay back" the incriminating silver underscores Judas's actual guilt. The move fails in part because the
chief priests do not accept it but instead divert it to the purchase
of a potter's field. This amounts to their own aversion to claiming
responsibility for events.

Also found in chapter 27 is the famous story of Pilate's attempt
to excuse himself from blame by washing his hands of the matter:

So when Pilate saw that he could do nothing, but rather
that a riot was beginning, he took some water and washed
his hands before the crowd, saying, "I am innocent of this
man's blood; see to it yourselves." Then the people as a
whole answered, "His blood be on us and on our children!"
(27:24–25)

This parody of the "purging" function belies his next move, which
is to condemn Jesus to death by crucifixion, something that only
he could do.

Together, the two stories of Judas and Pilate highlight the in-
adequacies of conventional modes of resolving conflict. However,
they favor contrasting images, with Judas throwing the silver
pieces back into the treasury (payback), and Pilate symbolically
washing his hands (purge). Together they serve to parody both of
the functions of typical narrative conflict resolution.

Because the purpose of the regulations on innocent blood is to
assign guilt for murder, Matthew is saying that murder has taken
place, but that no one accepts blame. Judas, the high priests, and
Pilate all refuse to take responsibility for the deed. But at this
point in the story that pattern changes. The response to Pilate's
action—the entire crowd says, "His blood be upon us and on our

children" (27:25)—is well known and has provided Christian tradition with a rationalization for condemning Jews. Only the crowd takes unambiguous ownership of the deed. With that we enter the realm of social responsibility, and the problem of pollution of the community.

## Innocent Blood and the Scapegoat

The disclaimers of Judas, the priests, and Pilate point to another strand of the innocent blood theme in Matthew's approach. He implies a certain remedy for spilling innocent blood. Because of the degrading social effect on the host community in cases of bloodshed of innocents, biblical law was particularly concerned about instances when the perpetrator was unknown. With his account of each party disclaiming guilt (except the people as a whole), Matthew's story evokes that situation.

In Deuteronomy 21:1–9 we find the ritual for purging a village community from the pollution of innocent blood when an unsolved murder occurs in or near its premises. This remedy applies to villages, but in Jewish tradition a ritual is in place for ridding the entire people of the pollution of social guilt. That is the scapegoat ritual of the Day of Atonement, detailed in Leviticus 16.

Two goats are a part of this ritual. One is sacrificed to purify the inner sanctuary, the tent of meeting, and the altar from the sins of the people (Lev 16:15–19, 20). The second, living but driven away, is intended to carry away the sins, guilt, and impurity of the people. This is the *scapegoat* (Lev 16:20–22). It is typical of Matthew to make his case from Jewish custom, and so it is here. The model for the scapegoat in Matthew's Gospel is not the literary version, as we find in the works of René Girard (as in the chapter on John, below); rather, it is the Jewish experience of the ritual.

Furthermore, if Matthew is invoking the Atonement ritual of Leviticus 16, it is likely not that of the sacrifice but rather that of the scapegoat. Twice Matthew introduces into his text a saying from Hosea, "I desire mercy, not sacrifice" (Matt 9:13; 12:7; cf. Hos 6:6). It indicates that sacrificial atonement is not how he imagines the story of Jesus working. We can conclude that he favors the biblical figure of the scapegoat as the model for Jesus's death. In absorbing evil the scapegoat becomes a ritual image of refusing to practice payback. By absorbing the hurt, non-retaliation stops a strain of violence from continuing in its spiraling course. Likewise, it ritually demonstrates nonviolent purgation. It becomes an image of non-retaliation and forgiveness, which refuse to return harm for harm, damage for damage.

Invoking the theme of innocent blood, which in turn evokes the theme of the scapegoat, Matthew is positioning Jesus's death as a salvation for the people, not a condemnation. His emphasis is on all the people, seen, for instance, in Matthew's preference for the term *Israel,* as in "all Israel" (Matt 2:6; cf. 2 Sam 5:5). Jesus's assigned task in Matthew's account is "save his people from their sins" (1:21). All Israel is freed from its bondage of sin and violence. It is on that basis that Jesus announces the mission to the world (24:16–20).

### Convergence in Matthew

In Matthew's ritually oriented vision of conflict resolution, certain themes converge:

1.  An emphasis on "all the people," connecting Matthew's story to the theme of the scapegoat. All Israel is freed from its bondage, fulfilling the commission of 1:12.

2.  A process of elimination involving Judas, the priests, and Pilate that simulates the situation envisioned in Deuteronomy 21—a crime without an identifiable perpetrator.

3.  The scapegoat ritual as a non-sacrificial model for drawing off the guilt of the whole people (Lev 16:10).

4.  The nonviolent pattern of being willing to absorb evil and violence rather than paying them back, thereby ending real or potential strands of reprisal.

5.  The practice of Jesus as a nonviolent model for the disciple in situations of conflict (Matt 6:38–43).[13]

---

[13] See Beck, *Banished Messiah,* 187.

**Resurrection and Final Commission**

At the end of the Gospel, Matthew's presentation of Jesus's resurrection is not greatly elaborated. The stories in Matthew 28 include (1) the empty tomb, with the addition of the encounter of the women with the risen Christ as they leave the tomb; (2) the dealing with the guards at the tomb; and (3) the final commission from the mountain in Galilee.

The Matthean report of guards placed at the tomb, as requested by the Pharisees, has already been discussed. It helped set up the counter charges of being an impostor and hypocrisy in this story. The contrast between guarding an empty tomb and the white-washed tombs full of bones has been mentioned. The model that uses guards, with its implication of force and violence, is power-less against the resurrection. What requires particular notice now is that we are at the cusp of the future for which Matthew is a contestant in a rivalry for the future of post-Temple Judaism. A new story is about to begin. The tomb is emptied to launch a new story, and that begins with Jesus summoning the eleven disciples to the mountain in Galilee:

> And Jesus came and said to them, "All authority in heaven and on earth has been given to me. Go therefore and make disciples of all nations, baptizing them in the name of the Father and of the Son and of the Holy Spirit, and teaching them to obey everything that I have commanded you. And remember, I am with you always, to the end of the age." (Matt 28:18–20)

The commission is the mandate, the narrative program, for a new story. This one begins here and moves into the time after the time of Jesus of Nazareth. In effect, this is the time of Matthew, the evangelist, and the time of the writing of his Gospel. It is the basis for Matthew's double focus in his Gospel, that is, seeing the story of his community in the story of Jesus. And so, we find in the earlier instructions to the Twelve as they are sent out, two by two, other words more suitable for the church of Matthew's time, a time when "you will be dragged before governors and kings because of me, as a testimony to them and the Gentiles" (Matt 10:18).

## RESISTANCE AS NON-RETALIATION

From the injunction to turn the other cheek (5:39) to the example of the scapegoat, Matthew presents a policy of non-retaliation for the disciples of Jesus. Non-retaliation, it should be noted, is not the same as nonresistance. As shown in Chapter 2 on Mark, the practice of nonviolent action, a form of resistance, includes a final moment of non-retaliation. This is the proper context of non-retaliation, and it should be seen here as such. Matthew's teaching of non-retaliation is expressed most famously in the Sermon on the Mount (5:38–42, 43–48), but it also shapes the narrative resolution of conflict, as we have seen. There the return to Judea and the confrontation in the Temple show that Matthew has not abandoned the need for resistance. In effect, Matthew has focused on the essential moment in nonviolent action that differentiates it from other forms of resistance—its signature moment of not retaliating to the harm it attracts from those accustomed to relying on force.

We can add that non-retaliation aligns with forgiveness, another emphasis of Matthew (18:21–22, 23–35). Here, too, we see the pattern of deliberately refusing to respond in kind. Hannah Arendt identified forgiveness as an instrument for resolving conflict in public life with the teaching of Jesus. It manages to end a cycle of violence by refusing to continue it, at the cost of seemingly ignoring the demands of justice.[14] In the Sermon on the Mount, Matthew shows Jesus concluding his teaching of love of enemies by the injunction, "So be perfect, therefore, as your heavenly Father is perfect" (5:49). But the picture is complicated by Matthew's portrait of a God who appears to favor retribution. That needs attention.

---

[14] Hannah Arendt, *The Human Condition* (Chicago: University of Chicago Press, 1958), 238–39.

## Matthew and Divine Retribution

Flannery O'Connor's novel *The Violent Bear It Away* borrows its title from Matthew:

> And from the days of John the Baptist until now, the kingdom of heaven suffereth violence, and *the violent bear it away.* (11:12, Douay-Rheims, emphasis added)

Her novel is also a homecoming story, as the boy Tarwater returns to the house in which he was raised by his stern grandfather and burns it down. O'Connor describes a Christian vision driven by righteous anger. A spirit of retributive violence pervades the novel and seems to characterize young Tarwater's destruction of his home. But, as the context of Matthew 11:12 indicates, the question remains whether this applies more to John the Baptist than it does to Matthew's portrait of Jesus.

And yet there are those troublesome endings in Matthew's parables. At the end of the age there will be weeping and gnashing of teeth. And these words, we ought to note, are directed toward disciples. Matthew's hard sayings at the end of the parables have suggested for many that this God acts with retribution, even while forbidding it to the disciples. The paradox of a God who will not tolerate intolerance, who insists on non-retaliation or else will inflict retribution, grabs one's attention.[15] The paradox can be seen clearly in the story of the unforgiving steward (Matt 18:21–35). Forgiveness, which puts aside a debt of injury, will absorb rather than pay back the harm received. It is without calculation. But in the parable, the servant who has already been forgiven has that forgiveness revoked when he, himself, fails to forgive. Just preceding this story we find Jesus telling Peter that he should forgive seventy times seven—in other words, unconditionally. So we find ourselves wondering in the parable how God can put conditions on our forgiveness, which is expected to be unconditional.

---

[15] Barbara Reid, OP, "Violent Endings in Matthew's Parables and Christian Nonviolence," *Catholic Biblical Quarterly* 66 (2004): 237–55.

And yet, the parable also points to a possible answer to the co-nundrum. On the other side of mercy is justice, and justice seems to be a concern here. The injunction to avoid retaliation invites the suspicion that justice will not be served. A just God will exact suitable consequences for injustices done, but the disciple need not worry about that. The disciple's task is to act nonviolently, without retaliation, and leave justice up to God, in God's good time.

Moral philosophers distinguish retribution from vengeance on grounds of proportion and limits—present in the former, lacking in the latter. Vengeance is free-flowing and subjective, whereas retribution tries to balance punishment against the harm previously caused. A concern for retribution is a concern for justice, and, when assigned to the final age, stands as an assurance of God's ultimate justice. Vengeance, which is often confused with justice, is short-circuited in the practice of the disciple. Mercy risks in-justice, it would seem, but Matthew assures his readers that is not the case. God will provide.

## Matthew and Non-retaliation

More than with the other Gospel writers, images of purgation com-mand Matthew's imagination. The stories of banished princes re-turning to rule are framed as cleansing the realm of all traces of the contaminating presence of the usurper. The theme of usurpation itself involves a comprehensive removal of all threats to power. The story of Herod slaughtering the boys of Bethlehem belongs in this mindset of comprehensive purge. The return of Jesus to Judea, and the city of Jerusalem, is placed in the context of this set of expectations, though those expectations are not realized.

In Matthew's hands the theme of purge is connected to that of payback, insofar as the success of the first requires the refusal of the second. The apparent need for comprehensive purging of en-emies is managed by the simple stratagem of refusing to pay back evil for evil. The return of Jesus to the city is not only a refusal to purge the element, but also a refusal to pay back what has hap-pened to him. He does not continue the harm, neither returning it nor passing it on under the delusion of returning it. This refusal is articulated most clearly in the story of his arrest in the garden, with its message of non-retaliation. "All who take the sword will perish by the sword" (Matt 26:52).

The theme of innocent blood is one of overcoming a contaminating influence. While presented more directly in the case of Pilate washing his hands of innocent blood, it also is presented under the rubric of payback, as Judas attempts to return the tainted thirty pieces of silver. But the theme of overcoming violated innocent blood is not resolved by rituals of shedding further blood, but rather by that of the scapegoat. This is an image of absorbing blood guilt rather than spilling more blood. It shows Jesus refusing the option of payback, thereby ending any further reciprocal damage on damage.

### Non-retaliation and Reinhold Niebuhr

Non-retaliation as a Gospel theme is frequently connected to the political theology of Reinhold Niebuhr. Consistent with his evangelical tradition, Niebuhr grounded his theological positions in the New Testament. This contrasts with those philosophical efforts largely consistent with his Augustinian realism, such as the just-war theory, which develops its positions apart from the witness of scripture. In Niebuhr's view any effective form of social pacification is coercive, and coercion is effective because of its harmful effects. It ensures compliance by making noncompliance too costly for the dissenting party. In Niebuhr's view, because the cost involved concerns the real or threatened destruction of life or property, even nonviolent coercion is ultimately violent in its effects. But he sees the authentic ethic of Jesus, described in *An Interpretation of Christian Ethics,* as beyond coercion. This universal ethical ideal is "love-perfectionism."[16] Jesus represents the absolute norm of virtue that allows anything less than perfection to be seen as sin, understood as self-interest. Love is negatively defined as lack of self-interest, and pure love is a complete

---

[16] Reinhold Niebuhr, *An Interpretation of Christian Ethics*, reprint ed. (Louisville, KY: Westminster John Knox Press, 2013), 27–28.

suppression of ego in favor of the service of others. The impossible ideal of nonviolence turns out to be pure nonresistance, and Niebuhr considers it to be the only authentic form of nonviolence.

In a short but influential essay Niebuhr focuses his objections to nonviolent methods in a pointed fashion. He insists that for Christians, pacifism is heretical, and the notion of nonviolent action is not to be found in the New Testament. "There is not the slightest support in Scripture for this doctrine of non-violence. Nothing could be plainer than that the ethic uncompromisingly enjoins nonresistance and not nonviolent resistance."[17] His assessment of Gandhi is instructive in this regard. Gandhi's campaigns are viewed as admirable work, but flawed as an example of nonviolence because they use coercion. Rather than perceiving an unfamiliar practice in new territory, Gandhi is viewed as blurring categories.

Niebuhr rooted his understanding in the teachings of Jesus, especially as found in the Gospel of Matthew, and not in the account of Jesus's ministry and practice. He neglected the evidence of the practice of Jesus as given in the narratives, in particular the larger narrative of the Gospel as a whole. While he has clarified the concept of non-retaliation, his theory begs to be completed by a consideration of the narrative context of the Gospel. There we find it is one part of a dynamic of exchanges between opposing parties. In practice, it does not stand alone, as it does in theory. And this is shown in the narrative.

When we turn to that narrative, as rendered in the hands of Matthew, we find a story that adopts Mark's nonviolent action. But it moves that story source toward an emphasis on non-retaliation. In treating the entry to Jerusalem as a return, Matthew positions it as a chance for retaliation that is denied. In greatly elaborating the moment of Jesus's arrest in the garden, he privileges the occasion in which retribution is readily available, and not only does he show it refused, but gives it a thematic statement in the sword saying.

At the same time, Matthew retains the theme of nonviolent confrontation. The entire motif of return to the scene of violation

---

[17] Reinhold Niebuhr, "Why the Christian Church Is Not Pacifist," *Christianity and Power Politics* (Hamden, CT: Archon Books, 1969), 9–10.

and loss is one of confrontation. This is not a story of nonresistance alone.

In its historical setting Matthew's Gospel fits into the context of Christian nonparticipation in the nationalist wars following the Great Revolt. Matthew teaches that the practice of answering violence with violence does not work. Within the biblical tradition the testimony of Second Isaiah tells of another way, now dramatized in the story of Jesus. Instead of resisting the force of the empire by employing the empire's means, Matthew's message is to enter into the world of the empire, resisting it through living by different values. For, in the arena of conflict, "all who take the sword will perish by the sword" (Matt 26:52).

# 4

## Luke-Acts

### LUKE'S PROJECT:
### A PATH TO THE GENTILES

The writer we call Luke is responsible for a Gospel and the Acts of the Apostles, here combined under the title Luke-Acts. Luke's contribution is significant. Of the 260 chapters in the New Testament, 52 are in Luke-Acts—fully one-fifth of the whole.

Luke's project complements the previous two Gospels. Where Mark and Matthew strove to retain a place for their Jewish tradition in the Roman world, Luke moves in the other direction. Luke wants to show the Gentiles of the Roman Empire that there is a place for them in the faith world of Judaism. Luke is not replacing a Jewish church with a Gentile church; rather, he is *showing Gentiles a pathway into the story of Judaism*. But that involves a double imperative. Not only must Judaism be parsed to show there is room for Gentiles, but it also must be shown how it confronts the imperial value system. In both cases, the way forward is through telling the story of Jesus of Nazareth.[1]

---

[1] Important sources for this chapter are these commentaries: Luke Timothy Johnson, *Sacra Pagina: The Gospel of Luke. Sacra Pagina*, vol. 3, ed. Daniel J. Harrington, SJ (Collegeville, MN: Liturgical Press, 2006); idem, *Sacra Pagina: The Acts of the Apostles. Sacra Pagina*, vol. 5, ed. Daniel J. Harrington, SJ (Collegeville, MN: Liturgical Press, 1992). Johnson takes a literary approach to the Gospel and Acts without subscribing to empire studies

When we turn from the other Gospels to that of Luke, we enter a different world. Luke is commonly recognized as a historian in the ancient literary manner. He calls his work an "orderly sequence" (1:3, author's trans.). He favors distinctly linear, chronological formats. In addition, the Gospel narrative is expanded by the addition of another book, the Acts of the Apostles. The result, the double work Luke-Acts, is treated here as a single project, one that Luke planned from its first conception. It represents another dimension of the chronological impulse in Luke's writing. Contrasting with the other evangelists' tendency to view the Gospel story as a representative figure of their own situation, Luke spells out that situation in a separate volume. Our first task will be to look at what Luke's "orderly sequence" means for his narrative.

A second matter concerns Luke's audience, the *implied reader.* In contrast to the Gospels of Mark and Matthew, with Judaism confronting the Roman Empire, Luke shows the empire, in the persons of friendly Gentiles, engaging with Judaism. We see this first in the dedication to Theophilus, who likely is both a reader and a sponsor of Luke's work. More specifically, Luke's readers are thought to be God-fearers or God-worshipers. These terms refer to prominent Gentiles who, although partial to Judaism, did not convert. Practices such as the food laws and circumcision, which served as Jewish identity markers, also inhibited outsiders from full inclusion. Our second task is to identify this implied reader.

Finally, the purpose of Luke's project, as given in the narrative conflict, upon which the work turns, needs to be unfolded. Luke presents Jesus as favoring the outward-looking Isaian tradition of the "light to the Gentiles" rather than the inward-looking community tradition of Ezra, with its insistence on identity markers.

---

or the position adopted here of the God-fearer as implied reader. See also, Sharon Ringe, *Luke* (Louisville, KY: Westminster John Knox Press, 1995). Ringe's approach is always insightful and opens new vistas by way of her standpoint outside the usual conventions. And for comprehensive information on positions taken toward the text, see Joseph A. Fitzmyer, SJ, *The Gospel according to Luke I—IX,* Anchor Bible 28 (Garden City, NY: Doubleday, 1981); and idem, *The Acts of the Apostles,* Anchor Bible 31 (New Haven, CT: Yale University Press, 2007).

Rather than shifting the salvation story from Jews to Gentiles, Luke shows Gentile readers a path into Judaism by way of the Jesus movement. However, a compensating demand is made of the readers, distancing them in turn from certain values of their native imperial culture—Luke's call to repentance. Here we will look at each of these topics in turn

## An Orderly Sequence: Luke's Narrative

In his prologue, Luke says, "I too have decided, after investigating everything accurately anew, to write it down *in an orderly sequence.*" What does Luke mean by an orderly sequence? The term *(kathexis)* sometimes refers to a *journey*, where it has the idea of successive stages (Luke 8:1; Acts 18:23). This step-by-step arrangement is essential to the idea.

He also uses the term to mean a *well-organized explanation*. After Peter's engagement with the centurion Cornelius, in Acts 10, which resulted in his abrogation of food laws for the Gentile convert, the apostle was invited back to Jerusalem to explain himself. It says that "Peter began to explain it to them, step by step [*kathexis*]" (Acts 11:4). Here it probably has the same implication as the step-by-step progress of a journey.

While this idea of an orderly sequence has been explored from many directions, the *narrative* significance of the claim emerges when we trace the course of the dramatic conflict of Luke's work. Again we find a sense of step-by-step progress.

Luke's sequential interest is expressed, first of all, in developing calendar sequences. He has given us the forty days until the Ascension and the fifty days of Pentecost. He also is concerned to tell things one at a time, in proper order. Examples include his account in Luke 3:19–20 of the arrest of John the Baptist—here not so much as the "signs prophet" of Mark's Gospel, but rather as one who represents one phase in the progressive revelation of God in history. John is arrested immediately before the account of Jesus's baptism, at 3:21–22. His reader was not bothered by this, nor should we be. He prefers to conclude one topic before he begins another. In this case the era of John ends before that of

Jesus begins. Another example is the report that while visiting the pregnant Elizabeth, Mary stayed three months and then returned home (1:56), seemingly right before Elizabeth gave birth (1:57). But we can assume Luke thought she stayed for the birth. One thing at a time.

Sequential concerns are also seen in the way Luke has set up distinct stages in his story. Each of the stages takes up a further dimension of the conflict and develops it, as if making a set of points in an argument. These are usually indicated by explicit beginnings and endings, so as to show a clear identity for each. In addition, each stage typically has its own set of characters. At the beginning we meet the villagers in Galilee, the ill and displaced persons who would benefit from Jubilee release, as well as disciples and opposing Pharisees. On the road to Jerusalem along with the crowd and disciples, a new group, the lawyers, enters the picture to head the debates with Jesus. In Jerusalem, the disciples share the stage with the Sanhedrin, the Jewish Council.

Each section of the story begins with an episode that sets the program for the action to come. The episodes are strategically placed by Luke to trace the ongoing conflict and how it proceeds from point to point in the narrative. These are similar to the major narrative contracts that introduce stories by engaging the main character and defining the coming action. Luke has one of these as well, in the Nazareth synagogue episode, but he has also provided a minor set of similar passages to establish each stage in his account. These key episodes provide a guide consisting of a thread provided by the programmatic statements.

Luke's procedure involves taking episodes from his sources, such as Mark's Gospel, and moving them into pivotal places to introduce separate stages in the narrative. Luke's sense of freedom in composing his narrative is seen in the ease in which he takes episodes found in Mark, a known source, and moves them to different locations in the narrative where they work better for his writing project. Important examples of these programmatic episodes include the following.

*The Synagogue in Nazareth (Luke 4:16–30).* At the beginning of his seven-chapter section about Jesus's ministry in Galilee,

Luke transposed and heavily edited Mark's account of Jesus's rejection by the people of his hometown of Nazareth (Mark 6:2–6). For Luke, this was useful as a programmatic event to set up the larger narrative contract for Luke-Acts. But at the local level it announces a set of Jubilee themes that introduce the Galilee section that begins Jesus's public life (Luke 4:16—9:50). It introduces the contest between Jesus's practice and that of traditional Judaism.

*The Great Commandment (Luke 10:25–37)*. The next major part of Luke's narrative is Jesus's long journey to Jerusalem (9:51—19:27). One strand of the narrative, important to what we are discussing here, is the ongoing series of debates between Jesus and the Pharisees. These debates shift the Gospel's attention to conflict from the practice of Jesus to a discussion of the theory behind it. Luke introduces the debates with a story transposed from its place in Mark—the debate about the Great Commandment (Mark 12:28–34). There it is one of the attempts to trap Jesus in his speech. In Luke the attempts to trap Jesus in his speech begin early, as he begins his travel toward the city (11:54).

*Parable of the Kingdom (19:11–27)*. A parable found in Luke, as well as in Matthew (Matt 25:14–20), but not in Mark, is commonly known as the parable of the Talents. In Luke's hands it might better be called the parable of the Kingdom, since it speaks of delegating governance rather than wealth. Luke places it just prior to Jesus's entry into the city, identifying the two groups with whom he will interact in a major way during the final days—the disciples to whom he will delegate authority, and the "rulers" who will oppose his own claims to authority.[2]

*Pentecost (Acts 2:1–11)*. At the beginning of Acts we have another example: Luke's use of the gift of tongues (1 Cor 12:4–11). Retaining its note of spiritual enthusiasm, he transforms glossolalia—enthusiastic spiritual speech—to specific foreign languages. This is to prepare the reader for the events to follow in Acts with the expansion of the spirit-filled community into the far reaches of the world.

---

[2] See Johnson, *Luke*, 292–94.

*The Ancient Genre of Historical Writing*

In the short prologue to the Gospel, Luke makes a claim about his work that suggests his sense of the *genre* of his writing. A consensus among Luke scholars is that his sensibilities are those of a first-century historian. N. T. Wright, for instance, finds a parallel in Josephus, the Jewish historian.[3] But once this is said, it is good to make the point that our notion of historical writing differs considerably from the days in which the discipline was first taking shape. Our concern about factual accuracy was not shared in the first century.

Ancient historians strove for a smooth, pleasing narrative style. This in itself calls for the use of narrative analysis. But this interest frequently took historians in a direction we today would not endorse. For us, accuracy is prized over other virtues; for them, other features were of greater importance, even while they clearly considered themselves to be delivering the truth of the story. One example, frequently noted, is the use of speeches, which were invented and placed in the mouths of primary characters. This convention was used to guide the reader to the meaning of events. A famous example is the Jewish historian Josephus's account of the final speech at Masada, inspiring the Sicarii to commit mass suicide. Josephus's readers knew that he was not there to record it, and no one survived to tell him the facts of the case. They understood it to be a convention, and they took it as such.

*A Wider Horizon*

An important effect of Luke's approach, not to be ignored, is the expanded *horizon* of his narrative. In the early chapters of his story he includes announcements that place events within a world horizon. When Luke announces the birth of John the Baptist, he

---

[3] On Luke's historical genre, see David E. Aune, *The New Testament in Its Literary Environment* (Louisville, KY: Westminster John Knox Press, 1985), chap. 3. For the parallels with Josephus, see N. T. Wright, *The New Testament and the People of God* (Minneapolis, MN: Fortress Press, 1992), 373–79.

situates the event "in the days of King Herod of Judea" (1:5). However, when he tells the story of Jesus's birth, he writes: "In those days a decree went out from Emperor Augustus . . . while Quirinius was governor of Syria" (2:1–2). And later, he dates the baptism by John "in the fifteenth year of the reign of Emperor Tiberius, when Pontius Pilate was governor of Judea, and Herod was ruler of Galilee . . . during the high priesthood of Annas and Caiaphas" (3:1–2).

Of course, history treats public events, and Luke situates Jesus's story amid the events of world history. In the Gospels of Mark and Matthew the story of Jesus is visualized as a movement within a branch of Judaism. It is of interest to a select group. In Luke, however, it is a public event from beginning to end. Jesus is a public figure, emerging at the early age of twelve. His work is widely known, and it grows in reputation as the story progresses. Furthermore, the wider horizon is integral to Luke's project. He is committed to showing the expansion of the Jesus movement out to the Gentile world.

Luke's interest in the public nature of his story even influences his use of the calendar, his "orderly sequence." To cite one example, Herod the Great died in 4 BCE. After his death his territory was divided into the four tetrarchies. The kingship of Judea was assigned to one of his sons, Archaelaus (Matt 2:23). His reign lasted only ten years, after which Rome resorted to the alternative plan of making Judea a Roman province with a Roman governor. Josephus tells of the census taken in Judea (not the whole world) at that time to apprise Rome of the sources of taxes in its new territory.[4] But this happened in 6 CE, some ten years after the death of Herod the Great. Did Luke get his dates wrong? Not likely, given his historical bent, especially regarding what were for him relatively recent events. It is more likely that he is providing a suitable historical *setting* for the incidents that he relates. In this way he can say that the Judean world is proper to John the Baptist's story. But the expansive world horizon is

---

[4] Josephus, *The Jewish Wars*, 2:117, in *The New Complete Works of Josephus,* William Whiston, trans. (Grand Rapids, MI: Kregel Pub., 1999).

appropriate for Jesus. His story, in Luke's hands, opens out to the entire world.

### "Most Excellent Theophilus": The Implied Reader

The first chapter noted that an important task for our reading is to identify the implied reader—the reader implied by the text itself. In this case Luke is explicit. He presents his "orderly sequence" to a certain "Theophilus" (Luke 1:3; Acts 1:1), a person addressed with a degree of formality otherwise reserved in Luke's account for the governors Felix and Festus (Acts 23:26; 26:25).

Was Theophilus an actual person, or simply a name chosen to represent Luke's reader? Critics dispute the matter. Because the work is dedicated to him, it would appear that Theophilus, if an actual person, is also a sponsor of Luke's work, though it doesn't actually say that.

*Theophilus* translates as "God-lover." This aligns with another feature of Luke's account. Unlike the other Gospels, Luke's narrative voice—and not simply persons in the narrative—calls Jesus "the Lord."[5] This suggests a faith commitment that the writer shares with his reader—that is, Theophilus, like Luke, accepts Jesus as "the Lord."

The term *God-lover* has reminded many commentators of a similar term, *God-fearer.* It should be noted that "fearing" God here is a positive idea, expressing a proper respect due the one God. In the New Testament context "fear of the Lord" or "fear of God" refers to reverence or awe. The term *God-fearer* is sometimes replaced by *devout* or *God-worshiper.* The meaning is the same. It is applied to the devout Jew, but less commonly to the devout Gentile. But it is that rarer usage, the devout, God-fearing Gentile, that draws our attention here.

What is a God-fearer? One place to look, in understanding the title in the larger culture, is to the evidence of archeology. In the small city of Aphrodisias, in present-day Turkey, archeologists

---

[5] Luke 7:13, 19; 10:1, 39, 41; 11:39; 12:42; 13:15; 17:5, 6; 18:6; 22:61; 24:3.

have discovered an inscription listing donations to the local synagogue. Included among them are several identified as *theosebeis*, or "God-fearers." These were Gentile sympathizers of Judaism and supporters of the synagogues. They were not full converts, which would require circumcision and adherence to the entire law of Moses, including food laws and Sabbath observance. However, they did share a faith in the one God, along with a devotion to the Greek Old Testament, the Septuagint. In Luke's view Jesus would offer them an entry into this story of God's people, whom they so much admired.

As commentators have noted, if we take into account all the various aspects of Luke's rich double work, from acquaintance with the Greek Old Testament to knowledge of the legal workings of the imperial provinces, and then ask ourselves what kind of reader could be expected to appreciate the many dimensions present in this writing, we have a clue to its implied reader. The answer that emerges is the God-fearer. Looking at it from the other direction, if we accept that Luke's sophisticated literary product was intended for Gentile readers, such a cultured, literate, well-disposed reader would match the image that Luke himself provides of the God-fearer, both in the Gospel and in Acts.

Among New Testament writers Luke is the one who alerts us to the presence of God-fearers. In the Gospel, for example, we meet a certain centurion whose slave was on the verge of death (Luke 7:1–10). The story also appears in Matthew's Gospel, but Luke's version has certain unique aspects. The fact that the man is a centurion makes it clear he is not Jewish. But he is esteemed enough by the Jewish community members that they agree to make an appeal to Jesus for him, "for he loves our people, and it is he who built our synagogue for us" (Luke 7:5). When Jesus goes to the centurion's house, another delegation of friends, presumably Gentile, intercedes for him. Luke doesn't use the term in this instance, but he clearly presents the centurion in the role of the God-fearer.

It is in the book of Acts that Luke makes explicit use of the idea of the Gentile God-fearer. Another centurion, Cornelius, is described three times as one who is devout, who fears God (Acts 10:2, 22, 35). The term is also found elsewhere in Acts.

In his speech at Antioch of Pisidia, Paul mentions God-fearers twice (13:16, 26). Lydia, Paul's convert in Philippi, is a Gentile described as "a worshiper" (16:14), as is a certain Titius Justus (18:7). In Luke's portrayal of his ministry, Paul does his work among the God-fearers.

A telling example of this is Paul's proselytizing attempts in Athens. It is one of only two instances in Acts when Paul appeals directly to pagans; the other was in Antioch (13:8–20). In Athens, however, his effort is deliberate. After first meeting with the Jews and God-fearers in the synagogue (Acts 17:17), Luke shows him proceeding into the public forum, the agora. Here Paul preaches about the one God, not the resurrected Christ. This is for a reason. He is addressing pagans, and for Paul (in the view of Luke), they must first accept the one God before they are ready to believe in Christ. They must become the equivalent of God-fearers before they can be baptized. This characterizes the entire viewpoint of Luke-Acts. In contrast, Paul's own account of his missionary activity mentions his outreach to idol worshipers (e.g., 1 Thess 1:9).[6]

### Luke's Narrative Contract: The Nazareth Synagogue

In the Nazareth synagogue Jesus reads a passage from the scroll of Isaiah to the approval of his hometown people. It begins, "The Spirit of the Lord is upon me" (Luke 4:18; cf. Isa 61:1–2). We realize the following will be under the direction of the Holy Spirit. It would not do to neglect the role of the Holy Spirit in Luke. While it is not developed in this chapter's description of the narrative plot, Luke gives an overriding role to the Holy Spirit as a director of the action. Like the Stage Manager in Thornton Wilder's *Our Town*, for example, the Spirit is Luke's guide for the action. The Spirit provides the guarantee that the program is divinely approved. We understand that the expansion of the

---

[6] As in Philip Francis Esler, *Community and Gospel in Luke-Acts: The Social and Political Motivations of Lucan Theology* (New York: Cambridge University Press, 1987), 43.

mission to the wider world is neither a mistake nor an accident, but divinely driven.

But there is more to the scene. There is an added note: "Today this scripture has been fulfilled in your hearing" (Luke 4:21). What was a divine voice heard at the baptism (Mark 1:11), and the angel of the Lord in Joseph's dream (Matt 1:21) is here represented by the word of scripture. This complex passage is crucial for Luke. It is the narrative contract for the Gospel and Acts. The protagonist, the main character, receives a commission to perform the task that defines the dispute at the center of the following narrative.

But quickly the tone of the assembly turns, and questions arise.

> They said, "Is not this Joseph's son?" He said to them, "Doubtless you will quote to me this proverb, 'Doctor, cure yourself!' And you will say, 'Do here also in your hometown the things that we have heard you did at Capernaum.'" And he said, "Truly I tell you, no prophet is accepted in the prophet's hometown." (4:22–24)

As in other places Luke reworks something from his sources to fit his own program. We recognize the source story in Mark 6:1–6, where Jesus is rejected by the people of his village, Nazareth. But it has been extensively elaborated by Luke. Jesus suggests that he will be performing his works elsewhere, citing the examples of Elijah and Elisha, who went to Gentiles. Upon hearing this, his neighbors turn against him. Despite their attempt to throw him from the brow of the hill, he walks away unharmed (Luke 4:16–30).

## The Narrative Program of Luke-Acts

Here some words of clarification are in order. We saw earlier that Luke begins each of his sections with a programmatic scene, the first of these being the scene at the Nazareth synagogue. We will look at that shortly, in discussing the stages of the story. But this particular scene, we see, is more than that. It also provides the program for the entire double work of Luke-Acts. It is that relationship to the larger work that we consider here.

In the story of the Nazareth synagogue Luke makes special use of the word *acceptable (dektos)*. It appears twice, first in the quotation from scripture, "proclaim a year *acceptable* to the Lord" (4:19, NAB) and then in the proverb, "no prophet is *accepted* in the prophet's hometown" (4:24). For the second, Luke had to rework Mark's version, "prophets are not without honor, except in their hometown" (Mark 6:4). Clearly, what is acceptable in the eyes of God is a concern for Luke. And so it is notable that the term reappears at a crucial moment in Acts, with Peter's vision that everyone who does what is right is "acceptable" to God—a key passage concerning the Gentile mission (Acts 10:35).

Acceptance is the other side of rejection. Luke is also working this theme, in connection (perhaps surprisingly) with that of *mission*. We can see this in two opposite ways. In one way, rejection leads to mission; in another way, mission leads to rejection.

In the first place, *rejection leads to mission:* Jesus tells of the rejection here in his hometown. He makes the case that he will not be acceptable in this place.[7] This is followed by the reference to Elijah and Elisha:

> But the truth is, there were many widows in Israel in the time of Elijah, when the heaven was shut up three years and six months, and there was a severe famine over all the land; yet Elijah was sent to none of them except to a widow at Zarephath in Sidon. There were also many lepers in Israel in the time of the prophet Elisha, and none of them was cleansed except Naaman the Syrian. (Luke 4:25–27)

For Luke, these two prophets are presented as emblems of the mission beyond Judaism to the Gentiles. And the program suggested here is that the rejection prompts the mission. This is the

---

[7] The use of the future tense helps to complicate the picture. Jesus is saying they *will* reject him when they discover he is going elsewhere. This points to our second reading.

case, for instance, with the stoning of Stephen (Acts 8:1–3). In terms of Luke's narrative program it describes the relationship of Luke-Acts. The Gospel shows Jesus's rejection; Acts shows that rejection generating a mission to the world.

But if we look again at the passage, we see that *mission also leads to rejection.* Jesus's example of Elijah and Elisha prompts the villagers to make an attempt on Jesus's life. And this also relates to the program of Luke's narrative. How is this so? To see this we need to look at the historical circumstances that underlie the story.

Luke's opens a space within Judean traditions for the God-fearing reader who has been strongly attracted to the faith in the one God with its ethical dignity and theological merit. Luke's narrative is not about Judaism being replaced by a Gentile church. Rather, it is a story of believers who happen to be Gentiles, who have committed themselves to the one God, who admire the stories of God's people in the Septuagint, and who are seeking a way into that story. This way is announced in the Nazareth synagogue. But to see that more clearly, we need to work back into the traditions underlying Luke's synagogue scene.

*Second Isaiah and Ezra*

In the common lectionary of Sunday readings shared by most mainline Christian churches, many of us will have heard the above story paired with that of Ezra's post-exilic renewal of the Judea community (Neh 8:2–10). On the surface, these seem to be similar renewal stories. Ezra begins a new day after the exile; Jesus launches the new era of Christianity.

Yet once we become aware of the historical events behind them, we discover a profound tension between these two stories. It takes us to Judea's struggle after returning from exile in Babylon. While the people were in exile, opposing interpretations of their experience competed for dominance. The prophets Third Isaiah (Isaiah 56—66) and Ezekiel presented contrasting visions for the exile community's predicament. Their work crystalized two visions of

Israel's presence to the world. On the one hand, we have the Isaian "light to the Gentiles," a vision of witness to the larger world (Isa 49:6). On the other, we have a community sealed against outsiders. One welcomed outsiders to worship the one God; the other restricted their participation (Isa 56:1–8; Ezek 44:6–9; 47:23).

The returning community was caught between these two visions. The followers of Second Isaiah brought back with them the tradition of witness to the Gentiles. It was a theme that would be severely constrained by the difficult conditions of reestablishing themselves in the land. Those traditions are found in the prophecies collected under the name Third Isaiah (Isa 56—55). The same sentiments were considered unrealistic and visionary by those with the responsibility of leading the returning community. The reforms of Ezra leading to a closed community, thought necessary for survival, prevailed. Identity markers for the beleaguered group became important. Sabbath, food laws, circumcision, marriage laws—these became powerful indicators of community identity. Rules originally designed to set the Jews apart from their neighbors had the secondary effect of barring outsiders from joining them.[8]

We sometimes speak of the various Jewish sects in the New Testament era—Pharisees, Sadducees, Essenes, and others. According to the Jewish New Testament scholar Jacob Neusner,[9] it is more accurate to speak of a plurality of "Judaisms" at this time. The tension between the traditions of Isaiah and Ezra are a part of that plurality. Luke's story of Jesus in the synagogue of Nazareth is in the midst of that tension.

Luke shows Jesus reviving a suppressed Isaian tradition, one that Luke's God-fearing readers would find "acceptable" (Luke 4:19, 24). He is providing his God-fearing readers with an

---

[8] For how the returning community was caught between these two, see Rainer Albertz, *A History of Israelite Religion in the Old Testament Period, Volume 2: From the Exile to the Maccabees* (Nashville, TN: Westminster John Knox Press, 1994), 311–470.

[9] Jacob Neusner and Bruce Chilton, *Judaism in the New Testament: Practices and Beliefs* (London: Routledge, 1995), xv–xvii.

expression of Judaism they can embrace, recovered in the discipleship of Jesus of Nazareth. But at the same time Jesus's proposal
would elicit firm resistance from those who would see here an
attack on their very way of life—those for whom the identity
markers are of guiding importance. Identity markers, whether
patriotic or religious, arouse passionate vigilance even today. The
Nazareth villagers' reaction to Jesus, which seems excessive and
largely unmotivated, stands here as both a forewarning and a parable of sorts about the kind of opposition that questioning identity
markers can and will receive.

In the Nazareth scene Jesus selects a text from the prophecies of Third Isaiah on the theme of release from bondage (Luke
4:18–19; Isa 61:1–2; 58:6).[10] This follower of Second Isaiah
shared the same openness toward the Gentile world and brought
it back to the post-exilic world of Judea, where it lay dormant,
as a vision for the future and a possibility to be activated when
its time came.

Here it merges with another biblical theme: the Jubilee vision of
Israel, with its message of "release" from debt and other forms of
bondage.[11] Leviticus 25 gives it classic expression. Although it is
promised there as a cyclical event, historically it would not seem
to have been implemented regularly. However, its enduring vision
of social justice remained "on the books," imagined typically as a
promise to be realized in the fullness of time.

It is in the writings of Third Isaiah that these two neglected
traditions—the vision of Second Isaiah, continued by Third
Isaiah, and the Jubilee vision of Leviticus—merge. Adding the
Jubilee theme of setting the oppressed free to the openness to
the Gentiles, the prophet of the returning community allows the

---

[10] This is from the part written by the anonymous prophet we today call
Third Isaiah (Isa 55—66), a disciple of Second Isaiah, the prophet of the exile
(Isa 40—55). Luke may not have been aware of the different authors as we
are today, but he would have been sensitive to the messages of the different
parts.

[11] Sharon Ringe, *Jesus, Liberation, and the Biblical Jubilee: Images for
Ethics and Christology* (Eugene, OR: Wipf and Stock, 2004), esp. 33–49.

two to coalesce in an ideal vision for the community.[12] Citing this passage, the Nazareth synagogue episode clearly leads into the ministry of Jesus in the villages of Galilee with its promise of amnesty, forgiveness, and release from bondages of debt, death, and disease.

However, lest we get the impression that Luke clears a way to discipleship for Gentile converts that makes no demands upon them, we are assured that this is not the case. Luke definitely challenges his reader. His response to historical circumstances is not a nonviolent campaign, as in Mark, but an entire way of life. With Luke, resistance takes the form of a call to *repentance*. While the call to repentance isn't the theme of Jesus's initial proclamation, as it is with Mark (1:15) and Matthew (3:2; 4:17), Luke does make it a major theme. It dominates the debates on the road to Jerusalem.[13]

Even more noticeably, he dramatizes the theme in a series of figures in a way unique to this Gospel:

- *Peter* is called from his boat. After a miraculous catch of fish, he makes a disclaimer—"Go away from me, Lord, for I am a sinful man" (5:8).
- The unnamed *woman* who washed Jesus's feet is contrasted with Simon the Pharisee, Jesus's host, and is commended for her "great love" (7:47).
- The parable of the *Prodigal Son*, the longest parable in the Gospels, presents repentance in a most memorable way. His rehearsed mantra is, "Father, I have sinned against heaven and before you; I am no longer worthy to be called your son" (15:21).
- The short tax-collector of Jericho, *Zacchaeus*, concludes the long journey to Jerusalem with an example of repentant restitution—"Look, half of my possessions, Lord, I will give to the poor; and if I have defrauded anyone of anything, I will pay back four times as much" (19:8).

---

[12] Ringe, *Jesus, Liberation, and the Biblical Jubilee*, 30–31.
[13] Repentance enters the debates on the journey to Jerusalem at Luke 10:13; 11:32; 13:3, 5; 15:7, 10; 16:30; 17:3, 4.

- The so-called *good thief* at the crucifixion provides a climactic example of repentance in the Gospel (23:42).

Further, the Acts of the Apostles presents Paul's paradigmatic conversion as an act of repentance. Luke manages to describe it three times (Acts 9:1–9; 22:6–16; 26:12–18), making it one of the more memorable scenes in the book.

In this way, the opening to the Gentiles is accomplished by appealing to an alternative tradition within Judaism, one without the onerous identity markers of the post-exilic era, but one that makes its own demands. The "narrow door" of the laws and customs is replaced with another, one that will invite many who "will come from east and west, from north and south, and will eat in the kingdom of God" (Luke 13:29).

## LUKE'S STORY:
## OPENING A ROUTE TO THE GOD-FEARERS

It is not customary to view Gospel stories in their entirety, and so it is useful to set out the action in the order in which it is presented. In Luke's case this is especially important because it is a double work, and the second volume is not usually given as much attention or read in direct connection with the first. In addition, it is important to notice what Luke is doing differently from the other Gospel writers.[14]

We are accustomed to viewing the Gospel and Acts separately, as distinct works, and so in some senses they are. But they also are continuous, and reward a reading that recognizes this. The following outline treats the double work as a single narrative, moving the action from Galilee to Jerusalem in the first volume, and moving from Jerusalem to Rome in the second.

---

[14] The departure from Jerusalem is more convoluted than the rhetorical plan of Acts would suggest. Acts 8:1—15:28, on closer examination, turns out to be two simultaneous missions, one near, and one far (Acts 11:19–20), treated alternatively.

*In the Gospel:*

| | |
|---|---|
| 1. Infancy narrative, 1:1—2:52 | Villagers and the Empire |
| 2. Galilee, 3:1—9:50 | "The Spirit of the Lord is upon me' |
| 3. Road, 9:51—19:10 | "The Law, how do you read it?" |
| 4. Jerusalem, 19:11—24:53 | Jesus in Jerusalem |

*In Acts of the Apostles:*

| | |
|---|---|
| 5. Jerusalem, 1:1—7:60 | The New Jewish Council: Apostles |
| 6. Leaving Jerusalem | Mission into the World |
|   a. Judea and Samaria, 8:1—11:18; 12:1–25 | Peter and Philip |
|   b. Antioch, 11:19–30: 13:1—15:28 | Barnabas and Paul |
|   c. Ephesus, 16:1—20:38 | Paul's Mission |
| 7. Back to Jerusalem, 21:1—26:32 | Mission Accomplished |
|   8. Rome, 27:1—28:31 | The Gentile mission established |

In this part of the chapter we look at Luke-Acts as a continuous narrative, building on the program announced in the Nazareth synagogue. We see how the ongoing conflict moves through stages indicated by shifting scenes, characters, and programmatic passages. Our procedure will be to trace this conflict through the stages of the story, with some description of the action as it unfolds.

## The Villagers and the Empire (Luke 1—2)

The opening chapters represent the link with the Jewish tradition as experienced by the God-fearers. The implied reader is allowed to enter into the story of God's people. It is the story as represented by the Greek Bible, in its idiom and its symbolic world. This is the story the God-fearers wish to join. The Gospel shows them that the Jesus story opens the door to them. Meanwhile, it also signals the transformation of their imperial world in the movement that begins among these remote villages in the hills of Galilee.

Luke begins his story by portraying village life among the ordinary people of the Judean world. Told in language imitating the familiar cadences of Septuagint Greek, his account evokes the lives of the devout, humble people of the land. For the God-fearers, who were the intended readers, one aspect of this was Luke's use of idiom. By the time of Luke's writing, this Greek translation of the Hebrew scriptures, produced in Alexandria, Egypt, around 250 BCE, would have the patina of an archaic language, experienced perhaps as many experience the King James Bible today. Similarly, the God-fearers would have an affection for this translation, their primary link with the Jewish tradition that they admired. An example would be the Ethiopian of Acts 8:27–28. At the same time, the implied reader, a cultured Gentile, would experience a dramatic difference between the portrait of the Judean villager and that reader's own circumstances. This would be a part of the reading experience intended by Luke, as he presents a picture in sharp contrast with the sophisticated imperial culture.

Of those populating this world, we meet the couples Zechariah and Elizabeth, Joseph and Mary, and their children. We also meet Simeon and Anna, figures familiar to those who frequent the Temple. These represent the humble folk whom the prophet Zephaniah celebrated as the anawim, the "humble and lowly people" who will prevail (Zeph 3:12–13). The anawim, according to Psalm 37, are those who trust in the Lord, who wait for the Lord, and who will inherit the earth (Ps 37:3, 9, 11).

Luke's characters in these opening chapters have certain traits. They are righteous and devout. Zechariah and Elizabeth are "righteous before God, living blamelessly according to all the commandments and regulations of the Lord" (Luke 1:6). Simeon is described as "righteous and devout" (2:25). In addition, they are waiting upon the Lord's initiative. The implication is that they are among the powerless. They are not in a position to shape the events that determine their lives. They are waiting on God to act. Simeon was "looking forward to the consolation of Israel" (2:25) and Anna spoke "to all who were looking for the redemption of Jerusalem" (2:38).

Jesus is presented as coming from this milieu, a pious but also precocious youth (Luke 2:41–52) who emerges in the Gospel as a prophet from the Jewish tradition and who also has the traits of a master teacher in the classic Hellenistic tradition. In this way Luke engages both the Jewish tradition and the Greco-Roman culture of the implied reader.

At the end of the Gospel story another representative of this pious group appears in Luke's presentation, Joseph of Arimathea, who placed the body of Jesus in a tomb. He was "a good and righteous man" who "was waiting expectantly for the kingdom of God" (Luke 23:50–51). He too is a member of the righteous who are waiting on the Lord. They are found at the beginning and the end of Luke's story, at the birth and the burial, framing the account of Jesus's mission to Israel.

Along with accounts of the angel Gabriel visiting Zechariah and Mary, with the stories of birth and circumcision, we are treated to canticles by the different characters in the story. The canticles of Mary, Zechariah, and Simeon, along with the song of the angels, all have their roots in passages of Old Testament poetry, which are not so much directly quoted as improvised. Mary's Magnificat recalls Hannah's song in 1 Samuel 2; Zechariah's Benedictus reworks Malachi's promise of Elijah's return (Mal 4:5), and Simeon's Nunc Dimittis plays richly upon the passage about the "light to the nations" in Second Isaiah (Isa 49:6; 42:6; 60:3).

Not only are these canticles evocative of known biblical passages, but they also preview themes for the coming narrative of Luke. In the narrative to follow Luke will call attention to three groups who interact with Jesus: the disciples, the crowd, and the opponents (Pharisees, scribes, lawyers, and rulers of the Jews).

*Mary's Magnificat (Luke 1:46–55).* This canticle introduces the theme of the reversal of roles and values so central to Luke's presentation of Jesus's story. Unfolding in two parts, it praises the raising up of the lowly, as shown in his servant Mary (1:46–50), followed by the fulfillment of the promises to the servant Israel, with its equivalent lifting of the lowly, while the mighty are brought down from their thrones. The image of reversals reappears in instructions to the disciples. In the Sermon on the Plain (6:17–49), Luke's version of the Beatitudes emphasizes the reversal of positions. Throughout, culminating in the instructions at the last supper, service is identified as the proper role of the leaders among the disciples (22:24–30).

*Zechariah's Benedictus (Luke 1:68–79).* This canticle previews the roles of Jesus as the messianic son of David and John as the new Elijah. Already given notice in the public setting of John's story in the reign of Herod the Great (1:5) and that of Jesus in the empire of Caesar Augustus (2:1–2), the canticle outlines the coming story of Jesus. The public role of the messiah king is especially of interest to the crowd, who are looking for an authoritative voice. They laud him and seek his opinion on various matters of concern to them.

*Simeon's Nunc Dimittis (Luke 2:29–32).* And this canticle anticipates the movement out to the Gentiles, to be related in the fuller narrative of Luke-Acts. Something of an improvisation on the passage from Second Isaiah about the "light to the nations" (Isa 42:6–7), it sounds a note that will be heard again as Luke's narrative nears it fullest expanse in the missions of Paul (Acts 13:47). But this mission to the Gentiles at the heart of Luke's Gospel is central to its conflict. Accordingly, Simeon warns about a "sign that will be opposed."

*The Angels' Song (Luke 2:14).* Meanwhile, the *angels'* song to the shepherds announces a time to come when there will be "on earth peace among those whom he favors!" (2:14). The favored are the humble villagers whose stories we are following in the narrative. The story of Jesus's birth, the familiar Christmas story of Luke, is set in deliberate contrast to the empire. The Pax Romana, which occasioned the census of "all the world," provided a model for peace established by force of military power. The census presumed this *pax,* since the purpose of a census was to determine who and what were available for military conscription, forced labor, and, of course, taxation. As if in ignorance of the present standing of the Roman peace, the angels proclaim peace on earth, preparing us for the story to come.

## Beginning in Galilee (Luke 3:1—9:50)

First, the stage is set. As with the other Gospel, Luke prepares for the story of Jesus with the mission of John the Baptist (Luke 3:1–20). However, he manages to tell that story to his own advantage. Not only does he set the story in the context of world history (vv. 1–2), but he expands the quotation from Isaiah to include "all flesh shall see the salvation of God" (3:6). This neatly fits the plan of the work to follow. In addition, John and his baptism are identified with repentance, which becomes an important part of Jesus's program.

After the opening chapters invite the reader into the story of Jesus, we come to the adult mission of the main character, Jesus. He has the characteristics of an Old Testament prophet combined with those of a notable teacher in the Hellenist tradition. Luke begins with the primary programmatic episode of the story—the announcement in the synagogue of Nazareth. We have considered this in its role as narrative contract establishing the narrative for the double work of Luke-Acts. But it also serves more proximately as the program for the first part of the story, the Galilean ministry.

Proclaimed in the Nazareth synagogue (Luke 4:18–19), the Galilean ministry of Jesus inaugurates his year of Jubilee, releasing a struggling people from *disease* through healing, from *debt* through repentance and forgiveness, and from *social injustices* through a teaching of reversing false values. This part of the account presents Jesus's *praxis* of liberation; the *theory* will follow as Jesus debates with the Pharisees on the way to Jerusalem (9:51—19:27).

As we've seen, the synagogue event establishes the program for the entire work of Luke-Acts, including the proclamation of Jubilee with its message of release from various constraints. The Galilee section of the narrative is where most of the healing stories are found. Here Luke establishes the meaning of Jesus's mission. Much of this is taken from his source in Mark's Gospel, although with distinct Lukan touches.

While the Nazareth reading is programmatic for the Galilee ministry in its evocation of Jubilee, such amnesty is not accepted readily by all. When the event takes an ugly turn, and the villagers

of Nazareth attempt to cast Jesus from the crest of the hill, it signals what is at stake. As noted earlier in this chapter, two Jewish
traditions are at odds. One is the welcoming tradition of being
a light to the nations, which originates with Second Isaiah in
Babylon and is continued back in the land by his successor, Third
Isaiah, and is adopted by Jesus in his citation of Isaiah 61:1–2.
But an alternative tradition, exemplified by Ezra, rejected this as
too risky and unrealistic. It opted for a more closed community,
guarded by the identity markers of food laws, circumcision, Sabbath rituals, and marriage laws. These came to be the indications
of observant Jews.

However, challenging identity markers is risky, as seen in the
reaction of the villagers in the synagogue of Nazareth. The opposition of the Pharisees, something Luke inherited from his source,
Mark's Gospel, is adapted by Luke to his purposes. And it begins
here. The involvement of identity markers is not explicit at this
stage. But in the story of the paralytic, the scribes in Mark are
joined by "scholars of the law" (something akin to law professors
in the Mosaic tradition, Luke 5:17). The legal implications of
Jesus's stance will be challenged.

This opposition begins a thematic strand that features lawyers
*(nomikoi)* who join the Pharisees in opposition to Jesus's teachings. Although the lawyers are most in evidence during the journey
to Jerusalem, they make a parenthetical appearance in Galilee. In
the story of John's sending messengers from prison, Jesus's answer echoes the earlier reading in the Nazareth synagogue, in that
way reviving the Jubilee message. In the midst of this we have a
parenthetical note from the author:

> (And all the people who heard this, including the tax-
> collectors, acknowledged the justice of God, because they
> had been baptized with John's baptism. But by refusing to
> be baptized by him, the Pharisees and the lawyers rejected
> God's purpose for themselves). (7:29–30)

This stands as a bridge between the Jubilee theme of the Nazareth synagogue and the debates to come, while on the road to

Jerusalem. Luke is telling his reader that the topic hasn't changed. On the journey, Jesus's current practice will then be elaborated in theory, in confrontations with his opponents.

In addition to the rise of the opposition, the Galilee section of the narrative introduces the group of disciples. Here we also have the apostles named and set up as a group as a distinct element in the narrative drama. The Twelve are named, selected as a cadre within the larger group (7:12–15). In Luke 6:17–49 their introduction is followed by an extended teaching as a discipleship program. A briefer version of Matthew's Sermon on the Mount, this Sermon on the Plain follows the call of the Twelve. These twelve apostles will assume a major role in the book of Acts, but they make their first appearance here. In addition, the sermon begins the instruction to discipleship, which carries forth the promise of reversals announced in Mary's Magnificat. Luke's version of the Beatitudes and the Woes makes this point succinctly (6:20–26).

In addition to the naming of the Twelve (6:12–16), the call of Peter receives special attention. This is not the first time the two have met. Jesus has already healed Peter's mother-in-law (4:38–39).

Luke has worked the story so that Peter is fishing, along with his companions, James and John. Having success upon following the advice of Jesus, Peter makes a significant confession: "Go away from me, Lord, because I am a sinful man!" (Luke 5:8). Peter becomes a prototype of repentance, a theme that entered the story with the Baptist. Repentance is a dominant motif in this Gospel, and Peter is the first of a series. Although Luke does not show Jesus announcing a call to repentance, as do Mark and Matthew, he does include a number of figures representing repentance. Apart from Peter, these include the repentant woman (7:36–50), the prodigal son (15:11–32), the Pharisee and the tax-collector (18:9–14), Zacchaeus (19:1–10), and the good thief (23:39–43).

Luke 7 is a good sampler of Luke's interests. It is unique to Luke and puts his basic themes on display in a set of stories. It begins with a nod to the Gentile reader. The centurion whose servant is healed (7:1–10) is described with the traits of a God-fearer who supports the synagogue of the Jews. This story is followed by that of the widow of Nain (7:11–17), which reprises the Elijah story of the widow of Sidon, earlier mentioned by Jesus in the Nazareth synagogue, where it was used to preview the turn to the Gentiles.

The sequence continues into the next story of John the Baptist sending messengers to Jesus (7:18–35). Jesus's response evokes the Jubilee tradition of release, as in the Nazareth announcement. The report includes a parenthetical remark that contrasts the public sinners, who listen to John and repent, with the Pharisees and legal scholars who ignore him, seeing no reason to repent (7:29–30). On the one hand, this introduces us to the lawyers who will make their presence known later, on the road to the city. On the other hand, it leads into the next episode, which contrasts Simon the Pharisee with the nameless repentant woman who washed Jesus's feet with her tears (7:36–50).

This woman's story, riveting enough in itself, shows us the basic themes in conflict in Luke's narrative. Simon the Pharisee has neglected the duties of the host, perhaps presenting Jesus to his guests as an interesting display. He personifies the resistance to repentance just signaled in 7:30, indicated in the refusal of John's baptism. In contrast, the woman represents those of 7:29, who accepted the baptism of repentance, and here is the image of repentance. In his small parable, Jesus equates this with love.

### The Law: How Do You Read It? (Luke 9:51—19:44)

The longest part of Luke's Gospel is Jesus's journey to Jerusalem. Luke builds upon that event as it is found in Mark's Gospel but introducing new material. It begins when Jesus "set his face to go to Jerusalem" (9:51); it concludes with a grand entry into the city. But that final triumphal procession simply caps this long journey, which itself seems like an extended procession. Jesus does not travel alone.

Following Luke's practice of introducing a distinct set of character groupings for each phase of his narrative, we find Jesus accompanied by three groups: his disciples, the growing crowd, and the Pharisees. Luke distributes his attention almost equally among them, creating three distinct ongoing conversations for Jesus.[15]

*The Disciples.* The dialogue with the disciples builds on the beginnings in Galilee and continues the instructions begun there. The parable of the wildflowers and the instruction on the Lord's Prayer remind us of the Sermon on the Plain. In terms of the developing narrative the disciples not only connect with their origins in the Galilee section, but Luke suggests the emergence of a distinct leadership group within the larger group of disciples. The parable of the Responsible and Irresponsible Stewards anticipates the conferral of authority that will come later at the supper and in the early chapters of Acts.

*The Crowd.* Meanwhile, certain parables, such as the Mustard Seed and the Leaven, are delivered to another of the groups with which Jesus interacts on the way to Jerusalem, the *crowd.* Throughout the first chapters that establish a route for the gentiles, the crowd remains largely in the background. But now they are shown to be present in the background of many of the interactions of Jesus with disciples and Pharisees. One of the more important roles of the crowd is to demonstrate the public nature of Jesus's mission, as various members of the crowd ask for him to make decisions for them and, in general, help to paint a picture of a large, and growing, movement making its way to the city.[16]

*The Pharisees.* The interaction with the Pharisees serves to draw our attention to the building tension in the narrative plot. It is here, in his debates with the Pharisees, that the practice of Jesus in the liberating Jubilee time in Galilee now receives a theoretical support.

---

[15] *Disciples*: 10:1–12, 17–23; 10:38—11:13; 12:1–12, 22–53; 16:1–13; 17:1–10; 17:22—18:8 (127 verses); *Religious authorities*: 10:25–27; 11:37–53; 13:31—14:24; 15:1–32; 16:14–31; 17:20–21 (133 verses); 18:8–14; *Crowd*: 9:57–62; 10:13–15; 11:14–36; 12:13–21; 12:54—13:30; 14:25–35 (100 verses).

[16] Often with the crowd we are shown another feature of these conversations on the road. They are depicted as overheard by other groups, who will at times interrupt and take the talk in a new direction.

A parable toward the end of the journey captures the issues involved. In Luke 18:9–14, we hear about the Pharisee and a tax-collector praying in the Temple. The Pharisee thanks God for giving him the wherewithal to follow the law and thereby reach a state of righteousness. The tax-collector simply beats his breast and asks for mercy, "God, be merciful to me, a sinner!" Here the fundamental terms of the narrative conflict of the Gospel are set out: self-achieved righteousness versus repentance.

This debate between Jesus and the Pharisees begins in Luke 10:25–37, in one of the programmatic scenes mentioned earlier. Luke has moved the passage about the Great Commandment from its place in Mark, in the final week in Jerusalem, to its place here at the start of the journey to Jerusalem. It sets the program for the debates to follow. He expands the role of the Temple, in effect, by beginning the debates earlier, making them a major activity on the long road to the city. And the motive of the Pharisees is the same: they were "lying in wait for him, to catch him in something he might say" (Luke 11:54).

And here we discover that the role of the Pharisees has been amplified by the presence of legal experts, the *nomikoi* (lawyers). It is probably significant that Strong's Greek dictionary, in defining a *nomikos,* cites the scribe Ezra as a good example. We recollect the programmatic dispute in the Nazareth synagogue that pits two visions of Judaism, that of Isaiah and that of Ezra, against one another.

When the lawyer asks about inheriting eternal life (10:25), the mention of a *nomikos* invites us to look back to 7:29–30, where the term is first introduced. That passage is about John and the reception he received. It is something of a bridge, as it takes us back to the original Jubilee message in the Nazareth synagogue. Responding to John's inquiry from prison, Jesus repeats some of the same scripture passages of the Nazareth scroll (Luke 4:18–19; 7:22–23). In this way a thematic line is traced from the program announced in Nazareth to this debate on the road to Jerusalem.

The consideration of God's purpose is revived in this encounter. The lawyer asks a question about eternal life. This allows Jesus to ask the lawyer, "What is written in the law? How do you read it?" (10:25–26, author's trans.). This is the first time the word *law* appears in Luke, and it is Jesus who introduces it. He is posing a question of interpretation and use of the law. In fact, the entire episode is about the uses of the law. The lawyer responds with the Shema and the passage from Leviticus 19:18 about love of neighbor, just as in Mark, except it is the lawyer instead of Jesus providing the information. Here Jesus simply adds, "You have given the right answer; do this, and you will live" (10:28).

The lawyer's question in response is sometimes seen as an attempt to weasel out of the implications of the law by narrowing the demands as much as possible. But it is a legitimate question about the law, with a history of debate about it. In the Hebrew Bible the law applied to fellow Israelites (Lev 19:18) but in a later passage was extended to the stranger in the land (Lev 19:33–34). The Greek Bible, the Septuagint (the Bible for our God-fearer), narrowed it again by translating it to refer to the stranger who was a convert to Judaism. At the time of Jesus the Essenes were absolute in denying to outsiders the status of neighbor; the Pharisees debated it vigorously.[17]

So here in the story the question concerns the application of the law. That the lawyer wanted "to justify himself" suggests that he wanted to keep the law so as to earn eternal life. The implication is that this would be placing the accomplishment on his own shoulders rather than the grace of God, hence the need to specify carefully and accurately the application of the law.

Jesus answers, perhaps disconcertingly for an advocate of precise definitions, with a parable. If the priest and the Levite were restrained by the ritual laws from attending to the dead, the purity law then determines their action. However, the Samaritan is not restrained by that law and so is free to help the man—which he does at considerable expense to his own energy and resources. If the priest and Levite were not free to do the same thing because of their position, then the issue is not about their lack of compassion, it is about the law that prevents them from exercising compassion. For Luke's polemic it is not primarily about the priest and Levite

---

[17] Johnson, *Luke*, 172–73.

or even the Samaritan, but about the law. And this has direct implications for the predicament of the God-fearers that Luke is addressing in his Gospel.

After all this, Jesus's final question does a switch on the original question. Where the lawyer asked, "And who is my neighbor?" Jesus asks who *acted* as neighbor (10:30, 36). The first talks about the receiver of the action; the second about the actor performing the action. In a moral reading of this story this question replaces the impulse to close down the possible recipients of neighborly help by opening it up again, showing how to *be* a neighbor, not how to *find* one. But what the conflict reading reveals is that Jesus is showing that being a neighbor is something involving compassion, good in itself, and that the purity law is interfering with it in certain circumstances. In the parable, being a neighbor is a good thing, and the Samaritan is applauded for that. The listeners understand that the law is getting in the way of doing the good thing, in the way of compassion, and that there is a conflict that may not have been perceived till now. Once again, it is about the law, not the morality of the persons. It is about the law that prevents the moral action from occurring.

The contrast between the priest and Levite, representing Jewish leadership, on the one hand, and the Samaritan, on the other, is still important. But taken in relationship with the law topic at the center of the story, the contrast is between those who keep the law, and are therefore prevented from doing works of compassion, and the one without the law, who is therefore freed to respond to his compassionate impulses. The central issue is the law, and how one reads it. The perspective offered by the sense of the conflict at the heart of the Gospel allows a reading of the story that puts the dilemma of the law at the center. It serves Luke's purpose as a proper way to begin the debates about the law, at the start of traveling the road to Jerusalem.

The road portion of the story, though concerned with the law, does not address the identity-marker laws directly. Rather, it considers the *concept* of the law and how it is used. The purity rules stand for the larger issue of the laws preventing the God-fearers from full participation. The purity laws that are addressed are those of meals and hospitality, but not circumcision or food laws directly.

Upon being invited to dinner at a Pharisee's house, Jesus uses the opportunity to criticize the legal practices of the Pharisees (10:37–54). After he delivers a series of woes against them, some lawyers intervene, pointing out that in condemning the Pharisees, he offends them as well. Jesus then offers a few woes directed at the lawyers. A final test involving the lawyers involves their questioning Jesus about appropriate actions on the Sabbath concerning healing a man with edema. This leads into a chapter concerning meals, which features a series of reversals, from advice to guests about seeking the higher or lower places at table, to advice to hosts about inviting those from the byways and highways.

The debates between Jesus and the Pharisees and lawyers come to a head in 18:9–14, in the parable of the Pharisee and the Tax-Collector, told to "some who trusted in themselves that they were righteous and regarded others with contempt" (18:9). Here we see made explicit the contrast that is implied in the debates on the road. On the one side is the righteousness that is achieved by successful adherence to the law. On the other is the act of repentance.

When we think of self-righteousness, we frequently associate it with hypocrisy, with the underlying implication that no one is truly virtuous, and those who claim virtue must be lying. This may be included in Luke's portrait of self-righteousness. But as the parable shows, he is also including those who *successfully* keep the commands of the law. Of course, as the context of meals implies, the ritual rules of food laws are prominent in his mind. Nonetheless, he is as critical of successful keeping of the law as he is of hypocritical pretense.

Against this self-achieved righteousness he positions the act and attitude of repentance. As we see in the parade of examples previously cited, with Peter's call a prime exhibit, repentance is more than an admission of sins. It is an admission of sinfulness itself. Rather than an acknowledgment of certain behaviors, it is a recognition of something more basic.

This is the lesson that we take away from the teaching of Luke's journey narrative. As a final instance, we conclude with the story of Zacchaeus, the tax-collector who climbed the tree (19:1–10). Here is one who is disregarded by the worthy because he lives outside the categories of ritual law. Now he finds himself invited to repentance. He mentions specific practices for which he faults himself, but his conversion represents a revolution in his way of life. The readers of Luke's Gospel find themselves responding to Jesus's question to the lawyer: "How do you read it?" For now a way of living opens up that does not depend upon the regulations of purity that characterize Pharisaic Judaism.

## Jesus in Jerusalem (19:45—24:53)

In Jerusalem two things occur in Luke's narrative: Jesus's story comes to fulfillment, and the disciples come into their own. The section begins with an interpretive parable, followed by the procession into the city, the Temple action, and the emerging opposition of the Jerusalem elite.

### The Parable of the Coming Kingdom

As previously, Luke provides a program for this part of the story. Right before the entry into the city, he positions a passage that serves a programmatic function. It is a parable that has acquired different names—the parable of the Pounds, or the Gold Coins, or the Minas. In Matthew, it is known as the Parable of the Talents (Matt 25:14–30), but there are no talents in Luke's version (19:11–27). His story features a nobleman becoming king rather than a rich merchant on a journey. In addition, the successful servants in the king's absence are rewarded with territories to manage rather than funds. It concludes the speculation during the journey about the coming kingdom, and it projects the following action in Jerusalem in two aspects. It rewards the faithful with delegated responsibilities, and it condemns those who rejected the king. On the one hand, it anticipates the *delegation* of authority to the apostles at the Lord's supper. On the other hand, its previews the *rejection* of Jesus, the king.[18]

*Entry and Temple Cleansing*

In the entry the provisional establishment of the kingdom occurs by the arrival of the king. The parable of the Coming Kingdom has alerted us to the roles coming up—those opposing Jesus and those delegated with his mission. In a grand triumphal procession Luke slows the action, as if to indicate that the long journey is ending. He marks stages of the entry, as Jesus comes to Bethany (19:28), then descends the Mount of Olives (19:37), approaches the city (19:41), and finally enters the Temple courts (19:45). It is during this time that the Pharisees, after warning Jesus to control his disciples, disappear from Luke's narrative. In Luke's telling the Temple action is the final part of the procession into the city, not a separate event. Notably, however, it is not the cleansing itself that prompts the antagonism of the Jerusalem authorities, but rather Jesus's teaching (19:47). Luke's adjustments in this regard are worth noting. Although he has removed the Great Commandment debates from the final week in order to supply a program for the journey debates, he has compensated for its absence. The farewell discourse of Mark and Matthew has simply become part of the teaching in the Temple for Luke (21:37–38). This is previewed earlier (Luke 17:22–37), and we can assume the Temple teaching to be a continuation of the matters debated on the way to the city.

At this point, following his practice of introducing a new set of characters for each major segment of the story, Luke alerts us to the antagonists for the drama in Jerusalem (20:1–8): the chief priests, scribes and elders. These are the rulers or leaders of the people. The narrative itself shows various authorities trying to catch Jesus in debate—in a continuation of the activity along the road—but losing face decisively. This, in turn, generates a response of insults and intense taunting of Jesus as circumstances change, and Jesus is taken into their hands.

---

[18] As in ibid., 272.

## *Delegation of Authority: The Lord's Supper*

Meanwhile, the apostles, for their part, are given authority. It is at the supper that the disciples become more prominent in the narrative. Luke's account of the supper differs notably from the other Gospels. One issue is the matter of the two cups. A closer reading, however, reveals that there are actually two moments in the meal, each involving a cup. One of these is about the Passover, and one is about the Eucharist. The first involves celebrating the Passover and sharing the cup. Jesus announces that he will not eat or drink again until the kingdom comes (22:15–18). This moment concerns the story of Jesus. The second concerns the subsequent story of the disciples. He offers as a remembrance the bread and the cup, the meal that will be theirs as the body and the blood of the Lord (22:19–20). The first looks to the past; the second to the future.

However, the delegates are not yet ready for their new role. When Jesus predicts his betrayal, it results in a dispute among the disciples about their relative importance. This passage recalls the first and last sayings during the journey to Jerusalem. But here Luke uses it to introduce his version of a farewell speech of Jesus to his disciples (24:22–30).

With language much like the Markan response to the ambition of James and John, Jesus insists that they not be like the Gentiles, where kings lord it over their subjects. He then translates this into the language of serving at meals: "I am among you as one who serves" (22:27). He adds, "You are those who have stood by me in my trials; and I confer on you, just as my Father has conferred on me, a kingdom, so that you may eat and drink at my table in my kingdom, and you will sit on thrones judging the twelve tribes of Israel" (22:28–30). Here Luke is preparing his reader for Acts of the Apostles, where the promises made here will be carried out.

After a dialogue with Peter that includes the prediction of his denial, they prepare to leave. The final conversation has generated much conflicting interpretation. Reminding them of the times they were sent out on mission, two by two, Jesus changes the instruction and encourages them to have swords. They have two, they say, and Jesus says, "It is enough!" (22:38)

*Rejection of the King: Trial and Death of Jesus*

Luke's account of the temptation in the garden is given the name *agony*, a term found only here in the New Testament (22:44). While we have our own meaning for this word, we should not forget that *agon* meant contest and struggle; this has given its name to the contestants in the narrative, the prot*agon*ist and the ant*agon*ists.

In the arrest that follows the disciples use one of the swords mentioned at the supper to cut off the ear of the high priest's slave. Jesus stops them and, in this Gospel, heals the ear (22:51). This is not only consistent with the proclaimed program of Jesus, but it dramatizes the exact opposite of the harm contracted by violent conflict. One can threaten with harm, but healing invites allegiance, not antagonism.

Luke, always interested in eliminating puzzling features (even while introducing others for us) shifts the trial before the Sanhedrin, the Jerusalem Council, to the following morning. The incarceration of Jesus following the arrest is not a trial but something of a preliminary investigation. And here a striking feature needs to be noted. Jesus and Peter are visible to each other, since in this Gospel Jesus has not been taken inside. When the cock crows, Peter abruptly recognizes how he has denied knowing Jesus. The two of them lock eyes, each knowing that the other knows (22:61).

While much of the rest of Luke's passion story is similar to the other Synoptic Gospels, a conspicuous exception is the inclusion of Herod Antipas in the proceedings (24:6–16). We are reminded that Luke did not tell the story of this same Herod's execution of John the Baptist. But now we see him involved in the execution of Jesus. Again Jesus is mocked.

*Mockery: The Theme of Luke's Passion Story*

Luke differs from the other Gospels in that the mocking of Jesus begins early and becomes a major motif of the passion. In Luke's account the trial is deferred to the morning, while Jesus is held overnight in the courtyard, where he is mocked. In the other Gospels the humiliation begins only after the verdict of condemnation. In Luke's narrative it continues with Herod, the Roman soldiers, the rulers of the people, the executioners, and even the criminal on the cross next to Jesus. Excluded from this list, however, is the crowd, passive but not opposed. And then, of course, another not joining in is the good thief, a final exemplar of repentance in the Gospel, bringing this part to a conclusion.

Upon Jesus's death not only the women who had accompanied him from Galilee but also the crowd gathered for the spectacle leave in sorrow, "beating their breasts" (23:48–49). At the end Jesus is buried by Joseph of Arimathea, whom Luke describes in language that recalls the faithful villagers in the first two chapters.

### Luke's Easter Stories

Luke's resurrection stories include his account of the empty tomb, again similar to the other accounts but slightly rearranged (24:1–12). And for the first time we have elaborated resurrection stories, most notably the Emmaus story (24:13–35). The account of the two disciples meeting the risen Christ while on the road to Emmaus is unique among the Gospels. Following their encounter, they return to Jerusalem to relate their experience to the disciples, for in this Gospel the disciples remain in Jerusalem (24:52–53). And so the reader is ready for the narrative of Acts of the Apostles.

The gathering of the disciples in Jerusalem, first seen here, is followed by an abbreviated account of the ascension of Jesus. Here, and in the Emmaus story, we first hear the announcement that the messiah must suffer, according to the scriptures (24:26, 44). Since the Old Testament never presents the messiah in this way it can be presumed to refer to the convergence of messiah and Suffering Servant, first encountered in the voice from heaven in Mark's baptism account, combining Psalm 2:7 and Isaiah 42:1. In effect, Luke's phrase summarizes in a slogan-like saying the theology of reversal seen throughout the Gospel of Luke.

*Conflict in Luke Reviewed*

In looking back over the Gospel narrative we note the conflict between the two strands of Judaism first announced in the synagogue of Nazareth, then working its way through the dramatic action. At the center is the teaching of Jesus and his debates with those who defend the traditions. These debates, articulated on the road to Jerusalem, become something more lethal when the opposition shifts from Pharisees to the "rulers" of the people, the Sanhedrin. At this point Jesus's adherence to an alternative view of the tradition produces not a set of counter-arguments, but rather the decision to silence him. The ultimate result, however, is not silence but a movement. And this is the story of the Acts of the Apostles.

## Acts of the Apostles: Introductory Remarks

Acts is Luke's second volume, part of his project from its original conception. As with the Gospel, it is introduced by a dedication (to Theophilus) and picks up where the Gospel of Luke leaves off—with the ascension of Jesus, now specified as having taken place forty days after the resurrection.

In Acts, the early chapters show the Apostolic Council, considered as a standing institution, replacing the Jewish Council. Initial moves into the surrounding areas follow this, raising troubling questions about the Jewish identity markers. The decision of the Apostolic Council (Acts 15) allows the convert Paul, now with a letter from the apostles (contrasting to that earlier, from the high priest) to launch his representative mission to the Gentiles.

Jesus's announcement at the moment of ascension sets out the program. He informs the Apostles, "You will be my witnesses in Jerusalem, in all Judea and Samaria, and to the ends of the earth" (Acts 1:8). In the first half of the work Luke presents a vivid image of mission as moving out to the wider world in a threefold division, following this directive (Acts 1—5, 6—12, 13—15).

These geographical indicators recur (1:12; 8:1; 13:47) shaping the story. Each part is characterized by a *list of names*: apostles (1:13), deacons (6:5), prophets and teachers (13:1); by a *rite* of commission (1:26; 6:6; 13:3), and by a major *speech,* delivered respectively by Peter (2:14–35), by Stephen (7:1–53), and by Paul (13:16–41). In the manner of ancient history writing, these speeches serve as interpretations of the ongoing narrative. Where the Gospel takes us to Jerusalem, the book of Acts leaves the city behind. Guided by the Spirit, it bears the "light to the Gentiles" from Jerusalem out into the larger world.

However, this is rhetoric. With help from clues given by Luke's text, we find a more nuanced pattern beneath the generalized outward movement suggested by Acts 1:8. A review of the outline given earlier is helpful:

| | |
|---|---|
| Jerusalem, 1:1—7:60 | The New Jewish Council: Apostles |
| Leaving Jerusalem | Mission into the world |
|    Judea and Samaria, 8:1—11:18; 12:1–25 | Peter and Philip |
|    Antioch, 11:19–30; 13:1—15:28 | Barnabas and Paul |
|    Ephesus, 16:1—20:38 | Paul's Mission |
| Back to Jerusalem, 21:1—26:32 | Mission accomplished |
| Rome, 27:1—28:31 | The Gentile mission established |

The narrative of Acts is best envisioned as stages centered in hub cities. In addition to Judea and Samaria, the outward mission includes stages identified with Antioch and Ephesus. And finally the narrative turns toward Paul of Tarsus, who carries the burden of the story to the end of the book.

As in the Gospel, the set of characters changes with each stage. It begins in Jerusalem with Peter and the apostles; and then Stephen, Philip, and their companions, who take it out of the city into the surrounding territory. As Jerusalem fades into the past, Antioch is the first replacement. At this point Paul and Barnabas become the main characters, with their mission to Asia Minor. After the council meeting in Acts 15, the spotlight moves to Paul's mission, with Titus and Timothy. This stage finds its center in Ephesus. Paul circles in the territories around it, establishing churches in Macedonia and Achaia, until he eventually finds his way to Ephesus.

When he leaves for his final visit to Jerusalem, his farewell address is delivered to the Ephesians.

The latter part of the book—Paul's arrest in Jerusalem, his detainment by the procurator, along with the visit of Herod—reflects back on Luke's passion account and the conclusion of the Gospel. The final move to Rome features Paul and the centurion Julius. It resembles another grand procession, moving the center of the Jesus movement from Jerusalem to Rome. It is an outward movement, but with a destination. Rome concludes the book of Acts, standing as proxy for the worldwide mission—the capital representing the whole.

Yet relocation is never simple. In a move from one house to another, for example, the old house is gradually abandoned, typically in stages. Luke's account in Acts shows this move accomplished in stages as well. It establishes a foothold "there" before it can let go of everything "here."

### Jerusalem (Acts 1—7)

After the dedication to Theophilus, Acts begins with the ascension of Jesus, forty days later. Here we recognize Luke's concern for placing theological events not only in a geographical context but also on a calendar timeline. In fact, Luke has Jesus announce the timeline of the book of Acts in 1:8. This describes the movement of the mission in Acts, although the narrative drama, when traced, gives a slightly different shape to the book.

The book opens with the Pentecost event taking place in the upper room (Acts 1:13). The descent of the Spirit upon the community recalls the baptism of Jesus. And just as Jesus interpreted his event with a text from Isaiah 61, so Peter employs the book of Joel to explain what is happening (Acts 2:17–21; Joel 3:1–5). For Luke, this event reverses the Tower of Confusion, as the Greek Bible calls it—or Babel, as we know it.

Meanwhile, of course, it previews of the story of Acts, to follow. This is behind the list of nations that stand proxy for the world of the mission to come. The entire tone of the story evokes an international community, with the universal horizon anticipated from the first chapters of the Gospel.

The part of Acts focused on Jerusalem in particular begins with chapter 3. Now, suddenly, the crowd is gone, the many languages put aside, and the focus narrows to the community in the city itself. We observe the community praying together, sharing goods, and presenting an ideal picture (2:42–47; 4:32–37; 5:12–16). Meanwhile, Peter, the primary figure in this part of the story, accompanied by John, continues to witness to the resurrection of Jesus despite attempts by the Jewish authorities to stop him. The first of many prison experiences enter the story (4:3; 5:18), and we have a programmatic statement for the many arrests to come: "But Peter and the apostles answered, 'We must obey God rather than any human authority'" (5:29).[19]

The delegation of authority in the Gospel illuminates an episode in these early chapters of Acts that typically troubles readers. The story of the accusation and deaths of Ananias and Sapphira, members of the community who pretended to share their goods but did not (5:1–11), seems especially harsh. However, we can see in this incident the apostles assuming their new role. Authority includes the power of correction as well as direction. Here we can contrast the report of the Jewish Council, the Sanhedrin. Gamaliel advises the Sanhedrin not to take action. His reasoning is familiar to us: if the upstart movement is from God it cannot be stopped; if it is not, it will fade of itself (5:38–39). In other words, the Jewish Council with no call to make no longer has a role to play.

In effect, for the narrator of Acts the *new* Apostolic Council replaces the Sanhedrin. It is this transfer of authority that is validated by the presence of the Holy Spirit, coming upon and residing in the community. Although the word *apostle* literally means "one sent," Luke has a special role for the apostles. They will remain in Jerusalem, as the new Sanhedrin, while others in the community are sent out.

---

[19] Acts presents a picture of disciples readily arrested by authorities. This deserves a volume in itself. The following survey of Acts, however, focuses on its continuation of the program begun in the Gospel.

## Leaving Jerusalem (8—20)

*Judea and Samaria (8:1—11:18; 12:1–25)*

The mission takes place in three stages: (1) mission in the territory proximate to Jerusalem, namely, Judea and Samaria; (2) the early Gentile mission based in Antioch; and (3) the mission of Paul and his companions, related to Ephesus. While the initial move outward from the city into the surrounding territory of Judea and Samaria takes the mission outside the city; that move is delayed. Although it begins in chapter 6, with the designation of the seven "deacons," the mission doesn't move beyond Jerusalem until the stoning of Stephen and the persecution that follows it (8:1). Stephen and Philip are Hellenist Jews, showing the movement beyond Jerusalem to be sociological as well as territorial. With Stephen gone, Philip is featured in this part of the narrative, taking the message to Judea and Samaria (8:4–8, 26–40). In his encounter with the Ethiopian on the road to Gaza, we meet our first God-fearing Gentile in Acts. We also note his devotion to the Greek Bible, characteristic of this group.

Paul is first introduced (9:1) as Saul, an enthusiastic reformer eager to expunge this excrescence from the world of Judaism. Paul, bearing a letter of authorization from the high priest, is portrayed as part of the stoning group, whose members place their cloaks at his feet. As seen at 4:35, where members of the community put donations at the feet of the apostles, this gesture signals authority. Paul is likely a young zealot in charge of the stoning of Stephen. But shortly we will hear of Paul being converted on the road to Damascus (9:3–9).

Peter is also still active as part of the Jerusalem church, now reaching out to the boundary of the territory. He takes the mission to the coast—Lydda, Joppa, and finally Caesarea (9:32–35, 36–42; 10:23–24). In a passage emphasized by its elaboration, Peter converts the centurion Cornelius and his family after having a vision in which all foods were declared ritually clean. Echoing the Nazareth synagogue event, Peter declares all things "acceptable" to God (10:35). And so another barrier is surmounted, that of the food laws.

## Antioch: Disciples First Called Christians
### *(11:19–30; 13:1—15:28)*

Meanwhile, others have been taking the message beyond Judean territory to Antioch in Syria, where some who were not Jewish were also being baptized. While Luke's program suggests an ordered program, with each stage describing a wider circle than the previous, he lets us know that the Antioch mission occurred at the same time (Acts 11:19, 20). Antioch marks the first steps beyond Judaism. With no ties to Judaism, we have the beginning of a new identification. In Antioch, the baptized are first called Christians (11:26).

Here Luke's narrative concentrates on the departure from Judea and the dominance of Jerusalem. It is a time of disengaging. It will culminate in the Council of Jerusalem, establishing conditions for the disengagement. This is still part of the leaving behind. Antioch now becomes the launching pad for a new set of missions. Barnabas (from Cyprus) and Paul (from Tarsus) are instrumental in this stage of the transition. Barnabas, having recruited Paul, begins to proselytize in Cyprus and the southern parts of Asia Minor. Paul makes a major speech that notes their mission is to the "ends of the earth" (13:47).

Just as the issue of food laws was raised by the mission of Peter, so now the question of circumcision is given attention by the work of Barnabas and Paul. We see Luke's narrative program at work, insofar as the proclamation of Jubilee release, announced at Nazareth and debated on the road to Jerusalem, now begins to be fulfilled. The last of the post-exilic identity markers preventing devout Gentiles from converting to Judaism has now been put aside. At the conclusion of this early mission we are told by the narrator that God "had opened the door of faith for the Gentiles" (14:27).

At this point, precipitated by the mission of Barnabas and Paul, it is time for the Apostolic Council to make some policy decisions. In Acts 15 the Apostolic Council, in its new role in the history of salvation as replacement for the Sanhedrin, considers the demands of the law as regards the Gentile converts. Peter, in his final appearance in Acts, gives testimony concerning food laws. Paul and Barnabas testify concerning circumcision. The council decides for abrogation of the laws, with the exception of a few for mixed Jewish-Gentile communities, to avoid undue disturbance of the Jewish members with a lifelong adherence to these practices.[20]

The council produces a letter confirming its decision, which provides the warrant for Paul's following ministry (Acts 21:25), just as the high priest's letter did for his earlier career persecuting the Jesus movement. Upon the conclusion of the council gathering, Barnabas drops out of the narrative, because he and Paul have a falling out. From here on we will follow Paul and his new companions, Silas and Timothy, in a continuation of the promise of a mission "to the ends of the earth" (1:8; 13:47).

*Ephesus: Paul and the Mission to the Gentiles (Acts 16—20)*

The account narrows now to the missionary work of Paul (Acts 16—20). The story begins in Antioch, but its symbolic center is Ephesus, the new narrative hub in the account. Paul's mission continues the movement outward on new footing.

Paul is a transitional figure, both Pharisee (23:6) and Roman citizen (16:37). Only Luke tells us that Paul was a Roman citizen. Paul's letters make no such claim. But it serves Luke's purpose to bring this out, as his story of Paul will effect a major shift from synagogue to civic hall, from a vantage point that looks to Jerusalem to one that looks to Rome.

Paul's mission is framed in the account by two visits to Troas, one launching him into Europe for his mission (Acts 16:9–10) and the other bringing this phase to a conclusion (20:4–12). Basically, Paul and Silas leave for western Anatolia, picking up Timothy along the way. But they are diverted by the "Spirit of Jesus" (16:7). Arriving at Troas, site of ancient Troy, Paul has a vision of a Macedonian seeking their help (16:8–10). A tour through Macedonia and Greece, founding churches as they go, leads them

---

[20] After leaving the house of John Mark's mother, in Acts 12:17, Peter departs from the narrative of Acts, heading toward parts unknown. Now he is called back; the council takes testimony concerning food laws from him, and testimony concerning circumcision from Barnabas and Paul.

through Philippi, Thessalonica, Berea, and Athens, to Corinth. An eighteen-month stay at Corinth ends with meeting a couple from the Roman church who fled Rome during a persecution under Claudius (18:18–19). They travel to Ephesus, capital of Asia.

Paul leaves Ephesus not long after they arrive, apparently having planned to leave for Judea all along. He also leaves the narrative spotlight. While he visits Jerusalem and Antioch before returning, we observe what is happening at Ephesus. A certain Apollos, a skilled rhetorician from the Alexandrian church, visits Ephesus and has his catechetical education completed by the pair from Rome (18:24–28). Then they return to Rome, while Apollos moves on to Corinth. When Paul returns, they are gone.

Paul remains in Ephesus for two years (19:10), after which he plans to visit Jerusalem. Considering the seven accompanying him from different provinces (Acts 20:4–5), this presumably was to deliver the collection for Jerusalem, though Luke does not mention it specifically. First, however, he needs to visit Corinth to put out brushfires. By this time we are in the closing phases of his mission. He stops at Troas, closing one circle (20:4–6), and then delivers a farewell address to the Ephesians at the port town of Miletus (20:17–35). Then, in a deliberate fashion, his travel to Jerusalem is traced in stages, island by island.

Paul's mission narrative is characterized by a number of features. One is the geographical pattern it describes. Paul travels in a large circle around Ephesus before he finally arrives there. From there he makes visits as needed out to the churches he has founded.

Another aspect is the attention given to the God-fearers. We've seen the evidence for the God-fearers earlier. Most of these references take place during this part of the story. Reaching out to the God-fearers seems a particular feature of Paul's activity as Luke wants us to view it. Consistently, the Gentiles involved are God-fearers, not pagans. The one exception (in this part) is Athens. Here his effort is first devoted to creating God-fearers from pagans, after which he can follow his usual procedure of reaching out to God-fearers.

And, of course, we cannot discuss Paul's missionary activity without mentioning the opposition he encounters. Acts records beating and imprisonment in Philippi (16:22–23), an attempt to seize him at Thessalonica (17:5–6), another attempt in Corinth (18:12–17), and seizing of his companions at Ephesus (19:29). The sources of Paul's opposition were threefold: (1) the Jews who felt that Paul was taking away their supportive God-fearers; (2) the Roman authorities who recognized the subversive potential of his movement; and (3) the more traditionalist fellow-Christians who felt he was abandoning the Jewish character of the movement.[21] The narrative of Acts stresses the Jewish opposition. It prepares us for the closing chapters of the book, and the trials of Paul.

In Acts 19:8–9 an incident occurs in Ephesus. Paul entered the synagogue where he "debated boldly with persuasive arguments about the kingdom of God." After three months of this, confronted by opposition, "he withdrew and took his disciples with him and began to hold daily discussions in the lecture hall of Tyrannus" (19:9). This might ordinarily be considered another example of Paul's strident engagement with his opponents. But when we place it in its larger context, we find a deliberate pattern established and then broken in Ephesus.

A key term that appears here is *reasoning (dialegomai)*, as in "reasoning in the synagogue." Luke uses it to describe Paul's activity in the successive cities that he visits:

| | |
|---|---|
| 17:2 | reasoning in the synagogue—Thessalonica |
| 17:17 | reasoning in the synagogue—Athens |
| 18:4 | reasoning in the synagogue—Corinth |
| 18:19 | reasoning in the synagogue—Ephesus |
| 19:8 | reasoning in the synagogue—Ephesus (on a later date) |
| 19:9 | reasoning in the lecture hall of Tyrannus—Ephesus |

---

[21] See, for instance, John Dominic Crossan and Jonathan L. Reed, *In Search of Paul: How Jesus's Apostle Opposed Rome's Empire with God's Kingdom* (San Francisco: HarperOne, 2004), 28–32. Crossan is inclined to dismiss the demand Luke makes upon Roman authorities. However, see below, on the centurions.

At 19:8–9 a decisive shift takes place. This is a watershed in the program of Luke. The mission is placed on new grounds, in the lecture hall instead of the synagogue. In its larger effect, Paul's mission is transitional, moving the narrative from departure to relocation, from leaving Jerusalem and its synagogues to Rome and its lecture halls. So when Paul returns to Jerusalem, new ground has been prepared elsewhere, and the narrative is free to move there.

Paul takes formal leave of Ephesus in Acts 20, first revisiting Troas, the city that provided the vision for him to travel to Macedonia in the first place. With his farewell address to the Ephesians, readers are ready to return to Jerusalem with the findings and the achievements of the mission. We find that Paul returns to the city on a different basis from when he left it, and that is our experience as well. Since we were last in Jerusalem, the tone has shifted from dissent to affirmation. Our place in the mission is on new footing, no longer in the position of denying the received mandate, for now we have one of our own. We are no longer leaving, but arriving.

In brief, the movement has now acquired purchase in the empire and no longer needs to stand in the synagogues of Jerusalem. But this new advantage has been won; it is not simply a case of adopting the imperial standard. Far from being a gift of the empire, it has been painstakingly worked out move by move, step by step, so as to retain the essentials of the given heritage and relocate them in the new territory. It is a matter of transplanting, but securely so.

## Back to Jerusalem (21—26)

When Paul returns to Jerusalem, in two adjacent passages, a circle closes in the narrative and another reopens. In the first Paul returns to the Jerusalem church with a report on his mission, completing that part of the story. In the other the Jewish Council, not heard from since the early chapters, reappears. Both involve the terms of conflict central to Luke's project—the regulations that serve to mark what is Jewish. In the first, Paul's doctrine of freedom from circumcision is challenged. In the second, a perceived violation of the Temple precincts reignites the fires of conflict.

Upon his arrival in the city, Paul is questioned by the Jerusalem church. What began with the meeting of the Apostolic Council in Acts 15 now comes to a conclusion, as indicated by Paul's insistence that he adhered to the terms of the letter earlier issued by the Apostolic Council (20:25) authorizing the mission.

We are further told that the Jerusalem church is reacting to rumors that Paul is relaxing the laws on circumcision for the Jews as well as the Gentiles (21:21). This is an issue for them since "how many thousands of believers there are among the Jews, and they are all zealous for the law" (Acts 21:20). Luke's narrative is not about leaving the Jews behind. Rather, it looks to the inclusion of the Gentiles. This story is not the same as that of Matthew, who is addressing the Jewish followers of Jesus. In other words, Luke's account is not anti-Jewish; rather, it is focused elsewhere, upon the emerging Gentile population who make up Luke's audience.[22]

That is the last we hear of the Jerusalem church. As soon as a circle is closed, putting to rest one set of concerns, another dispute returns. Once again we have a change in the cast of characters. The Jewish leadership, last seen in Acts 5 as the Sanhedrin, returns to the story. From this point on the parties that interact with Paul are the Jewish leaders and the Roman authorities. As the action unfolds, Gamaliel's warning is realized—"if this plan or this undertaking is of human origin, it will fail; but if it is of God, you will not be able to overthrow them—in that case you may even be found fighting against God!" (Acts 5:38–39). The continual guidance of the Spirit throughout the action shows the movement is "from God"; the final trials of Paul show that the Sanhedrin is "not able to overthrow them."

---

[22] Here we depart from studies that portray Luke as anti-Jewish, privileging Roman imperial institutions and authorities over Jewish ones. The mandate of the Nazareth synagogue continues, opening a gate for the Gentiles into the story of God's people. The feverish Jewish opposition to Paul in the final chapters of Acts, similar to that characterized by Paul himself, is not the Jewish people but the disestablished authority (according to the narrator) and the defenders of the laws and customs understood to be constituent of the faith, now under threat.

The concern raised by the Jews is a fear that Paul brought an uncircumcised Gentile into the Temple (21:28). We are again faced with the controversy that animated the first chapters of Acts and culminated in the stoning of Stephen. There, too, the bone of contention was the Temple and its legitimacy.

Once again the issues raised conform to the program of Luke-Acts, insofar as it concerns the laws and regulations that mark off the Jewish identity from the rest of the world. They not only work to affirm the community's identity, but they bar outsiders. They work in both directions. Here with the Temple we can surmise an allusion to Isaiah 56:1-8, cited in the Temple cleansing of Mark: "My house shall be called a house of prayer for all the nations" (Mark 11:17).

The opposition forces are those who are vigilant about the identity markers of Judaism. The attempts to ambush Paul (23:21) or present formal charges (24:1) can be understood better if they are seen as the kind of passionate concern that identity issues can arouse. The opposition viewpoint senses a threat to Judaism itself. We recall the concerns of Mark and Matthew, with their struggle concerning the threat to Judaism. Luke allows us to look at it from the other side.

As with the death of Stephen, Paul's trials are consciously described to evoke the trials of Jesus. They occur in two phases. First, he is arraigned before the governor, Felix, and then Festus, two years later. Throughout these adventures Paul appeals to his Roman citizenship and is saved by the Roman courts and guards. Festus brings the Jewish king, Agrippa, into the proceedings, and both agree that Paul is innocent. But his appeal to Rome must be honored, and he is sent there.

Throughout the story of Paul a gradual transformation has been taking place. Paul carries the weight of the narrative. In his success resides its success. He has taken the message to the Gentiles and reported back to Jerusalem. Now he brings a new confidence and presence to the situation. The Gentile churches are no longer dependent solely on Jerusalem; they can rely, within limits, on Rome. But at the same time they also are not accepting of Rome without reservations, mounting challenges to that cultural and political alternative base. Paul's trials and removal to Rome dramatize the new status.

## Rome (27—28)

The work of Luke's narrative project is all but complete. In the final two chapters of Acts the action shifts from Jerusalem to Rome, a reprise of the larger movement of the book.

Paul has a new traveling companion in the person of the Roman centurion Julius, who acts as his guard on the trip to Rome (27:1). He is the last of the series of Paul's companions that began with Barnabas and continued with Silas and Timothy. He also provides a final example of the centurions (and Roman soldiers in general) who figure prominently in Luke's work.

A definitive break from the past is established when a shipwreck occurs on the journey. The passengers wash ashore on the island of Malta, where they winter over (28:1, 11). We speak of burning bridges. But here we have a watery disruption, decisively breaking away from the previous, opening the way for a new beginning.

In the spring the party continues on to Rome. Having completed the departure from Jerusalem, the narrative finds the movement embedded in Rome, with Paul proclaiming the kingdom of God, the very thing that got Jesus killed (28:30–31). Paul, Luke tells us, is preaching "without hindrance," although under house arrest. The actual mission continues, but under an official suspicion of lawlessness. The challenge to Jerusalem is now replaced by a challenge to Rome. The various impediments have been removed, and now "the kingdom of God among you" (Luke 17:21), the seed and the leaven (Luke 13:18–21), are planted in the heart of the empire, ready to do subversive work from within. The Lukan narrative project is accomplished.

### A Look Back:
### Luke's Route to the God-fearing Gentiles

- The release from bondage proclaimed in the Nazareth synagogue turns out to include freedom from those prohibitions that were barriers to full communion for the Hellenist. In the successive course of the narrative, these are addressed one by one. Beginning with the evocation of the biblical faith of the Septuagint, in the stories of the birth of John and Jesus, we have the hopes of the God-fearer established. This evokes the story of the people of God that they desire to join.

- The Nazareth announcement promises the release of barriers, and the Galilee section of the Gospel shows Jesus releasing others from *bondages* of death and disease.
- The release from ritual barriers also begins here. The *Sabbath* is given a new reading and a new purpose.
- The new interpretation is reinforced on the road to Jerusalem, where the barriers of the *ritual laws* are confronted and replaced by the need for *repentance.*
- Upon reaching Jerusalem, Jesus faces attacks on his authority and his person. He makes provisions by investing his apostles with *authority* to carry on his work and teaching.
- In the Acts of the Apostles we see this taking shape—the first part, taking place in Jerusalem, concludes with Stephen's rejection of *Temple worship.*
- The next part, occurring in Judea and Samaria, comes to a climax with Peter's vision moving beyond the *food laws.*
- In the part centered on Antioch, Barnabas and Paul are shown refusing to require *circumcision* for the Gentile converts.
- Paul's mission, authorized by the Apostolic Council, takes the step that this "orderly sequence" of releases makes possible by shifting the arena of the movement from the *synagogue* to the Hellenist *lecture hall.*
- In a final move the Temple in *Jerusalem* is left behind, and the narrative shifts to Rome. It concludes in the heart of the empire, Luke's project of rejection to mission accomplished.

Luke's narrative is about the Gentile church and its place in the story of Jesus. It is not about replacing Judaism, but rather about joining the story of God's people. If we take this to be the whole story, and not just part of it, it opens to a reading of rejecting Judaism. However, we need to notice: (1) it is concerned with establishing a place for Gentiles in the church; (2) those in opposition are not all Jews, but those who act as guardians of the identity markers; and (3) Luke tells one side of a story; Matthew tells another.

One could argue that the story they hope to join is radically altered in their attempt to join it. Luke's account would take on a different meaning when the Gentile church adopted its procedures, originally described as concessions to an outrider group, now become the norm. The barriers that are overcome would for many continue to define the community that their adjustments would deny. And yet, ultimately, Luke's narrative remains an account of joining a faith story rather than replacing it with something new and better.

## CONFLICT RESOLUTION IN LUKE-ACTS

The Gospel of Luke alters the program of conflict resolution. Rather than a Jewish confrontation with the Roman Empire, as in Mark and Matthew, we find a challenge issued to the cultural values of the imperial reader. Here the conflict driving the Gospel story meets on a new front.

The resolution of conflict in Luke is further complicated by its double narrative. However, helping to hold this twofold work together is a continuously maintained point of view, anchored in its implied Gentile reader. This proposed reader is also challenged by Luke's work, and the challenge addresses something constitutive at the heart of the culture, namely, its love of honor.

With the aid of the cultural theme of *honor and shame*, we can understand the Gospel's preoccupation with the mounting and degrading mockery of Jesus. However, Paul's trials stand in stark contrast, insofar as he is presented as increasing in honor and status as the proceedings continue. Where Jesus was humiliated by this enemies, during Paul's trials they are themselves humiliated. The two attitudes toward honor might be seen as engaging the Gentile reader, the most excellent Theophilus and his contemporaries, so as to redefine *honor* with a challenge to that reader. The Gospel's demands for repentance, presented by the series of repenting figures in the story but directed toward the reader, become more vivid when understood in terms of the categories of honor and shame and the reversal of values made visible by them.

## Honor and Shame in the Hellenist World

In recent years numerous fruitful studies have applied the lessons of historical anthropology to the biblical texts. The categories of honor and shame in the ancient Mediterranean world have proven especially helpful. Much of the scholarly effort is to show how studies focused on Hellenistic culture also apply to the world of Judea. But since our concern is the Gentile culture shared by the implied reader, we can be confident of its presence in the world view of Luke and his reader.

Honor values dominated Greco-Roman culture. *Honor* has been defined as "a claim to worth that is socially acknowledged."[23] The definition emphasizes that there are two sides to the phenomenon. Along with the claim to worth, there has to be a confirming assent from society. Otherwise the claim is just foolish bragging. Love of honor shaped the world of the ancients. Xenophon describes Athenians as passionate for praise: "Athenians excel all others not so much in singing or in stature or in strength, as in love of honor, which is the strongest incentive to deeds of honor and renown." In a much later period the social demand remains much the same. Augustine reports, "For the glory that the Romans burned to possess, be it noted, is the favorable judgment of men who think well of other men."[24]

Honor was acquired by birth into an honorable family or by gaining honor through certain customary actions. Beneficent works

---

[23] Bruce Malina, *The New Testament World: Insights from Cultural Anthropology*, 3rd ed. (Louisville; KY: Westminster John Knox Press, 2001), 29.

[24] Xenophon, *Memorabilia* 3.3.13; Augustine, *City of God* 5.12. See Jerome H. Neyrey, *Honor and Shame in the Gospel of Matthew* (Louisville, KY: Westminster John Knox Press, 1998), 17.

gain honor, especially useful for prominent families needing to maintain their honorable position. At the supper Jesus dismissively cites this custom: "The kings of the Gentiles lord it over them; and those in authority over them are called benefactors" (Luke 22:25). And yet Theophilus, addressed as "Most Excellent," and to whom Luke's work is dedicated, is likely also its sponsor. This would count as a beneficent work. However, here it is likely that the message of this sponsored work, the Gospel of Luke, would subvert the intent of seeking honor for oneself. Barnabas is honored for divesting himself of his family property and donating it to the community (Acts 4:36–37).

More dramatically, encounters between males of equal social standing can become honor contests of *challenge and response.* Every encounter constituted a contest to be won or lost, whether engaging in verbal sparring or actual physical combat. The women's task, meanwhile, was to guard and preserve honor as caretakers of the group's status. The story of Simon the Pharisee, who neglected the courtesies of hospitality in his invitation to Jesus, constitutes an affront to honor. But the socially "shameless" woman repaired that neglect by performing the neglected gestures. The scene is an intricate study in the gains and duties of honor (7:36–50).

In the cultural categories of honor traditions, and especially in the contest of challenge and response, we find a new expression of the story strategies seen before, those of payback and purge.

*Payback and Purge*

Payback and purge are names we have adopted for two moves that are typically made in literary art, as well as in real life imitating art. The first, in an effort to achieve justice—closer to poetic justice—attempts to afflict the evildoer in the manner that person has been afflicting others. In life, it is the principle of revenge. But we have also seen how the Gospel narratives refuse such moves. Luke's is no different in this regard. And the Gospel's position on the matter is captured in one particularly illuminating statement: "Father, forgive them, for they do not know what they are doing"

(Luke 23:34).[25] Two sentiments are captured in this statement, one pertaining to payback and one to purge. The will to forgive implies release from the need to retaliate. Payback is highlighted in the narrative in Luke's account of the events on the Mount of Olives. In the garden arrest, one of the moments we understand as pivotal in the dramatic resolution of the Gospel plot, Luke shows this in another way. Jesus reverses the harm by healing the severed ear of the high priest's servant (22:51). Healing is in direct contrast to harming, and Jesus's action, echoing his entire mission, demonstrates that clearly at this particular crucial moment.

In addition to payback the saying on the cross speaks to purge. We have seen how in stories, as in life, this involves the need to identify the person with the sin, so that by eliminating the villain, we purge the world of the blight the villain represents. In saying they don't know what they are doing, Jesus separates the actions of perpetrators from their status as persons. The former can be condemned even while the latter are accepted as frail but true children of God. It is identification of evil with the character performing it that the Gospel refuses. As with Mark and Matthew, Luke refuses to make the conventional moves that lead to violence.

*Silence and Dishonor*

The silence of Jesus at his trials dramatizes this refusal. He remains silent or rejects self-defense (22:70; 23:3, 9). Hellenist readers would expect him to mount some kind of response. This expectation would be intensified by the humiliating mockery of Jesus, emphasized in this account. The taunts begin early, before Jesus is officially condemned, and continue to increase in intensity. At the time of his arrest, even before his trial, which occurs on

---

[25] The verse has a disputed history in Luke's Gospel. Though the early manuscripts by themselves are somewhat ambiguous, the sentiment is not alien to Luke's project, since we see something similar at the death of Stephen, itself shaped to reflect that of Jesus (Acts 7:60). We can see that the Gospel verse, whatever its claims to authenticity, speaks the language of Luke.

the following morning, he is abused and mocked. In the mounting tension of that Friday, the mockery intensifies as the ruler, the soldiers, and finally one of the thieves participate in the chorus.

For the early reader such a muted response would be disturbing. It stands in sharp contrast to the Greco-Roman traditions of the accused teacher. Luke Timothy Johnson cites famous accused teachers that Luke implies Jesus is equivalent to. Socrates defended himself vigorously before his judges. Johnson writes:

> Even more dramatic was the response of the Stoic philosopher Zeno when called before the tyrant; according to diverse traditions, he either bit off the ear of his judge, or bit off his own tongue and spit it at the judge, rather than betray his fellow conspirators against tyranny (Diogenes Laertius, *Life of Heraclitus* 9:26).

Jesus seriously disappoints in this department. For the Hellenist, this grave dishonor required redress. Johnson cites typical responses to the Gospel's account:

> And although taciturnity was highly regarded by the ancients in some contexts, it was expected of a philosopher to give expression in some fashion, verbal or symbolic, to his convictions at the end. Testimony to this perception is given by the pagan critic of Christianity Celsus, who in his True Word (an extended attack on Christianity) criticized this very silence by Jesus (Origen, *Against Celsus* 2:35).[26]

Honor absolutely required some response.

The mounting wave of vituperation concludes with the good thief. This scene, which culminates in the crucifixion account, deserves some attention. Like many of the isolated figures in Luke's account, this thief represents a type. One of his purposes in Luke's

---

[26] Diogenes Laertius, *Life of Heraclitus* 9:26; and Origen, *Against Celsus* 2:35. These these references to Diogenes Laertes and Origen are from Johnson, *Luke*, 367.

narrative is to conclude the series of repentance figures in the Gospel—figures representing the proper response to the movement of the Spirit. But he also stands at the end of the mounting strain of mockery and brings it to an end.

The good thief's statement cuts in different directions. In the first place, the mockery focuses on the kingship of Jesus. Accusations of blaspheming the Temple are omitted by Luke, this theme being deferred to the story of Stephen in Acts. So the thief's remark, "Jesus, remember me when you come into your kingdom," relates to this theme. Second, his response to the other thief is phrased in such a way as to alert the God-fearing reader: "Do you not fear God, since you are under the same sentence of condemnation?" (Luke 23:40). The God-fearer recognizes that the thief's question applies to the reader as well. With the good thief, the silent response of Jesus receives a voice.

## Repentance as Values Reversal

In addition to challenging the traditions of Judaism, Luke also challenges the assumptions of the Gentile reader. In Acts 17:6 a warning issued against Jason and the other Christians of Thessalonica reads, "These people who have been turning the world upside down have come here also." A reversal is taking place, as already anticipated in Mary's Magnificat—

> He has brought down the powerful from their
>     thrones,
>         and lifted up the lowly;
> he has filled the hungry with good things,
>     and sent the rich away empty. (Luke 1:52–53)

Values reversal is a theme in the Beatitudes: "Blessed are the poor. . . . But woe to you who are rich" (6:20, 24), and it is repeated in the debates on the road to Jerusalem (16:14–15), notably in the parable of the Rich Man and Lazarus (16:19–31). The language of social reversal implies a threatened class system, and in Luke it is often described in *economic* terms. The Roman world was sharply divided between a very few with wealth and a multitude of poor. No middle class existed as a buffer. But reversal is also asserted of *social* status as well, as seen in the stories of meals.

Meals are an important dimension to Luke's narrative. The Lord's supper was the occasion of the transfer of authority to the apostles. The recognition of the Risen Christ in Emmaus was during a meal. In Acts, meals provide the central experience of the emerging community. Prominently, in a stretch of text in the road narrative, Luke presents a series of passages about the first and last related to meals.

The meals are also the setting for teaching the reversal of values. If honor is to be defined as a claim to worth that is socially acknowledged, then it needs to be displayed for others to observe. One prominent way this was done was through elaborate meals. There is the time that Jesus, invited to a fine dinner, notices the guests seeking the highest places and advises them to take the lower places (Lk 14:7–11).

Further advice to the host follows this, to the effect that one should avoid inviting friends who can return the favor. Instead, he should venture outside the gates, invite "the poor, the crippled, the lame, and the blind" (14:12–14). This exchange sets the stage for the parable of the Great Feast, in which the instruction is continued. The host in the parable sends servants into the streets to invite "the poor, the crippled, the blind, and the lame" (14:15–24).

Here social reversal is realized in terms of the system of values defined by honor and shame. Elites were known as *honestiores* ("more honorable"), while the rest were the *humiliores* ("more lowly"). The differences were real, as seen in legal disparities. Not only were the upper classes less likely to be charged with wrongdoing, but their penalties, when they were actually convicted, avoided the more severe varieties. Crucifixion was reserved for the truly unvalued members of the society. We see in the final chapters of Acts that Paul's claim to honor as a Roman citizen, inherited and not purchased (Acts 22:28), provides him with special consideration before the law courts. Notably, the conclusion of Paul's story in Acts contrasts dramatically with that of Jesus. It is the good thief, also among the crucified, who discerns Jesus's true honor. In his repentance the thief is similar to the repentant woman, another without honor, who provides Jesus with the amenities without which he would be dishonored (7:36–50).

## Luke's Centurions

The treatment of Paul at the conclusion of Acts brings to our attention the role of the Roman military in Luke's account, represented here by the centurion Julius, who accompanies Paul to Rome. We need to pause a moment and consider the somewhat disquieting significance of the centurions in Luke's work.

Part of Luke's style is to create representative figures. The series of repentant persons is one example; the opposition represented by the lawyers *(nomikoi)* is another. One particular set of characters that sets Luke's writing apart is the Roman military. As Gentiles, they demonstrate Luke's story of outreach to the world. But as Roman military they represent the extreme goal of the mission. The distance to be traveled is cultural as well as geographical. Just as it crosses territories, it traverses populations—Judeans, diaspora Jews, God-fearers, pagans—each more remote from normative Judaism. In this vision of expansion the centurion occupies the far extreme, the sociological "ends of the earth." In the terms inherited from Mark and Matthew, the centurion represents the enemy. The centurions are not only foreigners, but they are officers in the military occupation of colonized Judea.

Two centurions have prominent roles as God-fearers, one in the Gospel and one in Acts. The centurion in Luke 7 is described in language that would be recognized as typical of the God-fearers. Joining him is the centurion Cornelius, converted by Peter, three times identified as one who "fears God" (Acts 10:2, 22, 35). Yet there are other centurions: the centurion who connects Paul with the Tribune in Acts 20—22; and Julius, the centurion who accompanies Paul to Rome, the only other centurion who is named.

While some, like the centurion in Luke 7 and Cornelius in Acts 10, are God-fearers, others, like the military tribune in Acts 21—22 and Julius in Acts 27—28, provide Paul with security, not merely confinement. With the mention of soldiers at the scene of John's baptizing as well as the crucifixion, and also appearing throughout Acts, we have an array of military that extends from troops to the commander of the local cohort, Tribune Claudius Lysias. But it is the centurions who get the most attention. They are representative of the group.

In general, the military personnel of Acts serve a peacekeeping function. We see them in prison settings, especially during Paul's time in Jerusalem. In addition, the centurion Julius is Paul's companion and guard on the trip to Rome. While the concept of a standing police force has perhaps not been yet articulated in the ancient world, the beginnings are seen in the assigned role of guards. The lictors of Acts 16:35 may serve that function. And the soldiers we encounter in the narrative serve as guards more than warriors. They typify the difference between policing and waging war. Recent trends to arm police with military equipment have raised the question about what distinguishes police from military.[27] An important matter mentioned recurrently is the relationship to the community. Police, presumed to be members of the community, are required to justify any act of violence. Not so with military actions. The relationship to community would seem to be the key to the role of the centurions in Acts. In some respects they have moved from invaders to peacekeepers. And with Luke, perhaps readers.

There is something more about the centurions of Luke that needs to be seen. The only God-fearers fully presented in the work are centurions—the unnamed centurion at Luke 7:1–10, and Cornelius in Acts 10. If we are to be consistent with our sense of Luke's project, they are like Theophilus: examples of the text's implied readers.

Two points can be made here. The first involves Luke's project. If his reader is a God-fearer, that project includes representatives of the empire. This fits with the Gospel's dedication to Theophilus, given the honorific "Most Excellent" (Luke 1:3), shared only with

---

[27] Gerald Schlabach, *Just Policing: An Alternative Response to World Violence* (Collegeville, MN: Liturgical Press, 2007), 69–92.

Felix and Festus, the Roman procurators (Acts 24:3; 26:25). Here, in a reversal matched only by the values inversion demanded of the God-fearing reader, Luke adopts a viewpoint poles apart from the imperial resistance of Mark and Matthew. Luke shows an open attitude toward the enemy. They are more than enemy. They are also fellow members of the human family. This, too, is contained in the saying on the cross, "Father, forgive them; for they do not know what they are doing" (23:34).

The second point involves us, the current readers of Luke. One part of competent reading is to place ourselves provisionally in the role of the implied reader. In the case of Luke's writing, does this mean that we might place ourselves in the role of the centurion, reading it as the centurion might? But placing ourselves in the position of the other requires an act of imagination. It recalls Thomas Merton's idea of nonviolent resistance as entering into conflict in the context of love toward the opponent.[28] Are we asked to look at the world through the eyes of the centurion? Coming to terms with that would seem to be a requirement of both peacemaking and Christian love. It appears that Luke's challenge to the reader extends beyond his day to ours as well.

## RESISTANCE AS LIFESTYLE

Luke, then, is taking the Gospel in a new direction when he writes for the Gentiles. Instead of taking his place among the Jews opposing the encroachments of the empire, he stands with the citizens of the empire looking to the world of the Jews, admiring and wishing to join their larger story. But if this is the case, then the meaning of the act of resistance represented in the story changes. And yet, in some ways it remains the same. While Luke is not writing with and for a community resisting imperial presence in a

---

[28] Thomas Merton, *Faith and Violence: Christian Teaching and Christian Practice* (Notre Dame, IN: University of Notre Dame Press, 1995), 8–10, 15–16.

political manner, he does adopt a stance in opposition to much of what counts as imperial values. In this sense resistance makes its appearance in another register, as a way of life, a lifestyle.

In Luke's Gospel, as seen in the parable of the Pharisee and the Tax-Collector praying in the Temple, the *terms of conflict* pit the self-achieved righteousness of the law against the act of repentance advocated by Jesus. Luke presents this struggle to show that the discipleship of Jesus offers an access to the admired Judaic tradition that bypasses the legal identity markers that characterized post-exilic Judaism. While these helped to preserve the character of a community under assault, they also closed off mission to the larger world, the "light to the Gentiles."

Although the theme of repentance occupies the foreground in his narrative, the radical call to resistance, which is found in Luke's principal source, Mark, was not lost on Luke. Here the method of nonviolence, implying as it does a trust in God's sovereignty and profound critique of violent force as the realistic foundation of social life, is nothing less than the proper program of a repentant community that finds itself in conflict with others. In this regard the centurions illustrate a conversion from militant force to cooperation, from violence to nonviolence, from the sword to healing.

Repentance is a fundamental reevaluation of one's life. This is not to leave behind the political meaning of the cross. Rather, it is to make it a foundational principle of one's faith life. When the Gospel speaks of taking up one's cross "daily" (9:23), Luke is not ignoring the political freight of crucifixion. Confrontation is no longer a single campaign, but rather the daily struggle to live out such resistance as a disciple of Jesus. Luke enlarges the narrative of resistance to the dimensions of a life story. More than being a matter of individual sins rejected, Luke's perception is rather recognition of sinfulness as a condition.

Repentance, for Luke, includes a sober consideration of one's own life project in relation to a God of justice and forgiveness. Consider the God-fearing reader. To fear God is about awe, not fright. It is the deep reverence that is a condition of discipleship.

The confrontation evoked in this Gospel is engaged with values absorbed from the culture against those presented by the Gospel narrative of Jesus of Nazareth. In this sense Luke, while moving away from the explicitly political, probes deeper into the alternative life of the Christian.

It is a Gospel calling for the depositions of the mighty from their thrones and lifting up the lowly that envisions an inversion of what counts as social worth. It is a Gospel written for the cultivated but favoring the poor, one that is "'good news to the poor' for the non-poor,"[29] a Gospel in which the humble are exalted and the exalted humbled. It is a Gospel that calls for a reversal of values. It is a Gospel that argues the precedence of repentance over righteousness that is claimed by careful adherence to performance standards.

It is this reversal of values that the German philosopher Friedrich Nietzsche bitterly protested in his denouncing of what he called the "transvaluation of values." For Nietzsche, there were originally two kinds of people—"the noble, the powerful, the superior, and the high-minded" and the "low, low-minded, and plebeian." He noted that the former had a sense of superiority justified by the fact they were superior. According to Nietzsche, the essential struggle between cultures has always been between the "Roman" (master, strong) and the "Judean" (slave, weak). He asserts that Christianity, not merely as a religion but also as the predominant moral system of the Western world, inverts nature, being "hostile to life":

> I call Christianity the one great curse, the one great innermost corruption, the one great instinct for revenge, for which no means is poisonous, stealthy, subterranean, *small* enough—I call it the one immortal blemish of mankind.
>
> And time is reckoned from the *dies nefastus* [impious day] with which this calamity began—after the *first* day of

---

[29] Sharon H. Ringe, "'Good News to the Poor' for the Non-Poor," in *The New Testament—Introducing the Way of Discipleship*, ed. Wes Howard-Brook and Sharon H. Ringe (Maryknoll, NY: Orbis Books, 2002), 62.

Christianity! *Why not rather after its last day? After today?*
Revaluation of all values![30]

It would seem that the author of Luke-Acts is Nietzsche's particular target. The philosopher's diatribe allows us to sense the
outrageous demand Luke makes upon his reader.

---

[30] Friedrich Nietzsche, "Conclusion," *The Anti-Christ,* in *The Portable
Nietzsche*, trans. Walter Kaufmann (New York: Viking Press, 1977), 656.

# 5

## John

John's story of the Word is one of "tabernacling" among us. The incarnation of the Word is not so much a presupposition to the story as it is the story itself. It begins with Jesus occupying the "tabernacles"—the sacred *spaces* of the Jerusalem Temple and Jacob's well in Samaria. This is followed by occupying, or repurposing, sacred *times*—Sabbath, Passover, and especially Tabernacles. Behind this pattern lies a resistance story that needs to be retrieved. Meanwhile, a hypervigilant Jewish authority maintains surveillance of emerging movements, seen at the first appearance of John in the narrative. It is from among these circles that the Jesus group surfaces.

The *difference* between John's Gospel and the others needs no argument. It begins in a different place, uses different language, and arranges its events in different order. It begins outside of time, in the mind of the Creator. Its language is poetic; speeches replace the parables we associate with the Gospels. The events cover a timespan of three years rather than one, and these three include fewer episodes, related at much greater length.[1]

---

[1] Influential narrative studies on John's Gospel include Warren Carter, *John: Storyteller, Interpreter, Evangelist* (Peabody, MA: Hendrickson, 2006); R. Alan Culpepper, *Anatomy of the Fourth Gospel* (Minneapolis, MN: Fortress Press, 1983); Robert Kysar, *John: The Maverick Gospel*, 3rd ed. (Louisville, KY: Westminster John Knox Press, 2007). Also valuable is Carter's study of John's narrative in the context of the Roman Empire, *John and Empire: Initial Explorations* (New York: T and T Clark, 2008).

The more urgent question is not the distance from the others, but rather the *connection* with them. The sense of the relationship of John to the other Gospels has varied over the years. The current consensus holds that there is little carryover from the other Gospels. It is largely based on identifying specific verbal similarities, and there are few of these. What degree of similarity can be noted between John and the Synoptic Gospels is attributed to his having used similar sources.[2]

But there are problems with that. One is the way in which John expects his readers to be familiar with the other Gospels. In the account of Jesus walking on the water (6:16–21), we hear that the disciples, troubled in the storm, were upset that "Jesus had not yet come to them." However, in 6:22 we learn that they had the only boat. Clearly, the reader, like the disciples, expects Jesus to walk on the sea. Another example is when he speaks of the Twelve as if the establishment of this group were common knowledge (John 6:76, 70). But we have not been made aware of the Twelve as an institution before this. Statements like this imply a familiarity with the story as it appears in the other Gospels.

More substantially, there is the problem of the Gospel as a *distinct form* in itself, shared by John despite his differences. There are only four writings in this narrative shape. While attempts to find a common genre outside these four has led most recently to the proposal of Hellenist biography as representing a possible underlying genre, this claim remains tentative. It provides a general background, but doesn't account for the distinct formal features common to the four works. These are substantive; the movement that begins in Galilee and ends in Jerusalem; the passion account of Jesus's final trial; the general framing of Jesus and his following confronting a hostile religious authority. These commonalities, and many others, suggest a specific story pattern that is shared, with differences amounting to nothing more than variations.

It is not likely there was a "Gospel" circulating, available to prospective writers. In the common consensus Mark's Gospel is

---

[2] See, for instance, Raymond Brown, *The Gospel according to John I–XII*, Anchor Bible 29 (Garden City, NY: Doubleday, 1966), xliv–xlvii.

the original, and others are versions of it. Add to this that Mark's has the shape and force of a resistance document. Its narrative is one that presents an alternative action to that characterizing the uprisings of the time. It is this fundamental form that the rest are reworking for other purposes. This, too, is the narrative that John has inherited. It is a story of Jesus and his movement resisting an unjust and alienating religious authority that obscures God's rule. John knows Mark's story and, to some degree, his language. His departures are intentional and instructive. That is the position adopted here. It serves as a useful hypothesis in observing how John's narrative works both in itself and in relation to the others.

One difference needs special mention. In John's handling of this story we encounter a considerable theological overlay in the form of extended discourses and narrative elaborations of events. Understandably, this theological layer has monopolized the attention of commentators. While important narrative studies have broken ground, there is still need to investigate the dramatic conflict. That means, for the present project, that we must excavate the "Jesus narrative" for examination. This will be the objective of the second part of the chapter. But first, we will consider the "Word narrative."

## JOHN'S PROJECT:
## THE STORY OF THE WORD

In terms of its narrative John's Gospel can be viewed from two different perspectives, from above and from below. For us, it can best be treated as two narratives. One is the story of Jesus of Nazareth, which will be discussed more fully in the next section of the chapter. The other story, that of the Word made flesh, is John's unique contribution to the Gospels, and will be treated here.

The story of the Word is one of "tenting" or "tabernacling" among us. This tabernacling, or incarnation, is not a presupposition to the story, put in place before the story begins. Instead, it is the story itself. It begins with occupying the tabernacles, the sacred spaces of, first, the Temple, and then that of Jacob's well. In the future they will be "neither on this mountain nor in Jerusalem" (4:21). The occupation of sacred places is followed by repurposing sacred times—Sabbath, Passover, and, of course, Tabernacles.

## Logos: John's Word

John begins by evoking Genesis and Wisdom writing. The book of Genesis—in the Hebrew Bible literally titled "In the beginning"—takes us back to beginnings, and John alludes to it to suggest new beginnings.

With that place of beginning, we find a prominent contrast with the other Gospels. The New Testament writers give different impressions as to when Jesus can first be called Son of God. The later the writer, the earlier the attribution. In Romans 1:1–7, Paul says that Jesus becomes Son of God at the resurrection. In Mark, the baptism at the start of his public life (Mark 1:9–11) is the crucial moment. Matthew and Luke push the moment back to the birth of Jesus, the beginning of his human life. But in John we travel back to the beginnings of creation itself, and the planning thereof, not only from all time, but from all eternity.

This beginning differs from the others not only in its occasion, set at the earliest possible moment, but also in its implication of a different *direction* of movement—in this case, from heaven to earth. With the others the imagination moves from the human to the divine. This person, Jesus of Nazareth, is the Son of God. But John begins with the divine and moves in imagination toward the human—the Word becomes flesh. It is an entirely different way of thinking about it, and we can see why high Christology—the theological emphasis on the divine in Jesus more than the human—is a prominent part of John's story.

The Greek word translated "Word" is *Logos*, which also gives us the English word *logic*. It has an honorable tradition in Greek philosophy. However, John's use of it differs. Behind his imagery most critics discern a reliance on the wisdom tradition of the Old Testament. The theme here is Sophia, rather than Logos. In the Hebrew scriptures the wisdom books differ from the historical and prophetic books in their more "philosophical" attention to the faith and well-being of Israel. In the wisdom writings we find the image of personified Wisdom present at the creation, as a guide and helper in the divine plan of creation (Sir 24; Prov 8—9; Bar 3—4; Wis 6; Job 28).[3]

John's Gospel has links with wisdom concerns. It favors reflection on the deeper meaning of events, and that suggests a different role for this Gospel. While it is basically a narrative, it is also a meditation—a reflection on the meaning of the narrative. Such reflection is what scholars call theology, and most of their commentaries on John focus on the theological message. It is necessary here to rehabilitate the narrative itself in order to examine how it chooses to represent Jesus as the Word.

The Jewish philosopher Philo of Alexandria is credited with first making the move from Sophia to Logos, from female to male. Apparently, John takes advantage of this shift in applying the tradition to Jesus of Nazareth. Not only Philo but the locales of Alexandria and Egypt in general hint that they have a connection with the Gospel. Along with the presence of a wisdom movement, as seen in the book of Wisdom, and the Septuagint itself (indicating Alexandria's role as a circle of deep learning), some commentators suggest that Alexandria might be the location of the community that produced this book.[4]

We can add to this the discovery of Gnostic texts in Egypt. In Gnosticism we discover a habit of mind similar to John's, one in which the spiritual enters the domain of the material, like a traveler entering a strange country. In Gnostic thought salvation means reversing this move, leaving physical matter behind to return to pure spirit. Not so long ago, television specials featured the Gnostic Gospels of Judas and of Mary Magdalene, promoting them as lost or suppressed documents. What we saw in these documents was a pronounced distaste for the physical, which in their view must be left behind. This habit of thought, with its theme of civilizing benefits (or dangers) arriving from another realm, is neither new

---

[3] Sharon H. Ringe, *Wisdom's Friends: Community and Christology in the Fourth Gospel* (Louisville, KY: Westminster John Knox Press, 1999).

[4] For example, ibid., 14.

nor outdated. We see it in myths as early as Prometheus bringing his gift of fire. At the same time it is as current as Superman from the planet of Krypton, or Erich von Däniken's *Chariots of the Gods*. In these, outer space replaces the realm of the gods. What they have in common is the theme of external sources, outside ourselves, bringing the boons of their civilization to us.

John's Gospel moves imaginatively in a similar frame of mind, but no convincing connection has been made with Gnosticism as an influence on John. Current thought favors the counter-theory that John was a source of Gnosticism rather than a product. A convincing argument for the location of John's writing is not available. Lacking definitive alternatives, the traditional choice, Ephesus, is still favored. Consequently, the helpful information of time and place for understanding the occasion or crisis to which the Gospel narrative responds is not available to us. However, we can note that a certain habit of imagination is at work, philosophical and akin in some ways to Gnostic thought, and markedly different from the other Gospels. This may supply all we need, despite the incomplete information.

### Narrative Contract in John's Gospel

As we have seen in the other Gospels, narratives typically begin with a commissioning moment in which the main character is given a task. Since characters are bound to complete the task, the commissioning has been given the name *narrative contract.* In John's Gospel we find a narrative contract at 1:14—"And the Word became flesh and lived among us."

*"The Word became flesh . . . ":* This describes what doctrine calls incarnation—its literal meaning is "to be made flesh." But an important implication is that the Incarnation is in some ways to be unfolded in the narrative itself. We are accustomed to thinking of the moment of incarnation as happening before the story of Jesus begins. But instead we are invited to think of it as a process, an ongoing project, unfolding in narrative time. In John, incarnation is not a prior given, but a narrative project. With that in mind, we can look to its unfolding.

*"and tabernacled among us"*: The continuation of the verse provides the remainder of the narrative contract of the incarnation story. The Greek verb in this verse, usually translated "lived" or "dwelt," is more literally rendered "tented" or "camped," related to the noun "tent." Translating it literally, to glimpse some of the overtones available to the original readers, suggests that John is evoking the original tabernacle (the tent and movable shrine that traveled in the wilderness with Israel) in Exodus and Numbers. The Temple is its successor, the tabernacle of Jesus's day. We now can see why John places the account of the Temple cleansing at the beginning of Jesus's story, rather than at the climax of Jesus's action, as in the other Gospels. Not long after Jesus is found at the site of another sacred site, Jacob's well, in the story of the Samaritan Woman. In this way the narrative of the incarnate Word begins as he "occupies" sacred spaces, altering their meaning. First it is the Temple, the successor of the desert tabernacle, a stone monument that is a "tent" in name only. Then, the shrine of the Samaritans follows ("Woman, believe me, the hour is coming when you will worship the Father neither on this mountain nor in Jerusalem" [4:21]).

Following these scenes, which alter the meaning of sacred *places,* the Word inhabits sacred *times* in order to repurpose them as well. First, the Sabbath (John 5) and the Passover (John 6) are targets of his attention. Reinterpretation of the Sabbath is seen in all the Gospels. In Mark, for instance, Jesus declares the Sabbath to be servant, not Lord, of the human community of believers: "Then he said to them, 'The sabbath was made for humankind, and not humankind for the sabbath'" (Mark 2:27). And in all the Gospels the last supper changes the meaning of Passover when it is presented as the occasion for the feast. In John these changes are also present, though in a different manner and with the added note that the death of Jesus on a Friday evening brings together in one moment both Sabbath and Passover.

But it is the feast of Tabernacles that John presents as the primary focus of Jesus's revision of sacred times. This marks the intense struggle of John 7—10, and its relevance clearly relates to the "tabernacling" of the Word. In the Temple debates on the feast we discover that the movement of incarnation is an occasion of conflict.

The story of Jesus's rejection at Nazareth in Mark 6:1–6 offers a privileged moment in the Gospel tradition for treating the theme of rejection. Already brought to our attention was the use made of it in Luke's opening event in Jesus's public life (Luke 4:16–30). Earlier it was mentioned that John had some awareness of the other Gospels, and in particular, Mark's. Now we see John's more radical employment of the same story. Of the few instances John shows verbal similarity to the other Gospels, most are from this story in Mark.

John borrows from this story to give shape to the opposition that Jesus encounters ("he came to what was his own, and his own people did not accept him" [John 1:11]). These elements from Mark are reused by John:

- the question about where he received his wisdom (Mark 6:2),
- the remarking upon his humble origins as a carpenter, and son of Mary (6:3),
- the reference to his brothers (6:3),
- the proverb "prophets are not without honor, except in their hometown" (6:4).

John makes use of each of these:

- citing the proverb as regards to Jerusalem (John 4:44), which Jesus identified as the location of his Father's house (John 2:16), identifying Jesus as the son of Joseph in the confrontations in Galilee (6:42),
- beginning the pivotal Tabernacles debates with the skepticism of his brothers (7:3–5),
- continuing with questions from the crowd about how he gained his knowledge (7:15).

In short, the rejection of the character of Jesus among "his own" in Nazareth provides language for describing the resistance of the Word among "his own" in John's Gospel. In this, we see the narrative of the incarnate Word in John's account enmeshed with another, the story of Jesus of Nazareth. This prompts us to reclaim the narrative of Jesus that has been eclipsed by the theological interpretation John has provided. The retrieval of the Jesus story is the subject of the second part of the chapter.

## Word and Voice

The Word requires a voice, and the Baptist identifies himself as that voice. Replying that he is neither the messiah, nor Elijah, nor the prophet, John insists, "I am the voice of one crying out in the wilderness, 'Make straight the way of the Lord'" (1:23).

The work of the voice is to give testimony. The Baptist testifies. So do others, including the narrator, whose voice continues throughout the text. We can imagine the entire story as the narrator speaking, even the reports of what the characters say. At times John's narrator speaks as a distinct voice in the text. At other times the narrator interrupts the story with parenthetical information.

In general, everything we know in any story is told to us by the narrator. And this has implications for our reading of John's Gospel. The Prologue (1:1–18) is usually discussed in terms of its characteristics as an early hymn, attached as an introduction to the beginning of the Gospel: "In the beginning was the Word . . . " But from the point of view of the work as a narrative, this is the narrator speaking and should not be considered outside or added to the account. Here the narrator introduces us to the story, announcing the themes and initiating the action. John's narrator is omniscient, knowing what is hidden in the minds of the characters. (This is worth remembering when we come to scenes that the narrator deliberately does not relate to us.) Furthermore, this narrator is not only omniscient but is aware of the original moments before creation. In this way, the narrator becomes not only omniscient, but tantamount to divine.

Furthermore, John's narrative voice blends into that of the Baptist (3:28–36). More important, the narrative voice shares the quality of Jesus's speech, as seen, for instance, in 3:16–21, where translators are not agreed as to whether this is Jesus or the narrator speaking. Jesus's voice carries the same authority as the narrator's. Notably, the voice of Jesus expresses itself in extended poetic discourses instead of parables. Typically, the theme in these discourses is Jesus's intimate relationship with the Father.

If we are looking for what constitutes the *terms of conflict,* as in the other Gospels, no better candidate is available than these claims of Jesus. They are contested by the religious authorities in Jerusalem. The established authorities are insecure, viewing any development of a religious person or group as a threat. The theme of testimony or voice presents just such a development in the appearance on the scene of Jesus and his group of followers. But it anchors its claims in divine authority.

Just as the Gospel begins with the testimony of the Baptist, so it concludes with that of the Beloved Disciple. This mysterious figure, popularly associated with the apostle John, first appears at the supper (13:23–25), reappears at the crucifixion (19:26–27), and is in the Easter stories (20:1–10; 21:7, 21–22). Since he appears only in the final chapters, some identify him as Lazarus, whom Jesus loved (11:6, 36). Though his identification remains uncertain, we do know that he is credited with authoring the Gospel.

The author is not necessarily the same as the narrator, and this has a bearing on John's Gospel project. Whereas Luke, for instance, highlights an implied reader, even naming him—Theophilus— John's text instead highlights the *implied author.* Certain passages at the end of the Gospel (20:30–31; 21:20, 24) speak explicitly about the writing of this Gospel. Although 21:24 reads like promotional material on the back cover of a book, all of this takes place *within* the text, and it is the author implied by the text. This, too, aligns with the emphasis on testimony and expresses itself as part of the theme of the voice. The implied author is unmistakably present.

The situation with John is more complex than that, however, since the "we" of 21:24, who is speaking in testimony of the implied author, is someone other than that author. We have something of a nest of testaments. Some unknown "we" is testifying to the disciple who wrote these things down and who is the implied author. This implied author, in turn, is identified as the Beloved Disciple. The story that begins with the testimony of the Baptist ends with the testimony of the Beloved Disciple.

In sum, the voice throughout the Gospel is one of testimony to the claims of Jesus. It begins with the narrator, who is so omniscient he is present at the deliberations before creation. It concludes with the author of this Gospel, according to the text (implied author). But at the center of it all is the testimony of Jesus himself, at the heart of the conflict in the Gospel.

## John's Word as Language

Having placed the Word in this prominent position, John inevitably makes us alert to his own words and language. While in many respects it is very simple, in other ways it is complex and subtle.

*It is simple.* John's Greek is considered extremely simple, not only in its limited vocabulary, but also in its simple grammar. John doesn't use some of the more sophisticated opportunities offered by the Greek language, in marked contrast to Luke, for instance. His writing has been called "primer Greek." But primers are produced by sophisticated users for the sake of learners. So such a claim may say more about the reader than the writer. In any case, while the language is simple in some respects, it is sophisticated in others.[5]

*It is symbolic.* John's language consistently moves at more than one level, seen in what the text calls "signs." In the rising action of John's plot—John 1—12, conventionally called "the book of Signs"—we are shown that Jesus's miraculous actions point beyond themselves to something greater. In essence, signs are indicators that point elsewhere, but the term has many meanings in the Gospel. Unsympathetic onlookers demand signs of Jesus (2:18; 6:30); Jesus refuses to produce signs on command (4:48; 6:26). Signs become an index of faith, present or lacking (2:11; 12:37). But one dominating theme is the identification of Jesus's works as signs rather than simply as wonders or miracles (2:11;

---

[5] Ringe notes, "Indeed, the simple constructions of most sentences and the limited and repetitive vocabulary make it an ideal choice as a first text for students of Greek to tackle" (ibid., 12). While some view it as translation Greek, she opts for the language of "a community in transition."

4:54; 6:2, 14). John's practice was to take one example of each kind of miracle and explore it further through the use of dialogue or discourse. The language of this Gospel reflects two levels—that of the action, and that of its further meaning as a sign.

In a similar way dualistic language pervades John's text, insistently presenting contrasting values—truth and falsehood, life and death, belief and unbelief, light and darkness. Typically these describe the tension between Jesus and his opponents. An especially important example of dualistic imagery in relation to the plot is that of light and darkness. Jesus operates in the public eye, in the light, while his opponents do their work hidden from view. It is John who tells us of Judas, noting that at the supper, "after receiving the piece of bread, he immediately went out. And it was night" (13:30).[6]

*It is double.* Beyond matters of dualistic language, doubleness in general is found throughout John's account. For our purposes an especially revealing aspect of this is his *word play.* His puns typically involve the intersection between the two narrative plots or the two levels of the plot. Some instances that are important for outlining the drama of the story are these:

- *anothen.* An early instance is in the story of Nicodemus coming to Jesus at night. "Jesus answered him, 'Very truly, I tell you, no one can see the kingdom of God without being born from above *[anothen]*'" (John 3:3). The Greek word *anothen* can be taken in different ways, perhaps similar to our phrase, "from the top." Jesus intends "from above"; Nicodemus takes it to mean "again." But introducing Jesus's first discourse in the Gospel with word play, misunderstood and corrected, John is alerting us early on that ambiguity will have a place in this text. Furthermore, this ambiguity may affect the storytelling. A couple of things are worth noting about this pun. First, it works only in Greek. Since it is unlikely that Jesus and the Jewish leader Nicodemus would speak in Greek, this indicates that John himself is at work here. Second, this passage sets

---

[6] On dualistic language, see, for instance, Carter, *John,* 86–104.

up another confusion later on, when Pilate, in his encounter with Jesus, is entangled in another misunderstanding involving the same word (19:11). In this case the same word complicates the resolution of conflict in the story.

- *topos*. The word *topos* appears at a critical moment in the story: "If we let him go on like this, everyone will believe in him, and the Romans will come and destroy both our holy place *[topos]* and our nation" (11:48). Here *topos,* commonly translated "holy place," referring to the Temple, can mean both a physical place and a social position. While theological exegesis sees here only a reference to the Temple, sensitivity to the narrative plot alerts us to another meaning of the word. It also can refer to social position, and in this case, the Jewish authorities' precarious place in the leadership. The two meanings combine in the passage showing the Jewish Council trying to solve its problem with Jesus.

- *Prince of this world.* Attuned to theological dimensions of John's work, we generally take the phrase "prince of this world" to refer to Satan. While this is certainly the case, there is a double meaning. It also refers, in the logic of the narrative, to Pilate, whose presence is looming when this term appears in the text (12:31; 14:30; 16:11).[7]

What these selected instances have in common is a doubleness that evokes two levels of narrative. One has to do with the Word at the theological level, while the other has to do with the action of Jesus in his struggle with his opponents.

## JOHN'S STORY:
## JESUS OF NAZARETH

In his story of the Word, John gives prominent attention to the interpretation of events; commentators have responded with theological explanations. As a result, the underlying story has tended to be

---

[7] For a development of this idea, see Carter, *John and Empire,* 290.

neglected and needs to be reclaimed. These two levels may be identified as the *theological* story of the Word and the *political* story of Jesus of Nazareth. It is to the political story that we now turn.

It helps to read Mark, with its "signs prophets" and popular messiahs as reported by the historian Josephus, when reading John's drama of Jesus of Nazareth. The crisis of the Great Revolt was the occasion for the loss of the Temple. That loss has not been forgotten in the writing of John's Gospel. Seen in this light the Word story of incarnation, as an interpretation of the story of Jesus, also interprets the events of the Jewish Revolt. With the failure of the Great Revolt, that Word story sees in the Jesus story a new beginning.

## John as Dramatist

John is a skillful storyteller, with a dramatic flair. He deftly develops particular episodes, such as that with the Samaritan woman, with its growing awareness of the persons and stakes involved (4:4–41).[8] The story of the man born blind dramatizes the increase in animosity between Jesus and the Pharisees (9:1–41). Then there is the almost cinematic way in which Peter's denial is juxtaposed with Jesus before the high priest, as we cut back and forth between them (18:15–18, 25–27). The account of the empty tomb plays out the growing realization of the resurrection (20:1–10). One might presume a similar skill in the narrative as a whole.

Not only does John develop scenes skillfully, but he manipulates them in interesting ways. A common feature is to repeat a scene in a different register. Twice, on subsequent days, the Baptist identifies Jesus as the Lamb of God—once for the reader and another time for the disciples (1:29, 36). Twice, on subsequent weeks, the Risen Jesus appears to the disciples in the locked room,

---

[8] Raymond Brown's masterful analysis of this scene is found in *The Gospel according to John I–XII*, 175–89. Brown's description of the scene as fulfilling the agenda set out by Jesus ("If you knew the gift of God and who is saying to you, 'Give me a drink,' you would have asked him and he would have given you living water" [John 4:10]) is enriched with the inclusion of the woman's agenda as well ("How can you, a Jew, ask me, a Samaritan woman, for a drink?" [John 4:9]). It also determines the direction of the conversation.

once without Thomas, and once with Thomas and his testimony (20:19–23, 24–29). In many cases this technique of doubled scenes addresses the two levels of the drama. Upon arriving at Bethany after the death of Lazarus, Jesus meets each of the sisters in turn. Each upbraids him—"Lord, if you had been here, my brother would not have died" (11:21, 32). First is the discussion of resurrection life; second is the distraught response, "Jesus began to weep." At the garden the scene of Jesus's arrest plays through twice, once for the Word ("I Am"), and once for the human event (18:4–6, 7–11).

But there is more. In something of a contrast to having the scenes that play out twice, some scenes are missing altogether. They play out in our absence. The main instance is the unsettling matter of the hidden encounter with Caiaphas. As Jesus is leaving the court of Annas, headed for Caiaphas (18:24), our attention is turned to the denials of Peter. When we return to Jesus, he is already leaving Caiaphas's court (18:28). We discover the charge against him only when Pilate asks Jesus if he is a king (18:33). The narrator chooses to keep us in the dark. In other cases we are not told when the authorities decide to implement the Roman solution, though we know they are running out of options (12:19). And in the beginning of the narrative the efforts against Jesus are only made explicit in chapter 5, though there are hints that they begin much earlier ("were seeking all the more to kill him" [5:18]).

In general, our experience with John's handling of individual scenes gives us confidence in his ability to fashion a larger narrative. And once alert to that possibility, we notice features that shape the larger drama.

## The Characters in the Drama

### The Protagonist: Jesus

Jesus of Nazareth ("can anything good come out of Nazareth?" [1:46]) is, of course, the main character, the protagonist of the drama. In his actions Jesus is characterized by openness and transparency. This is stated clearly in the dialogue before Annas, in which Jesus protests, "I have spoken openly to the world; I have always taught in synagogues and in the Temple, where all the Jews come together. I have said nothing in secret" (18:20). While he speaks openly, he frequently needs to leave the scene due to threats mounted against him. Nevertheless, he continually returns.

## The Antagonists: "The Jews"

The main conflict encountered by Jesus the protagonist is a hypervigilant Jewish authority, which maintains surveillance of emerging movements (1:22).

"The Jews"—a tendentious label in this Gospel—are functionally equivalent to the Jerusalem elite, caught in the precarious position of mediating between the Roman imperium and the people of Judah.[9] In chapter 11 we see the Jewish leadership in its role of negotiating unrest. The local leaders are the go-between leaders who manage the people for the Romans. They are the despised elites in the accounts of Josephus, though Josephus was himself part of such a group. As regards the apparent animosity toward Jerusalem, the conditions during the Great Revolt might offer a good example of the difference between the countryside and the city. In that case the city was a refuge from the dangers of the countryside, at least for the brigands.

In this Gospel, Jesus's opposition is characterized by *surveillance*, *intimidation*, *violence*, and *covertness*. The Jewish leader-

---

[9] A feature of John's text that has created considerable concern is the use of the term *the Jews* (some sixty times), compared to *Pharisees* and *(chief) priests* (twenty-one times each). Except for the story of the lake of Galilee in John 6, the Jews are always associated with Jerusalem. Even in the case of the Galilean event, it would appear they are delegates, as in John 1:19 (or Mark 3:22). Except in chapters 11 and 12, where Jews are mentioned as among converts to Jesus's movement, the term is used negatively, meaning the opposition party. Here, too, the exception does not demand a revision of the term since it serves to show the seriousness of the threat Jesus implies—even their own number have begun to turn away. So, while the term is used flexibly, generally "the Jews" are associated with Jerusalem. And when involving opposition to Jesus, the term refers primarily to the Jewish leadership.

ship is compromised in its need to serve Rome and the Jewish tradition at the same time. In contrast, Jesus and his group are seen to represent light and truth, which we might characterize as *transparency*. It is the truth that is shown in the light.

- *Surveillance* of the opposition is shown in the opening scene with John the Baptist, where the authorities send delegates to interrogate him. "Let us have an answer for those who sent us" (1:22). A hypersensitive authority is working to control and suppress dissident movements. The implication is that there is a tendency for such movements to arise, evoking the situation that Josephus describes. Something similar occurs when guards are sent to arrest Jesus (7:32, 45–53). A control center is sending out enforcers from a remote and guarded location.
- *Intimidation* is seen in the persistent threats to kill him, in the attempts at stoning. These are designed to quiet his efforts, persuading him if not physically ending him.
- *Violence* is behind the attempts at intimidation. The threats are violent, and they do not work, since he repeatedly escapes. But they are intended to harm him and let him know that he is a target.
- *Covertness* is a primary characteristic of the opposition—working in the dark. That implies controlling from a distance, keeping its workings hidden. This is behind the repeated call for openness and the theme of light and darkness. It is related to surveillance.

These traits, contrasting with those of Jesus and his people, provide the platform for the central conflict in the Jesus story. This allows us to recognize the legitimacy of Jesus's side despite its being opposed by the religious leaders. It is this authenticity that is reinforced by the Word story, with its clear endorsement of the work of Jesus.

*Jesus's Disciples*

While the main conflict of the narrative concerns Jesus's engagement with the Jewish leadership, the story also carries a subplot of the relation between Jesus and his disciples, a movement that begins with John the Baptist, already under observation (1:22). This story begins with their call (John 1:35–51) and proceeds to a crisis and sorting out in Galilee, at which time the group of disciples is reduced to a cadre of true believers (John 6:60–71).

The most extensive exposure we have to this group is in the speech Jesus delivers at the last supper (John 14—17). Jesus's farewell to his disciples ushers in a long series of discourses that differ markedly from those in the first part of the Gospel, in that they put forward a teaching of love for one another. The story of the disciples comes to a positive conclusion in the final chapters as the Risen Jesus meets with, forgives, and reinforces the group of followers (20—21).

Based on the characterization of Jesus's movement in the narrative, Bruce Malina and Richard Rohrbaugh suggest that the Johannine community that produced this Gospel was an "antisociety." They describe this as

> a hollowed-out social space within the larger society over against which it stood in opposition (in structure, not unlike modern big-city gangs). . . . Members remain in the society but are opposed to and in conflict with it (in John's terms, they are in the world but not of it).[10]

Projecting back from the narrative in front of us, this analysis posits the community that produced it. In other words, it properly characterizes the group given in the text.

**The Plot: The Rising Action—The Book of Signs**

Comparison with the other Gospels is a useful method for determining through contrast what is happening in John's Gospel. So it is with the rising action of the plot, often called the book of Signs. Here John has accomplished something remarkable.

---

[10] Bruce Malina and Richard L. Rohrbauch, *Social Science Commentary on the Gospel of John* (Minneapolis, MN: Fortress Press, 1998), 59.

The evangelist frames the rising action of the plot by separating and reversing the stories of the triumphal entry to the city and the Temple cleansing. These two events are closely connected in the other Gospels. In Mark, they take place on subsequent days. In both Matthew and Luke they are presented as one narrative sweep, occurring on the same day as part of the same move. John has separated and reversed the two while making sure that we understand they are connected.

In this Gospel they are marked with certain features that pair them. They are among the few instances that involve scripture quotations and, in these cases only, are identified as quotations his disciples remembered after the resurrection (2:16; 12:17, 22). In the triumphal entry the quotations involved are common to all the Gospels—Psalm 118 and Zechariah 9:9. In the story of the Temple cleansing, however, the quotation is unique to John: "It is zeal for your house that has consumed me" (Psalm 69:9). John, however, changes it to the future tense ("zeal for your house *will* consume me" [John 2:17, emphasis added]), looking forward to the time of entry into the city and the events that the move will initiate.

John strongly signals his intent that we connect the two episodes. What they mark off is the rising action of the plot. With the Temple cleansing the action begins. Jesus makes a claim for it as his Father's house (2:16). The claim is provisional; it cannot reach fulfillment until certain measures are taken. Getting the story from one to the other shows Jesus confronting opponents who try to arrest him and even seek to stone him to death. Moving in and out of the city as need demands, he finally returns to Bethany to raise Lazarus to life. At that time, the entry into the city recounted in John 12:12–19, can be officially performed.

The sequence of events that intervenes between the Temple cleansing and the entry is influenced by Jesus's persistent attraction to the city and its Temple. His occupation of this site generates initial opposition (John 2). But because of this opposition from "his own," Jesus is forced repeatedly to leave the city. Yet he keeps returning.

After the Temple cleansing he returns to Galilee by way of Samaria. Following the Cana healing of the official's son, he finds himself back at Jerusalem at the pool of Bethesda, where it is clear that the Jewish authorities are trying to kill him. A second Passover finds him back in Galilee, multiplying loaves and crossing the lake without a boat. He then leaves Galilee for good, departing belatedly for Jerusalem and the feast of Tabernacles. After four chapters and two stoning attempts, he leaves the city, but not for Galilee.

He is away when he receives the message from Mary and Martha, the sisters of Lazarus. He returns to Bethany, on the outskirts of the city, but not to Jerusalem itself. Once more he moves away and then back to Bethany. But only after the Lazarus episode does he formally enter the city. Only then is it possible.

## Stages in the Building Story

The drama of Jesus and his enemies develops in stages. Four of these can be discerned in the rising action: the opening week in which the action is called forth; the initial action in the Temple; the period of mounting crisis; and the culminating crisis of this part with the story of Lazarus.

*The First Week (1:19—2:10).* As with the other Gospels, the story begins with John the Baptist, who serves as the catalyst to set the following story into motion. Twice he calls Jesus "Lamb of God," though at this point the meaning of that title is unknown. John is under surveillance by the Jerusalem authorities, who are shown to be hypervigilant, with a defensive posture that stimulates suspicion. The Baptist is being watched, and the watchers need to report to the authorities (1:19, 22). As in other Gospels the Baptist has the task of setting Jesus on his way. He points him out to Andrew and another (1:35–36), who summon Simon (1:40–42), whom Jesus renames Peter. Here we see Jesus establishing a counter-society, the "antisociety" of the social sciences.

Numerous titles are applied to Jesus in these first days. But of these, two are emphasized. As previously noted, twice John identifies Jesus as "Lamb of God" (1:29, 36). The other is the kingly title Messiah. In this case the title is emphasized instead by the dramatic buildup of the scene. It leads to the recognition of Andrew and Peter, with echoes of the messianic recognition scenes in Mark and Matthew (Mark 8:27–30; Matt 16:13–20). In turn, it is confirmed by the acclamation of Nathanael—"Rabbi, you are the Son of God! You are the King of Israel!" (John 1:49)—which brings the scene to a conclusion. These two titles, Lamb and King, will reappear at the crucifixion scene with the title on the cross and the interpretive scripture citing the Paschal Lamb.

*The Initial Action (2:13—4:54).* Cleansing the Temple is an action performed only once. In the other Gospels it serves as the singular culminating offense that becomes the catalyst for the passion. In John, however, it initiates the action. But just as in the other Gospels, it generates a concern on the part of the city officials, with questions about his authority. Nicodemus, "a leader of the Jews," comes under cover of darkness to inquire (3:1). Shortly afterward, when the Pharisees learn that Jesus (or his disciples) are baptizing in the manner of John, Jesus decides it is time to leave for Galilee (4:1–2). A note of menace is already detected here. Prompted either by haste or by need for discretion, Jesus finds it necessary to travel through Samaria rather than the more common route by way of the Jordan valley (4:4). The die is cast.

*Mounting Tensions (5:1—10:19).* In the subsequent chapters leading up to the crisis in John 11, we experience a mounting conflict between Jesus and his opponents. The dialogues in this part of the Gospel focus on the question of Jesus's authority, asserted by Jesus and contested by the religious authorities. The themes of his relation to the Father and the testimony thereof are sounded in John 5:16–47 and are picked up again at a more acrimonious level in the Tabernacles debates of John 7—8. The response he evokes is extreme, including threats to take his life (5:18; 7:19, 20, 25), attempts to arrest him (7:32, 44; 10:39), and even attempts to stone him to death (8:59; 10:31). As stoning is a Jewish method of execution, it shows that in this part of the drama the effort to contain him is still restricted to Jewish circles. They have not yet turned toward Rome for a solution. That will come with the story of Lazarus.

*The Crisis (10:22—11:44).* After Jesus calls the leaders false shepherds, their attempt to stone him leads him to leave the area once again. While he is away he receives word of Lazarus's impending death. After delaying, he returns. Thomas alerts us to the danger of death this involves: "Let us also go, that we may die with him" (11:16).

The moment of arrival at Bethany is complicated. Two independent encounters with the sisters of Lazarus allow the narrative to establish two sides of the moment—the promise of life eternal and the devastating diminishment of death (11:25, 35). In his exchange with Martha we witness the Word speaking through the veil of the Jesus story. In the moment with Mary we see the human Jesus overcome with grief. While Jesus encounters the full devastation of death in the dying of his friend, he likewise confronts his own death as a consequence of what he is about to do.

Among the many deeds of Jesus the miracleworker, John singles out the one that causes the story to peak and then change direction. In restoring a person who is dead to life, something other Gospels mention but do not develop, John finds the key to unlock the story of Jesus himself. This scene concludes the rising action, as it prompts the authorities to make their definitive move against Jesus. And yet, it nullifies their move at the same time by disarming the threat of death. In a deeply symbolic sense, Jesus has unmasked death by demonstrating that it is not the last stop. Lazarus returns from somewhere and, in so doing, destroys death's dread reputation of being a final end, the place of no return.

## The Conspiracy

At this point the leadership, including the Sanhedrin, displays concern that the growing movement, which includes many Jews, will attract the attention of the Romans, and the leaders will lose their place (*topos*) and nation (11:48). While the theological meaning of the term *topos* suggests the Temple, we know by now that the overly suspicious leadership is concerned about its own political position, precariously situated between Roman demands and restive Judeans. This is not to say that the term does not include reference to the Temple, which as we have seen is already compromised by the claims of Jesus. Once again we encounter a richly loaded term in John's text.

Jesus himself has not been seen in the city since he left it following the second attempt to stone him (10:40). When he returns in response to the news about Lazarus, he returns to Bethany, a village east of the city. While he will leave the vicinity again, and return to Bethany again (11:54; 12:1), he will not enter the city until he enters in triumph. One last scene at the house of Lazarus dramatizes the victory of life over death, as Mary anoints the feet of Jesus (anticipating Jesus's own washing of feet in the next chapter). The aroma of the burial ointment fills the house, replacing the stench of the tomb.

Its work complete, the rising action concludes with the official entry into the city. After this, the unfolding events will take place in Jerusalem.

## The Plot: Falling Action

The final stages of action against Jesus are arranged by his opponents privately, out of our sight. They abandon the attempts to stone him and turn to the Roman solution, but the reader is not told when and where this happens. After the dinner at the house of Lazarus and his sisters, we learn that the leaders are disturbed because "the world has gone after him" (12:19). And yet we are not told what measures they are contemplating to get the situation under control. Similarly, the Caiaphas trial will occur in secret, with the reader barred from witnessing. Having learned little, we take leave of the enemies of Jesus in order to spend some time with the disciples.

*The Supper (13—17).* In his farewell to the disciples Jesus is shown presenting another vision, alternative to that of the paranoid opposition. It is one in which love for one's friends prevails. Echoing the discourse about the Good Shepherd (10:1–21), it culminates in the teaching that there is no greater love than to lay down one's life for one's friends (15:13). This unfolds in the narrative as the program for Jesus's alternative to the strategies of control of his enemies.

*The Forces Converge (19—21).* It is in the passion account that the various strands come together. In the arrest scene two disciples featured in the supper reappear in active roles. Judas comes with the guards, and Peter wields the sword in Jesus's defense, demonstrating the violent option for each side. As in the other Gospels, Jesus refuses this approach.

After the arrest scene, doubled to show Jesus as both Word and human person, he is brought to Annas, the father-in-law and surrogate of Caiaphas, the high priest (18:12). This is a surprise, since we were expecting Jesus to be taken to the high priest, not to his proxy.

Then we come to a part of the story in which the tale switches back and forth between Jesus and Peter. First, we shift to Peter for his first denial (18:15). We learn he is with another disciple who was known to the high priest and enabled the entry into the courtyard. We return our attention to Jesus and Annas to hear Jesus speak to the matters that surface in the arrest scenes in the other Gospels—how he has spoken openly in the Temple and no one confronted him there. Before we return to Peter, we learn that Jesus is being sent to Caiaphas (18:24).

After Peter's second denial we return to the scene with Jesus, only to discover that the hearing before Caiaphas has already terminated and that Jesus is being sent to Pilate (18:28). We are kept in the dark about what happened in their secret meeting.

*The Involvement of Rome.* After this we turn to the part of the story that features Pilate. Even though John has given us little preparation for the Roman participation in the action, John's passion account is dominated by Pilate. The majority of the verses involve him.[11]

The entire trial scene consists of seven smaller scenes, justified because the accusers would not enter the Praetorium due to their purification for the feast. So it was necessary for Pilate to shuttle between the scenes with Jesus inside and the Jews outside.

---

[11] Of the eighty-two verses of chapters 18 and 19, Pilate is given thirty-two, compared to eleven for the garden arrest, sixteen for the council trials and Peter's denial, eighteen for the crucifixion (without the discussion of the title on the cross), and five for the burial. The crucifixion account is remarkably abbreviated.

| Outside | 18:28–32 |
|---------|----------|
| Inside  | 18:33–38 |
| Outside | 18:39–40 |
| Inside  | 19:1–3   |
| Outside | 19:4–7   |
| Inside  | 19:8–12  |
| Outside | 19:13–16 |

In the course of these interactions Pilate has two lengthier scenes in conversation with Jesus, which are not part of the other Gospels (18:33–38; 19:8–12). The first dialogue revolves around the charge "King of the Jews." This is the first we learn of the charge of kingship. The accusers have chosen this language to have a charge against Jesus that involves Roman interests—something that they hope will force Pilate to act. It allows Jesus the chance to tell Pilate that his kingdom is not from "this world." We understand this to be Pilate's world, as illustrated by Jesus noting he lacks followers rushing to spring him loose (18:36). His kingdom is not that kind. Instead, he comes to testify to the truth. Pilate asks, "What is truth?" (18:38).

Pilate returns to the accusers, pointing out that he finds no fault in Jesus. He knows what they are trying to do. They insist Barabbas be released instead. Barabbas is identified as a revolutionary (*lestes*), which suggests that Jesus, to be considered a suitable substitute, is somehow comparable (18:40). Pilate has Jesus flogged and mocked as a king, and then returns Jesus to the accusers, insisting that he has no charge against him. At this point they respond with their true objection, that Jesus has violated *their* law by calling himself Son of God (19:7). Pilate is alarmed, suspecting that there are dimensions to this matter that he hadn't expected. Returning inside, he questions Jesus as to where he is from (19:9).

In the second dialogue (19:8–12) Jesus begins with silence, and Pilate points out that he has the power to crucify him. To that, Jesus answers: "You would have no power over me unless it had been given you from above *[anothen]*." With the Greek word we return to the ambiguity seen earlier in the dialogue with Nicodemus (3:3). Again it causes confusion. Where the reader, aided by the narrator, sees a reference to God, Pilate sees a reference to Caesar.

When Pilate attempts to release Jesus, the Jewish authorities object that if he does so he will be no "friend of the emperor," a title of favor indicating special patronage for certain Romans. The narrative assumes that Pilate possesses the honor. The charge of the Jewish leaders follows from the discussion of *anothen*, just previous, and constitutes a threat: They will let it be known in higher circles (those "from above") that he is not properly protecting Roman interests. They threaten Pilate by promising to interfere with his relationship with the emperor.

Pilate responds by asking, "Shall I crucify your King?" (19:15), eliciting from the chief priests the reply, "We have no king but the emperor!" In response to their pressure upon him, he exerts his own upon them. If they want to doubt his loyalty, he can question theirs. Their response makes evident what was implied all along—they stand in a delicate position, negotiating between the people and the power, which at the same time trying to retain "their place" (11:18). He not only unmasks the precariousness of their position, but he also forces them to state their allegiance to Rome. This is a bitter pill. They reluctantly invoked the Roman option in order to dispose of Jesus, and now they are required to profess full loyalty, whether they want to or not.

With the title on the cross—"Jesus of Nazareth, the King of the Jews"—Pilate drives the point home. The unusually extended dispute that follows (19:19–22) underlines the fact that this is also in response to their earlier threat. Before, when he presented Jesus to them as their king (19:14), they denied it, swearing allegiance to Caesar. The accusers react, requesting that he replace that title with, "This man said, I am King of the Jews." It would be sufficient for Pilate's purpose that Jesus professed to be king, in defiance of the imperial authority. But Pilate makes a point of saying that *they* claim him as king. This enables the narrator to make a theological point—Jesus is indeed their king. But in terms of the narrative unfolding, Pilate is pushing a point that dramatizes their impotence. They want no part of Jesus or of any claim that he is their king. Pilate can afford to ignore them. With this rancorous dispute between Pilate and the Jewish authorities, the narrative of Jesus's opponents dwindles out.

*The Crucifixion.* Meanwhile, Jesus proceeds to his death. The description is brief and remarkably free of anguish, especially considering that Rome prized crucifixion as the ultimate deterrent, given its degree of cruelty and humiliation. In this Gospel, Jesus carries his own cross. His belongings are accounted for, and the soldiers gamble for his cloak. His family obligations are also discharged, as he places his mother in the care of the Beloved Disciple. He thirsts. And then he dies. In conscientiously fulfilling his responsibilities to family and property, then calling for a drink to quench his thirst, we witness a death that in other circumstances could well be features of a deathbed account. In John's narrative the suffering is downplayed, even unmentioned.

The finality of all these moves, almost methodically discharging one responsibility after another, drives home the reality of Jesus's death. As with the exchanges with the sisters of Lazarus, death is presented as real, something one must pass through. It is not evaded; it is not finessed. And although it has not been stressed here, the shadow of Gnosticism hangs over this Gospel, as a mindset, if not by way of a formal relationship with its teaching. But that, too, is negated. This death is real, and in Sharon Ringe's words, it is "not the shedding of a human disguise by a Gnostic redeemer."[12]

The rest of the crucifixion account—fully seven of its thirteen verses—is given over to interpretation. The title on the cross at the beginning affirms the kingship of Jesus for the believer, the ironic claim occasioned by a stalemate between Pilate and the Jewish leaders. The biblical quotations concerning the pierced side and unbroken bones that conclude the account interpret Jesus's death in light of the Passover lamb, symbol of the birth of Israel. Jesus is the Passover lamb (Exod 12:43–48), like those being prepared for the Passover meal later that evening.

*Final Convergences.* At the end of John's story of Jesus, a grand sense of convergence takes over. Concluding this dramatic

---

[12] Ringe, *Wisdom's Friends*, 55.

narrative with its tensions and divisions, its crises and concerted opposition, and a distinct tension even with the main character himself, the various strands come together.

- The titles of Lamb and Messiah, announced in the first chapter, reappear in the elaborate interpretive texts that frame the crucifixion. For the believer, the title on the cross, King of the Jews, announces the Messiah. The text from Exodus identifies him as the new Paschal Lamb, dying to liberate his people.
- The sacred times of Sabbath and Passover, subject to reinterpretation in the debates between Jesus and his opponents, comes together in John's passion account. Both occur on the same day, the day following Jesus's crucifixion. Both are reinterpreted in the light of the final chapters of Jesus's story.
- The two stories—the theological story of the Word and the political story of Jesus of Nazareth—are shown to be one. At times, especially in the scene at Lazarus's tomb, the very movement of the incarnation itself seems in jeopardy, as the main figure seems torn between the assured Word and the vulnerable Jesus. But now the threatened rupture is resolved.
- Any Gnostic division into spirit and matter, with its disregard for physical reality, is emphatically denied in the scene with Thomas in the locked room. When invited to view, and even to touch, the physical wounds of the Risen Christ, Thomas responds, "My Lord and my God!" (20:28). Rather than being despised, the physical is the sign of the divine.

Any argument for division is overcome. Much of the sense of completion at the conclusion of John's story comes from this experience of diverse elements coming together.


## CONFLICT RESOLUTION IN JOHN

The resolution of the narrative conflict in John's Gospel is as individual as the Gospel itself. It follows a line unlike that of Mark and favored by Matthew and Luke. But with the help of narrative models in the letters of Paul along with the theories of René Girard regarding violence, we gain a better understanding what John's Gospel is doing.

## Interpreting the Jesus Story by the Word Story

Narratives interpret narratives. And two crucial plot lines in Paul's letters assist our understanding of John. The first is the well-known *kenosis* ("emptying") hymn of Philippians 2:6–11. It provides a sketch of the incarnation story, of the Word becoming flesh. As in the hymn, John's incarnation story is not complete until Jesus accepts death, including death on a Roman cross.

A second plot line, which can justifiably be called the master narrative of the New Testament, underlies the vision of Galatians and Romans. It is a story of reconciliation that lies at the heart of the New Testament understood as a new covenant. John, in his own way, affirms this master narrative as the theological meaning behind the story of Jesus. John's political resistance story of Jesus of Nazareth finds a place here as the unique turning point in the Word's narrative of salvation.

### Emptying to Death—Even Death on a Cross

In the *kenosis* hymn of Philippians 2:6–11, a narrative sketch of the incarnation unfolds. First, Christ "empties" himself of the prerogatives of divinity, becoming "obedient to the point of death—even death on a cross." In this diminishment, he experiences the full extent of the human condition, including the tragic limitation of a life that concludes with death. The second part of the hymn reverses direction, answering the humiliation with an exalting cry, as Christ rejoins the Father. John's Gospel is structured analogously, with "descent" followed by exaltation, as the book of Signs precedes the book of Glory.

We have followed the story of the Word Incarnate and how it concerns the occupation of sacred places and times. Viewing the story of Jesus from above, it offers a theological interpretation. In the incarnation project of John, the story of the Word takes on the human condition, even to the point of death. With his death Jesus completes the task assigned him, though the story is not over.

During the course of the story this movement is repeatedly opposed and the very project of incarnation itself is threatened. A troublesome division enters into the very character of Jesus at the tomb of Lazarus. On the one hand, he speaks brave words of resurrection and life to Martha. On the other hand, he weeps with Mary. On the one hand, he utters confident words of purpose to his Father; on the other hand, he is deeply troubled in spirit over the death of Lazarus.

The victory over death then follows, first made manifest in the raising of Lazarus, later reaching its completion with the death and rising of Jesus himself. Insofar as incarnation means the "enfleshment" of the human condition, the drama of incarnation would not be complete without the experience of moving through death and beyond it. In the Lazarus episode we see the struggle between the diminishment of death and the victory of life, dramatized in the exchange with the two sisters as well as in Jesus's own troubled spirit. We witness the victory over death. This is the pivotal point in John's story, insofar as it means the end of death's finality. In the unfolding narrative that follows, the primary weapon of the forces moving against Jesus is their option to inflict death; they are unaware that death is no longer effective.

The *kenosis* hymn of Philippians reminds us that this victory is not only over death, but even death on a cross. Paul is advocating Christian humility in the passage in which he cites the hymn. Extending the experience of death to death on a cross takes the experience beyond humility to humiliation, since that is the purpose of crucifixion. In its intent to deter resistance to the authorities by violence and humiliation, it contains a political content that we cannot easily appreciate today. Paul knew this in a way that we do not.

Consider for a moment the needs that this practice met for the empire. Crucifixion was an attempt to discipline and control those who had nothing to lose, who presented problems to the administration of the empire. It was a practice borrowed from the Parthians because it handled difficult cases effectively. Such difficult cases included insurrectionists, who were revolting against the very controls that the cross was intended to reinforce. But when those difficult cases were rebelling against the imperial controls themselves, the cross acquired a double meaning. In addition to the meaning of control intended by the empire, and precisely because of that, it becomes for the resister a supreme example of rejecting imperial control.

Death on the cross is more than death as death. It is a violent death perpetrated by hateful enemies. It is not only death, but it also is the coercive use of violence to dominate. Once it is adopted as an emblem of resistance, it represents the refusal to be intimidated by the threat it intends to communicate. In this way the resistance story of Jesus interprets the Word story. The political content of the execution of Jesus becomes part of the *kenosis* pattern.

John's Gospel agrees with this. Not only does the story of the Word interpret the story of Jesus, but the process of interpretation also moves in the other direction. The political content of the cross, added to the death, modifying the death, makes that death explicitly political. And when this is said of the Word story, it is because the political content of the Jesus story has been included. The story of Jesus, with its resistance content, expresses a rejection of violent coercion for controlling populations. With the cross as the reality that is interpreted by the incarnation narrative of the Word, we see that an endorsement of the Jesus narrative is taking place. It is not only a victory over death, it is a victory over injustice and violent coercion.

This is put in positive terms in the farewell speech to the apostles at the supper (John 14—17). Jesus tells them: "This is my commandment: love one another as I have loved you. No one has greater love than this, to lay down one's life for one's friends" (15:12–13). To die for one's friends is to conquer death. Its value as a threat is replaced with another value entirely, that of love. And so John introduces the vocabulary of love as the counter to that of violence and death. Death is redeemed because it has a new meaning; the old meaning is now eclipsed. In this Gospel story this is expressed by the extraordinary absence of suffering for Jesus. Death has no control over him.

And part of the meaning of Jesus's kingdom not being of "this world," as shown to Pilate when discussing his kingdom, is that it is not part of the lethal machinery of forced domination. It is unable to be forced. In a way it is akin to suicide bombers, who have nothing to fear. The basic commitment of the followers of Jesus is that they no longer have anything to fear. The victory over death means that they cannot be intimidated.

This freedom is dramatized in John's passion narrative as freedom from violence as well as from death. In John's crucifixion scene Jesus is in control; perhaps a better way to frame it is to say that he is not controlled. A problem with describing Jesus in control of events is that this evokes the specter of a kind of divine suicidal violence. Instead, John gives us an image of the powerlessness of violence to reach him. Violent coercion is no longer part of his story, and in this sense it is not so much that he is in control as that the dominant no longer are. He and his people are no longer under the sway of violence. Fear no longer imposes an external, determining control over them.

### The Master Narrative of Reconciliation

Again, narratives interpret narratives. John's narrative of Jesus is placed within the context of the narrative of the Word. For Paul, the *kenosis* narrative also takes its place within a larger narrative. This larger narrative can be called the master narrative of the New Testament. This foundational narrative has three features.

First, it is a story of reconciliation—the return and restoration of the lost children of God, the story of God reaching out and "reconciling the world to himself" (2 Cor 5:19). It is a key part of an overall drama that is sometimes called salvation history. Which is to say, the foundational story of the New Testament, as a narrative of reconciliation, is itself a form of conflict resolution.

Second, in Paul's hands the narrative is marked by three primary moments: a beginning, a middle, and an end. Paul's instances of this narrative are found in Galatians, repeatedly, and in Romans, decisively. The narrative is signaled by three phrases:

- *We were . . .* It begins with the moment when "we were" lost, alienated, sinners, slaves under the law—the human family in history.
- *But now . . .* In this second moment, the coming of the Christ changes everything.
- *If so, then . . .* The third moment follows as a consequence, as we are joined with this narrative through baptism and become adopted children of God.

This story is first told in Galatians, twice. In Galatians 3:23–29, it is told in connection with Abraham and those of Jewish background. Immediately after, in Galatians 4:1–7, it is told again, in terms of Gentile converts. In this telling Paul thinks in terms of a coming of age, as seen in his example of the Roman tutor, a slave who had authority over the child until the child reached maturity. For Paul, Christians are now to be seen as free, responsible adults.

Even more impressively, Paul used this narrative to structure the doctrinal part of his masterpiece, the Letter to the Romans, chapters 1—8. After an initial elaboration of the alienation of both Gentiles (1:18–32) and Jews (2:1—3:20), we arrive at the great "but now" moment: "But now, apart from law, the righteousness of God has been disclosed" (3:21). Shortly after, Paul defines this moment in the language of reconciliation: "For if while we were enemies, we were reconciled to God through the death of his Son, much more surely, having been reconciled, will we be saved by his life" (Rom 5:10). It is this "but now" moment that is elaborated in a different register with the *kenosis* hymn of Philippians 2.

John shares this perspective. While it is largely implicit, it does find explicit expression, for example, in widely known and quoted passage:

> For God so loved the world that he gave his only Son, so that everyone who believes in him may not perish but may have eternal life. (John 3:16)

This is the very moment that is occasioned by the Word becoming flesh that John unfolds in the story of the incarnation that is his Gospel.

The third feature of the master narrative is the pivotal place it occupies in salvation history, through which the New Testament recognizes itself as a new covenant. An understanding of this central salvation moment underlies the idea of the Word narrative as a reading of the story of Jesus.

## René Girard and the Gospel of John

René Girard's interpretations share the master narrative's high Christology and sense of its singular moment in history. His theorizing is distinctive, however, in its focus on the role of violence in society as well as the Gospel. He offers a useful perspective for our reading of John.

The Word narrative in the Gospel puts the resistance story of Jesus in the theological context of the incarnation, with the implication that that story is a privileged moment in time and history. The theories of René Girard are helpful in reading the Gospel in the context of this privileged moment. Alone among contemporary theorists of violence and its resolution, René Girard claims the historical uniqueness of the Gospel. Girard is often invoked in theological circles for his teachings on social violence, its causes and its prevention. These, among other reasons, suggest our turning to his ideas for understanding the resolution of conflict in John.

Girard's theory is socially conservative insofar as it prefers a hierarchical system that reduces rivalry between equals by limiting equality. Similarly, in what can best be described as a generalized conception of the Gospels as a single narrative, it favors a high Christology. Among the Gospels, John fits that mold best. Girard views nonviolence as an option reserved to the Son of God, at least initially. A similar role for Jesus beyond the common person's capability is part of John's vision as well. Where Mark presents discretion concerning the Sabbath as a common human prerogative (Mark 2:27), John restricts it to Jesus as the Word.

Girard's rich and complex theory resists easy summary. But for our purposes we can view his thought as built upon three overarching ideas: (1) mimetic desire and rivalry; (2) the scapegoat mechanism with its ritual reenactment in sacrifice; and (3) the historical uniqueness of the Gospel.

## Mimetic Desire and Rivalry

The first idea highlights the role of imitation in generating violence. We learn what is desirable by observing what others desire. Seeing that, we want it too, and so we compete for possession of it. Mimetic desire leads to mimetic rivalry. This, according to Girard, is the root of violence. In John's Gospel such behavior is typified at the arrest of Jesus. The former companions in discipleship, Judas and Peter, are shown standing in violent opposition, one with the guards, the other with the sword (18:1–11).

In the larger narrative, imitation appears in terms of uses of power itself. The complicity of the Jewish leadership is seen in the contradiction between their traditional role as religious leaders and their imitation of Roman methods of using and maintaining power. But this is integral to the position in which the local authorities find themselves. They have to answer to both the people and the empire. The objection on the part of the people is not simply that they are subject to a foreign power, but that the local authorities have replicated the methods that maintain that power. They have abandoned their traditions to imitate those of the empire. The law of Moses names the covenant that is constitutive for their self-understanding as Jews, a shorthand symbol for their own culture. It carries within it an attitude toward social justice that is brought out by the prophets, who viewed themselves as defenders and promoters of the Mosaic covenant. The tradition of Jubilee is another expression of this understanding of the people God calls them to be. The Roman system stands in violation of this.

*The Scapegoat Mechanism*

For those trapped in a dynamic of mutual payback, a common expedient is to identify a third party to blame—often accompanied by a conspiracy theory. They blame this "scapegoat" for their difficulties, which means that party must be powerful enough to have caused them. But a hidden contradiction lurks in the scapegoat mechanism. For if the remedy is to work, the party accused must not only be strong enough to cause the problems troubling the accusers, but also too weak to continue the pattern of reprisals. This is necessary if the pattern is to come to a halt. At a subconscious level those who do the blaming must know both of these contradictory traits, since they guide the choice of a scapegoat that will produce the necessary effect. Both weak and powerful, this is the contradiction of the scapegoat that needs to be kept out of awareness. It needs to be hidden from the consciousness of the participants if the mechanism is to work for them.

Girard takes another step. Religious *sacrifice* adds a ritual dimension to the pattern. The ritual sacrifice borrows the power of the scapegoat mechanism to recreate an emotional sense of catharsis that was first experienced with the release from violence that the original scapegoating experience produced among the participants. Sacrifice is the religious expression of the scapegoat, in Girard's view.

The scapegoat mechanism is visible in John, in the maxim of Caiaphas, the most explicit articulation of it in the Bible:

> But a certain one of them, Caiaphas who was high priest in that year, said to them, "You know nothing at all! You do not understand that it is better for you to have one man die for the people than to have the whole nation destroyed" (John 11:49–50)

This is interpreted immediately by John's narrator:

> He did not say this on his own but being high priest in that year he prophesied that Jesus was about to die for the nation,

and not for the nation only, but to gather into one the dispersed children of God. (John 11:51–52)

This interpretation is provided by the text itself. It identifies the high priest as a prophet, and the prophecy promises that Jesus will die for the nation, as the scapegoat. And it takes it further, naming that death as necessary for the children of God to be gathered into one. But the prophesying person is also the high priest, and the mention of the high priest evokes the Temple sacrifice, which would also involve the ritual imitation of the scapegoat, perhaps as ironic commentary on the larger role of Jesus as the Word.

The interaction between Pilate and the Jewish leadership, as described earlier, shows the same principle at work. Pilate finds Jesus innocent but allows him to be executed despite that in order to appease the Jews who confront him. Jesus serves as a scapegoat whose death will bring about the satisfaction needed to quiet the Jewish leaders. This is symmetrical with the actions of the Jewish leadership, as expressed by the high priest.

## The Historical Uniqueness of the Gospel

It is here in particular that Girard's theories come into contact with the Gospels, especially John's. In Girard's view, the Gospels turn the tables on the mechanism of the scapegoat by revealing its contradiction. Girard is saying that the scapegoat mechanism works only when it is hidden from those who depend on it. Once the truth is out, that the victim whom they consider powerful enough to be the cause of their difficulties is actually too weak to have that role, they can no longer pretend their use of violence against the scapegoat is effective. They are aware of their violation.

Girard says it is the Gospel that unmasks the scapegoat mechanism by adopting the perspective of the victim, in all his helplessness and innocence. Blaming the victim is shown to be a lie. Once the lie is unmasked, any effort to believe it fails. Therefore, it is no longer useful as a way of ending cycles of violence. Lacking an alternative, this is a precarious situation.

All of the Gospel narratives profess the innocence of Jesus in his trials and public execution. In each of them the legal apparatus that condemns him is itself presented as guilty instead. In John's Gospel the innocence of Jesus is further elaborated in the supper discourses (14—17). We learn that the name given Jesus's motivation is love, and that there is no greater love than to lay down own's life for one's friends (15:13). The good shepherd passages present the same teaching. The shepherd gives his life in defense of the sheep, against the wolves and marauders (10:11, 17–18). How does this metaphor work in the narrative of John? That takes us to Girard's notion of the two logics.

## Two Logics: Resolving the Conflict in John

While Girard's theory is useful for understanding the various dimensions of the closing moves in the conflict of John's plot, it is Girard's idea of the two logics that offers the most important contribution.

In a section of the book that first presents his idea of the uniqueness of Christianity, *Things Hidden Since the Foundation of the World,* Girard specifically turns his mind toward John's Gospel and its theme of the Logos. He contrasts the Greek source of the word, where it is usually translated "reason," with John's meaning. He argues there is an undercurrent of violence in the Greek tradition of reason that is absent in John's understanding of the Word. He contrasts these two understandings as a logic of violence and a logic of love.

> Once it has been possible to detect the operations of violence and the logic underlying them—or, if you prefer, the logic of violent men—confronted by the logic of Jesus, you will realize that Jesus never says a word that cannot be deduced from the events that have already taken place within the perspective of these two types of logic. Here and elsewhere, the "gift of prophecy" is nothing but the detection of these two logics.[13]

---

[13] René Girard, *Things Hidden Since the Foundation of the World* (Stanford, CA: Stanford University Press, 1987), 212.

The logic of violence shown in the narrative is driven by a rivalry for power. We have seen how John concludes his story in a complex three-way interaction. While the Jewish authorities and Pilate are engaged in a competition of honor, Jesus is shown calmly moving toward his own death. The vigilance of the Jewish authorities shows an awareness of the threat of rivals. Once Jesus and his group enter the picture, we see the unsuccessful attempt to close him down. A repeated pattern is the reaction to Jesus as that of division. His presence seems to spark rivalry. This pattern continues into the climax of the narrative, as the Jewish leaders and Pilate struggle against one another, while Jesus is calm and self-possessed. They are displaying the logic of violence; he shows the logic of nonviolent love.

Meanwhile, the final chapters show Jesus as remarkably at peace. As noted earlier, this is not so much a matter of being in control as of not being controlled by the dynamics of the violent interactions. In terms of the narrative it is the depiction of the nonviolent gift of a life lived without violence coming to a successful completion. This is similar to the notion advanced in Matthew of refusing to return harm for harm, and so dying without paying it back. But in John's hands it is also presented as a gift to his friends, the disciples. Again, to borrow from Girard, the gift is one of maintaining the logic of nonviolence to the end and making it available to his followers. In John's words, it is love:

> "As the Father has loved me, so I have loved you; abide in my love. If you keep my commandments, you will abide in my love, just as I have kept my Father's commandments and abide in his love. I have said these things to you so that my joy may be in you, and that your joy may be complete.
>
> "This is my commandment, that you love one another as I have loved you. No one has greater love than this, to lay down one's life for one's friends. You are my friends if you do what I command you." (John 15:9–14)

The account of Jesus's death as life-giving, as dying for others, as laying down his life for his friends, can be seen within the narrative. His gift is that of not only eschewing violence, but also finding life in so doing. *Their* commitment is to the promise of an alternative that resists the mechanisms of violence.

So it is that in the conclusion of John's Gospel we see the two logics unfolding, each in its own register, as it were. The opponents of Jesus end in a standoff of mutual rancor, each trying to best the other, meanwhile using Jesus as their scapegoat, but without success. Jesus, on the other hand, experiences peace. His life is not taken but rather given for others. His death is not a disaster but a gift. In the final scenes of the Risen Jesus with his disciples, his victory is literally made tangible.

The resurrection stories demonstrate the life-giving power of this logic when lived out. Jesus's "return" to the Father is in triumph, but his gift to the community is the continuation of his life. In the final chapters we return to the group to which we were introduced in the opening chapters. Where in the beginning they were recruited to an alternative action, we see at the end that they are now carrying it forward.

In short, John's narrative concludes in a manner different from the other Gospels. At the level of dramatic interaction, it resolves in a three-way opposition. We no longer have the simpler two-sided action and response, as we find first in Mark, unfolding in the reciprocal exchanges of nonviolent challenge, repressive response, and non-retaliatory counter-response. Instead, we find the two themes of violence and nonviolence each playing out to the end, each according to its own logic. Those in a rivalry for power, the Jewish Council and Pilate, both of whom favor the use of Jesus as a scapegoat, find no satisfaction. Each finds itself in an unsatisfactory place, in a standoff with the other, unresolved. On the other hand, the pattern of nonviolence unfolds in a confident move through the hazards of being the target of accusations and blame, the victim of scapegoating, to emerge into new life. The fear of death having been removed, life is available to be given as a gift for others. And in this, the new life is given its day.

For John, this dynamic of narrative resolution is made possible by its dependence on an underlying faith narrative. This supporting story is that of the incarnation of the Word, as a definitive turning point in God's relationship with the human family. In the Incarnation story that unfolds in the Gospel, the Word, incarnate in Jesus, is shown adopting the human condition even to death, death on a cross. In this encounter with death the full disarray of human loss is experienced and redeemed. But also, in the acceptance of the cross—the instrument of extreme control by which the imperial forces maintained their hegemony—the methods of violence were also taken on and rendered futile, their threat no longer effective.

## RESISTANCE AS LOVE

Thomas Merton makes the point that the ethic of love demands that we consider the good of our opponent as well as our own.[14] In practice, this means that we invite our opponent to conversion to our concerns, even while remaining open to our own conversion to that of our opponent. Girard's notion that John's Gospel contrasts the logic of violence with the logic of love makes a similar point. While love has many implications in this Gospel, we are interested in those implied for times of conflict.

When we examine the Gospel with these thoughts in mind, we are rewarded with certain findings. The first concerns vulnerability and risk. To love means to allow oneself to be vulnerable, open to the word of the other. In nonviolent action, as many will hasten to point out, personal risk is at a premium. In the Gospel, Jesus speaks of the authentic love shown when one would give one's life for one's friends. The vulnerability of love is clear in this. In the discourse on the Good Shepherd we hear the same idea. True shepherds lay down their life for the sheep.

Against this we have a second finding—the recognition of the futility of violence in achieving its objectives. Here also we find the Girardian idea that the scapegoat mechanism that presumes to protect us is founded on the lie that violence achieves the work we demand of it. In the Gospel this is dramatized in the closing

---

[14] Thomas Merton, *Faith and Violence: Christian Teaching and Christian Practice* (Notre Dame, IN: University of Notre Dame Press, 1968), 8–9, 12.

chapters by the useless rancor between Pilate and the leaders of the Jews, which produces nothing more than a standoff. Their feuding stands in dramatic contrast to the equanimity of Jesus moving toward his final days in peace.

This leads to the third finding. At one level it demonstrates the assurance that overcomes the risk, the confidence that comes from the knowledge of resurrection life. Jesus moves toward death knowing that it is not a final act. But on another level, it takes us further. In the story of the Word we are to understand that this is the love that is risked by God as well. In Jesus, as the Word, the risk is taken, the *kenosis* experienced, and the cross accepted. The human experience of Jesus is adopted by God. Here we find an answer to the question that our reading of Matthew raised: Is God nonviolent, or does God simply require Jesus's followers to be? In John's account, the Word enters the risk and offer of nonviolence in conditions of conflict. And in that example, we discover it to be life-giving.

# 6

## Narrative Conflict in the Gospels

### COUNTER-NARRATIVES AND THE ACCUSED WOMAN

In the preceding chapters we have seen how approaching the Gospels as the literary creations that they are—presenting the mission of Jesus of Nazareth as narratives—allows us to discern a crucial part of their message. We saw that compelling narratives are similar to dramatic works in their use of conflict development and resolution, and that this also applies to the Gospels. With that, a window opens into the Gospel writers' views of conflict and how it is to be resolved. Each Gospel differs, but all affirm nonviolence.

We further noted that the Gospels manage this by being counter-narratives. They depart from certain conventions typical of dramatic narratives. In particular, some conventional moves expected in the final resolution of conflict are refused, even reversed. Two that proved important are the impulse to exact revenge in the name of justice and the attempt to cleanse the world of the story of the evil invading it. The first we have called payback, noting that it is driven more by the impulse toward revenge than justice, in the manner of poetic justice. The second we called purge, noting that its attempt to rid the story of its perceived evil took the form of eliminating the persons associated with it, in the manner of ethnic cleansing.

A well-known scene in John's Gospel, often called the woman accused of adultery (John 8:10–11), is a paradigm of such non-violent action. The entire scene is charged with drama. During a moment of heightened tension caused by the imminent threat of stoning, Jesus writes on the ground, even as everything hangs in the balance.

Most likely the law that the scribes and Pharisees, representing the elders of the community, bring to bear on the situation is Deuteronomy 22:13–21. Caryn Reeder has shown that such laws of harsh reprisal are to be seen in a context of maintaining the covenant obligations of Israel by firmly preventing violations. She notes the many ways in which the harsh sentences were softened or commuted in practice.[1]

In John's story of the accused woman two methods of dealing with the aberration are dramatized—one by stones, and one by conversation. As the story unfolds, the tension is dispelled, but not by recourse to the traditional story formulas.

First, it is not about payback. The story says that Jesus is the main target of their efforts: "They said this to test him, so that they might have some charge to bring against him" (John 8:6). Yet this is not only a story about self-defense. In it we see Jesus defend someone else and do so without using force. Not only is Jesus defending another through nonviolent means, but he also does so at considerable risk.

Neither is it about purge, cleansing from evil by eliminating one's opponents. During the event Jesus takes the chance of inviting the elders to consider their own positions. He invites reflection in a situation that seems ill designed for it. In doing so he undertakes classic nonviolent action, inviting those in opposition to make a moral decision, opposing them with nothing more than his own vulnerability—and in this case, it seems, the woman's as well.

---

[1] Caryn A. Reeder, *The Enemy in the Household* (Grand Rapids, MI: Baker Academic, 2012), 45–57.

In the story of the accused woman we have a lens into the strategies of the four Gospels, their distinct solutions to a violent story. With her help we can look back upon the main moves of each.

## Mark and Nonviolent Action

*Like Mark's Gospel, the story of the accused woman presents a drama of nonviolent action. Jesus confronts a social situation that derives its effectiveness from the threat of destructive force.*

As we saw in Chapter 2, a similar and ongoing confrontation with the deleterious effects of a system is dramatized in Mark's Gospel. A campaign that begins by addressing the needs of the villages in Galilee takes a turn toward Jerusalem, from the edge to the center, from the effects to the causes of the troubles. Mark shows us resistance as nonviolent action. He presents a program of nonviolent confrontation as a means of addressing unjust social structures. Jesus's action involves a deliberate nonviolent confrontation that produces a repressive counter-reaction. This ends with a refusal on Jesus's part to retaliate.

## Matthew and the Refusal to Retaliate

*Like Matthew's Gospel the story of the accused woman dramatizes the refusal to retaliate. Not only does Jesus refuse to defend himself with force, but he also depends on the power of nonviolent response to preserve the life of the woman.*

Matthew's Gospel develops for its own particular purposes the key moment in Mark's nonviolent action, and that is the refusal to retaliate in kind. It is seen in how he frames the triumphal entry and Temple cleansing, the moment of nonviolent confrontation in the narrative plot (as Mark has shaped it). For Matthew, it is a case of returning and responding without repeating the harm done. Matthew insists on this pattern of action in his teachings on non-retaliation (for example, Matt 5:35–48), and forgiveness, also seen as not responding in kind (18:15–20, 21–35). Hannah Arendt has attributed the possibility of forgiveness in human relations and public life to Jesus of Nazareth. Her argument is that the refusal to pay back in kind is one of the few solutions to ending a cycle of violence.[2]

## Luke and the Call to Repent

*Like Luke's Gospel, the story of the accused woman turns upon an act of repentance. After he writes on the ground, they consider his words. As they gradually disappear, we can assume that they have come to some kind of recognition of their own complicity in many things.*

Luke's theme of repentance involves a cold, clear look at oneself. It includes the resolve to alter the circumstances of one's life. Luke shows us resistance as lifestyle. In emphasizing Jesus's demand for repentance, he shifts the work of resistance from any particular action to a continuing way of life. In a violence-prone culture, this is counter-cultural. The structures that regularly require forceful maintenance in society—social status, economic inequality, legal privilege—are undercut in the new society envisioned in Luke. At the same time the radical program is shown lived out, in Acts, perhaps in a series of compromises, yet maintained as a principle of Christian decision-making in life.

## John and the Call to Love

*Like John's Gospel, the story of the accused woman identifies the principle of nonviolence in the logic of love. The elders are not demonized, but rather are invited to look within. They are treated as sons of Abraham, as they claim to be. The woman also is treated as fully human, as the dialogue at the end indicates.*

---

[2] Hannah Arendt, *The Human Condition*, 2nd ed. (Chicago: University of Chicago Press, 1998 <1958>), 238–42.

John shows us resistance as love. The inner spirit of nonviolent struggle is foregrounded. As Joan Bondurant has insisted, proper nonviolent opposition is bringing truth to a situation in a spirit of love. Bondurant, in exploring the nonviolent practice of Gandhi, emphasizes the place of openness to the opponent, avoiding "symbolic violence," in the coercive use of nonviolence.[3] Authentic nonviolent action in conflict refuses to demonize the opponent and thus leaves open the possibility of the opponent's change, even conversion. Love is open to the truth of the other; love offers one's own truth as an option for the other to consider and adopt. It hopes for conversion.

## IN THE END . . .

Jesus of Nazareth is widely recognized as a nonviolent person involved in a violent story. How are we to understand that? The Gospels offer four scenarios, related and yet distinctly different. In the dynamic of the narrative plot, each depicts Jesus entering into conflict and resolving that conflict nonviolently. Each finds a way to resolve conflict in a manner that offers instruction to the reader.

It is not uncommon to hear instances of instrumental violence justified by appeals to the Gospels. Perhaps it is a verse from Luke, arguing Jesus's approval of the disciples' possession of two swords. Perhaps it is the image drawn from John's account of the Temple cleansing, involving a whip of cords. Many are eager to find verses that justify their own violence. The Gospel plots show that the underlying meaning of Jesus's life is otherwise, however. It is a witness to nonviolence.

---

[3] Joan Valerie Bondurant, *Conquest of Violence: The Gandhian Philosophy of Conflict*, rev. ed. (Princeton, NJ: Princeton University Press, 1988), 42–43: idem, *Conflict: Violence and Nonviolence*, ed. Joan V. Bondurant and Margaret W. Fisher, rep. ed. (Piscataway, NJ: Aldine Transaction Pub., 2008), 236–37.

Or, on the other hand, we might hear some say that "the Gospel teaches an ideal love that stands apart from the real world," that "we need not take literally its lesson of non-retaliation," that "Gospel teaching is just for inspiration, just an analogy for acting in the real world, where things are not so forgiving." Despite such thinking, despite the appeal to isolated sayings of Jesus, the Gospels in their narrative plots portray Jesus's nonviolence as active and engaged in struggles of the day. His nonviolence is *not* abstract. The testimony of the four Gospels in terms of their narrative plots is clear:

*Entry into conflict
and its resolution through nonviolence
is the praxis of Jesus and the will of God.*

# Index

Acts of the Apostles. *See* Luke-Acts
Arab Spring, 68, 86
Arendt, Hannah, 113, 226

Bar Kochba rebellion, 84–85
Barabbas, 43, 70, 205
Barnabas, 136, 155, 159–60, 166, 167, 170
Bartimaeus of Jericho, 35, 59–60, 62
biblical studies, new perspectives in, 2–11
Bondurant, Joan, 74, 227

Caiaphas, 125, 195, 203, 204, 216
conflict resolution
    conflict ethics, 11–12
    dramatic conflict in the Gospels, 21, 26
    foundational story of New Testament as a form of, 212
    in John, 193, 208–14
    in Luke-Acts, 168–69
    in Mark, 66–68, 68–70, 73, 75
    in Matthew, 103, 108, 109, 111, 113
    terms of conflict in the Gospels, 22–23
Cornelius the centurion, 121, 127, 158, 175, 176

David
    as ancestor of Jesus, 78, 87, 88–89

bloodguilt, David placing upon Joab, 107
family of David not returning to power, 100
genealogy of, 80
    son of David concept
    in Luke, 139
    in Mark, 51, 59–60
    in Matthew, 83, 93, 94, 101–2
    royal status of messiah, 62–63, 81–82
    Son of Man supplanting title, 64

Eleazar ben Ananias, 44
Eleazar ben Simon, 44, 45
Essenes, 77, 83, 132, 146

Felix and Festus, governors, 42, 126, 165, 177
Fiscus Judaicus tax, 77, 84
forgiveness
    Jesus and, 53, 65, 177, 198
    in Jubilee year, 140
    Matthew, as theme in, 104
    non-retaliation, aligning with, 111, 113, 225–26
    in payback and purge dynamic, 170–71
    unconditional forgiveness, 114

Gamaliel, 84, 157, 164
Gandhi, Mohandas K., 12, 70, 73, 74, 117, 227

genre, determining, 14, 32–33, 35,
    90, 124, 182
Gentiles, 59, 125, 144
    as God-fearers, 126–27, 158
    identity markers of the Jews, by-
        passing, 135, 159, 167, 178
    in Isaiah, 132, 133
    Luke, as audience of, 119–21,
        137, 164, 168, 169, 173, 177
    master narrative of New Testa-
        ment and, 213
    mission to the Gentiles, 55, 129,
        130, 136, 139, 154, 155, 158,
        160–63, 165
    purity rules, expanding due to
        growing Gentile population,
        46, 49
    repentance, called to, 134
    rulers, lording over Gentile sub-
        jects, 58, 151
    Septuagint text, as admirers of,
        131
    Servant Song, mentioned in, 103
    synagogues, supporting, 18, 127,
        142–43
    unclean territory of, 60
Girard, René, 110, 209, 214–18,
    219, 221
Gnosticism, 185–86, 207, 208
God-fearers, 131, 167, 178
    centurion God-fearers, 175, 176
    as Gentile believers, 126–27,
        158
    as implied readers of Luke, 137,
        147, 173, 177
    Isaian tradition, resonating with,
        132–33
    Jewish tradition, linking with
        through Luke, 136–37
    pagans, becoming God-fearers
        before baptism, 128
    Paul, missionary work with, 161,
        162

reverence, not fear, for the Lord,
    126, 178
Septuagint as bible of choice,
    146, 158
synagogues, supporting, 18, 127,
    142–43
as unconverted sympathizers of
    Judaism, 120, 127
Gospels as narratives
    apocalyptic writing, 64–65
    characters, two camps of, 19–20
    counter-narrative departures,
        23–25
    dramatic irony as a common
        technique, 50
    era of writing, taking into ac-
        count, 25–27
    fact *vs.* fiction, 15–16
    implied readers, determining,
        17–18
    literature of resistance, 29
    narrative contracts of Jesus,
        21–22
    narrative voice, 19
    narrator not the same as author, 17
    rising and falling action, 47–48
    terms of conflict, 22–23
    type-scenes, 90–91
Great Revolt of 66-70 CE, 65, 85,
    194
    dangers of the countryside dur-
        ing conflict, 196
    as a failure, 83, 86
    Jewish nationalism, beginning
        rise of, 84
    Josephus, writing on, 42, 43, 60
    Mark's Gospel written during,
        32, 45, 64, 75
    as second wave of revolts, 44–46

Herod Agrippa II, 156, 165
Herod Antipas, 40, 42, 52, 55, 152,
    153

Herod the Great, 33, 40, 139
  genealogy, importance of
    branched version, 79, 80
  Josephus, writing on, 41, 81, 125
  replacement by son Archaelaus,
    91, 125
  slaughter of the innocents in
    Bethlehem, 88, 105, 115
Horsley, Richard, 41

implied readers
  determining, 17–18
  as God-fearers, 137, 147, 177
  of Luke, 18, 28, 127, 136–38,
    168, 169
  of Mark, 34
  Theophilus, 120, 126, 154, 156,
    168, 170, 176, 190

Jacob's well, 181, 183, 187
John, Gospel of
  accused woman story, 224–25
  divine image, re-theologizing,
    28
  doubleness of narrative, 192–93,
    194–95
  Gnostic thought, writing as akin
    to, 185–86, 207
  implied author of text, 190, 191
  intentional departure from prior
    Gospels, 183, 184
  Jesus, portraying as calm at end
    of life, 219–20, 222
  Jews as antagonists, 10, 20,
    196–97
  kenosis and death of Jesus,
    209–11
  master narrative of New Testa-
    ment, affirming, 209, 212–14
  narrative contract as incarnation,
    186–87
  narrative voice, blending with
    characters, 189

Nazareth rejection story, rework-
    ing, 188
  passion account, 203–8
  prior knowledge of Gospel sto-
    ries, expecting from readers,
    182
  René Girard on violence in John,
    214–18, 221
  resistance as love, 227
  rising action in Book of Signs,
    198–203
  scapegoat mechanism, use of,
    215, 216–17, 221
  Word made flesh theme, 183,
    184
John of Gischala, 33, 41, 45
John the Baptist, 114, 167, 198
  arrest of, 58
  authorities on the scene, 176,
    197
  baptism with water as precursor
    to baptism with fire, 37
  birth of, 124–25
  execution by Herod Antipas,
    42, 152
  Jesus, initially identified with,
    75
  Lamb of God, identifying Jesus
    as, 194, 200
  in Mark, 43, 53, 55
  as mentor to Jesus, 94–95
  as the new Elijah, 139
  prison message, 98, 141, 143,
    145
  repentance, identified with, 140,
    142
  as a signs prophet, 42, 97, 121
  testimony of, 189, 190
Johnson, Luke Timothy, 172
Joseph of Arimathea, 70, 138, 153
Josephus, Flavius, 44, 124, 197
  on brigands, prophets and mes-
    siahs, 41–42, 43, 67, 194

on Great Revolt of 66-70 CE, 42, 43, 60
on Herod the Great, 41, 52, 81, 125
as a member of the elite, 196
Roman establishment, favoring, 26, 41
Jubilee, 123, 144, 215
Jubilee release, 122, 133, 143, 159
Nazareth synagogue, proclaiming from, 140–41, 145
Judas, 68, 192
in Matthew, 110, 111
in passion account, 70, 204, 215
thirty pieces of silver and, 108–9, 116
Julius the centurion, 156, 166, 175–76
just-war theory, 11–12, 24, 116

*kenosis,* 209, 210, 211, 212, 213, 222
Kitos rebellion, 77, 84, 85

Lazarus, 190, 203, 208
impending death of, 195, 200, 201–2
Jesus, raising from the dead, 199, 202, 210
Luke-Acts, 4, 188, 227
Apostolic Council, 154, 157, 159–60, 164, 167
centurions, significance of, 166, 175–77
genre of the Gospel, 124
Gentiles, focus on, 119, 164, 167, 177–78
Gospel and Acts as continuous narrative, 135–36
Greek language, sophisticated use of, 191

Holy Spirit, role in Gospel, 128, 157
implied readers, 18, 28, 127, 136–38, 168, 169, 177
on Jesus Christ
ascension, signaling the end of Jesus's appearances, 71
Isaian tradition, Jesus reviving, 132–33
Jerusalem, Jesus's journey to, 143–44, 147, 149, 199
Jesus movement, 121, 125, 156, 160
mission of Jesus, 93–95, 140
Son of God, Jesus proclaimed at birth, 184
kingdom of God proclamation, 166
lawyers as antagonists, 20, 141, 145–48, 149
Lord's supper and transfer of authority to apostles, 149–50, 151, 174
Mark, borrowing from narrative of, 27, 34, 35, 74, 122–23, 129, 130, 141, 143, 145, 146, 150, 175, 178
mockery during passion story, 152–53, 171–73
narrative contract as scripture fulfillment, 129
order, favoring for narrative sequencing, 120, 121–26
parable of the Coming Kingdom, 149–50
on Paul, reasoning in the synagogues, 162–63, 165
*Pax Romana* in Christmas story, 9, 139
Q document as a Gospel source, 40
repentance theme, 121, 134–35, 142, 145, 148–49, 167, 169, 173–75, 178, 226

resistance as a lifestyle, 177–78
Rome, favoring over the Jews,
    10
Sermon on the Plain, 142, 144
synagogue of Nazareth, narra-
    tive contract set up in, 123,
    128–30, 131, 140
Theophilus as implied reader,
    120, 126, 154, 156, 168, 170,
    176, 190
*See also* God-fearers

Magnificat of Mary, 138–39, 142,
    173
Malina, Bruce, 198
Mark
    anti-Jewish sentiments, 10
    apocalyptic writing style, 64–65,
        95
    baptism of Jesus, 22, 50, 52, 56,
        58, 59, 153, 184
    call to repentance, 134, 142
    chiastic pattern use, 37–39
    conflict resolution, 66–68, 68–70
    dual features technique, 36–37,
        47
    empty tomb sequence, 71–73
    genre of the text, 32–33, 34, 35
    Great Revolt, text written dur-
        ing, 45, 64, 75
    holy and unclean imagery, 4, 23,
        46, 47, 48–49, 53, 66, 108
    imperial resistance of, 177
    Jesus as people's messiah, 32,
        50, 51, 65, 74, 81, 93
    John, intentional departure from
        Gospel of Mark, 183
    Luke, adapting text of Mark, 27,
        34, 35, 74, 122–23, 129, 130,
        141, 143, 145, 146, 175, 178
    Matthew, borrowing from text of
        Mark, 27, 34, 35, 74, 77, 89,
        92, 94, 105, 106

messianic recognition, 200–201
Messianic Secret as a narrative
    strategy, 32, 49–50, 56, 93
nonviolent approach, 32, 35, 46,
    51, 65, 66, 69–70, 73–74, 86,
    117, 225
omniscient narrator style, 17
original version of Gospel narra-
    tive, 27–28, 31, 77, 78, 182–83
passion predictions, 58, 70
Pharisees as antagonists, 20, 46
popular messiahs, 32, 42, 51,
    62–63, 194
purity concerns, 4, 23, 46, 48–
    49, 53, 54, 55, 60, 66, 67
Q document, not consulting, 40
rejection at Nazareth, 188
resistance approach, 35, 48, 49,
    73–75, 225
on the Sabbath, 187, 214–15
signs prophets, 32, 41, 51–53,
    55, 75, 121, 194
social bandits, 32, 40, 41, 42–43,
    51, 55, 67
Son of David theme, 51, 59–60,
    62–63, 64
Temple cleansing and entry into
    Jerusalem, timing of events,
    199
threat to Judaism, contending
    with, 165
two-sided action and response,
    220
master narrative of New Testament,
    209, 212–14
Matthew
    banished and returning prince
        formula pattern, 78, 88–89,
        89–91, 91–92, 93–94, 100,
        102, 103, 105, 115
    bloodguilt and innocent blood
        themes, 10, 101, 107–8,
        108–10, 110–11, 116

call to repentance, 134, 142
centurion with ailing slave, sharing story with Luke, 127
commission of disciples to the nations, 72, 112
genealogy, importance of, 78–80, 80–83
imperial resistance and, 177
on Jesus Christ
Jesus as royal heir, 78, 81, 82, 88, 93, 100, 102
Jesus as Son of God at birth, 184
Jesus movement, 28, 77, 99, 125
Jewish followers of Jesus, addressing, 164
Messianic Secret as reveal of Jesus's royal heritage, 93
John the Baptist, conveying sense of urgency, 97–98
Mark, borrowing from narrative of, 27, 34, 35, 74, 77, 89, 92, 94, 105, 106
messianic recognition, 200–201
narrative contract as salvation from sin, 82
nationalism, Gospel written during growth of, 85
neo-rabbinic Judaism as competition, 84, 88
non-retaliation stance, 88, 105–6, 113, 115–16, 225
nonviolence of God, questioning, 222
parable endings as troubling, 114–15
Parable of the Talents, 123, 149
payback and purge motif, 104–6, 108–10, 219
Pharisees as rivals, 20, 87, 88, 96, 99
postcolonial criticism as a framework, 86–88

Q document as a Gospel source, 40
Son of David theme, 81, 83, 93, 94, 101
Temple cleansing and entry into Jerusalem, 199
threat to Judaism, contending with, 165
type-scene entrances into Jerusalem, 90–91, 105
Merton, Thomas, 29, 177, 221
Messianic Secret, 32, 49–50, 56, 93

Neusner, Jacob, 132
Nicodemus, 192, 201, 205
Niebuhr, Reinhold, 73, 116–17
Nietzsche, Friedrich, 179–80
nonviolence
absorption of violence vs. payback, 111
accused woman, Jesus defending through nonviolent means, 224
community repentance and, 178
Gospels as refusing moves towards violence, 171
Jesus, maintaining nonviolence to the end, 219
nonretaliation, 111, 113–18, 225–26
nonviolent action theory, 68–70, 74, 113
nonviolent approach in Mark, 32, 35, 46, 51, 65, 66, 69–70, 73, 86, 117, 225
nonviolent resistance, 12, 32, 35, 73, 74, 106, 117, 177
pattern of nonviolence at end of John, 220
as the praxis of Jesus, 228
Sermon on the Mount as prime example of, 104, 113
Temple cleansing not a violent act, 63

O'Connor, Flannery, 114

pacifism, 11–12, 73, 117
Paul
    Barnabas as missionary partner,
        155, 159
    on Jesus as Son of God at the
        resurrection, 184
    Julius the centurion, accompany-
        ing Paul to Rome, 156, 166,
        175–76
    master narrative of New Testa-
        ment and, 212–13
    mission to the Gentiles, 154,
        158, 160–63, 165, 167
    pagans, outreach to, 128, 161
    as a Roman citizen, 160, 165, 174
    trials of, 162, 164, 165, 168
payback and purge
    Christian Jews, not engaging in
        payback, 107
    ethnic cleansing, purge akin to,
        223–24
    Judas and Pilate, exemplifying
        theme, 108–10, 116
    mutual payback dynamic and
        scapegoating, 216
    payback as poetic justice, 24,
        170
    purge as elimination of a villain,
        25, 104, 171
    purge as partner to payback, 25,
        104–6, 115
    revenge, payback as drive to-
        ward impulse of, 170, 223
    scapegoat ritual as purging com-
        munity from ritual pollution,
        110–11
Peter, 71, 130
    in Acts, 155, 156–57
    blind man from Bethsaida and,
        55–56, 59
    Cornelius the centurion, convert-
        ing, 175

defense of Jesus by the sword,
    204, 215
denial of Jesus, 57, 72, 151, 152,
    194, 195, 204
food taboos and, 121, 159, 167
forgiveness, instructed on, 114
in Mark, 43, 51, 56–57, 58
messianic declaration, 43, 56,
    63, 72, 95
as a pillar disciple, 36, 53, 64,
    200
purity laws, declaring all things
    as acceptable, 158
sinfulness, admitting to, 134,
    142, 148
Pharisees
    debate with Jesus and lawyers,
        148
    guards at tomb of Jesus, request-
        ing, 99, 112
    as hypocrites, 88, 100
    in Jerusalem journey of Jesus,
        140, 144–45
    in John, 10, 194, 201
    Josephus as a Pharisee, 41
    in Luke, 122, 123, 141, 142,
        146, 150, 154
    in Mark, 58
    parable of the Pharisee and the
        tax-collector, 178
    Paul as a Pharisee, 160
    post Temple-destruction, 77, 84
    purity rules and, 46, 49, 54, 55,
        149
    repentance, not interested in, 143
    as rivals to Gospel writers, 20,
        87, 88, 96, 99
    Simon the Pharisee, 134, 143,
        170
Philo of Alexandria, 185
Pilate
    Barabbas and, 43
    in chiastic pattern example, 39
    hand-washing incident, 109, 116

in John, 212, 219, 222
kingship of Jesus, questioning,
    195, 205
in Matthew, 111
in the Passion account, 65, 70,
    204–7
Pharisees, requesting a guard
    from Pilate, 99
as "prince of this world," 193
scapegoating of Jesus, 217, 220
*Portrait of the Artist as a Young
    Man* (Joyce), 7
postcolonial criticism
    empire studies, 5–9
    hybridity concept, 7–8, 86,
        103
    Judaism studies, 9–11
    Matthew, understanding text
        through, 86–88
purity laws
    for attending to the dead, 146
    God-fearers, preventing from
        full participation, 147
    in Mark, 4, 23, 48, 53, 54, 60,
        66, 67
    neighborliness, as interfering
        with, 147
    Peter, declaring all things ac-
        ceptable, 158
    Pharisees and, 46, 49, 54, 55,
        149

Q document, 40
Quietus, Lusius, 85

Reeder, Caryn, 224
repentance
    good thief as a repentance fig-
        ure, 153, 173, 175
    in Luke, 121, 145, 167, 178, 226
    in Mark, 52
    Peter as a prototype of, 142

Pharisees and legal scholars, not
    interested in, 143
Ringe, Sharon, 207
Rohrbaugh, Richard, 198

Sanhedrin, 83, 122, 202
    apostles as the new Sanhedrin,
        157
    Apostolic Council, replacing,
        159
    early Christians, inability to
        overthrow, 164
    in Luke, 152
    as the opposition, 154
Sepphoris, city of, 5, 18, 40, 42
Sharp, Gene, 66, 68–70, 73, 74, 86
Sicarii, 41, 44, 45, 83, 124
Simeon, 137, 138, 139
Simon bar Giora, 42, 45
Stephen, 131, 155, 158, 165, 167, 173
synagogues
    Gentiles, supporting, 18, 127,
        142–43
    Paul, reasoning in the syna-
        gogues, 162–63
    synagogue culture as replacing
        Jerusalem Temple, 84
    synagogue of Capernaum, 47,
        53, 59, 61, 67
    synagogue of Nazareth, 143, 158
        conflict between competing
            visions of Judaism, 145,
            154
        Jubilee message announced
            from, 140–41, 145
        in Luke, 122–23, 128–35,
            136
        release from bondage procla-
            mation, 166, 167

Tabernacles, 181, 183, 187, 188,
    200, 201

Temple of Jerusalem, cleansing of
   act of violence, not a depiction
      of, 63
   as confrontational, 36
   in John, 196, 201, 204
   in Mark, 49, 60–62, 66, 165
   in Matthew, 105, 113
   rising action in narrative, as
      culmination of, 47–48, 59,
      67, 69
   timeline reversal, 187, 199
      Theophilus, 120, 126,
      154, 156, 168, 170, 176, 190

*Things Hidden Since the Founda-
   tion of the World* (Girard),
   218
Tiberias, city of, 18, 40
Titus, General, 45

unclean spirits, 23, 47, 48, 53, 54

Wright, N. T., 124

Zacchaeus, 134, 142, 149
Zealots, 41, 44, 45, 77, 83
Zechariah, 137, 138, 139